IAN THORPE

THIS IS ME
IAN THORPE

and Robert Wainwright

SIMON &
SCHUSTER

London · New York · Sydney · Toronto · New Delhi

A CBS COMPANY

First published in Great Britain by Simon & Schuster UK Ltd, 2012
A CBS COMPANY

3 5 7 9 10 8 6 4 2

Simon & Schuster UK Ltd
1st Floor
222 Gray's Inn Road
London
WC1X 8HB

www.simonandschuster.co.uk

Simon & Schuster Australia, Sydney
Simon & Schuster India, New Delhi

A CIP catalogue for this book is available
from the British Library.

Hardback ISBN 978-1-47110-122-9

Designed by Blue Cork Design
Typeset by Midland Typesetters, Australia
Printed in the UK by CPI Group (UK) Ltd, Croydon, CR0 4YY

For Patrick and Sarah,
so that you know the tales
your uncle used to tell you
are actually true.

'There is no need of any competition with anybody. You are yourself, and as you are, you are perfectly good. Accept yourself.'

Osho

CONTENTS

WATER

I've come to the conclusion that I'm not going to win against the water, that I'll drown eventually. Because it doesn't matter how good you are – there's only so far you can swim before it takes over.

When I first dive into the pool I try to work out how the water wants to hold me. If I let it, the water will naturally guide me into a position; a place for my body to settle, resting with my head down, almost meditating.

This is the starting point for me, not just floating but lying flat on top of the water. Then I begin to initiate movement; lifting myself, pushing with my chest and engaging my muscles. That's the basis of the way anyone should swim, although it's not the way we learn because we're not taught to connect so intimately with the water.

As I begin to swim I allow myself to feel where the water is moving around me, how it flows off my body. I listen for any erratic movement which means I'm not relating to the water and I have to modify my stroke, change it until I feel the water moving smoothly past me. I can do this at low speed or very high speed.

It's really rewarding because I receive constant feedback without stopping. I don't need someone to tell me that my stroke looks great or that it looks terrible because I have an inner sense of the water and the environment is already communicating with me.

If I'm swimming next to someone and they aren't swimming properly, I can hear it, even without looking at them – although I prefer to swim by myself. Elite swimmers tend to become very territorial of the water around them, as if we own it. We don't want anyone else messing up our water.

At times, especially when I feel as though I've swum well, I'll turn around at the wall and look back to see what the water is doing. I look for telltale signs; little whirlpools which mean that I've created the right amount of turbulence as I've moved through it.

This is why I've returned to the pool; not for medals and records or to relive past triumphs as most people assume. If that happens then I'll be happy, but if not it doesn't mean I've failed. I'm doing it because swimming was an integral part of my life that I felt forced to abandon.

Now I want it back.

1 AUGUST 2011

There are fireworks across Lake Maggiore tonight. It feels like I'm back in Sydney but I'm not. It's Swiss National Day and, although beautiful, the water in front of me ain't Sydney Harbour. Home seems so far away at the moment with so many reminders of what I've left behind.

I've been in the Swiss Alps since March, in a town called Tenero, just across the northern border of Italy, churning out 60 kilometres a week in the swimming pool a few hundred metres from my apartment, under the guidance of former Australian Institute of Sport coach Gennadi Touretski.

Training's been good. I'm tired but am finally getting somewhere with changes to the new stroke Gennadi and I have been working on. Still, I know I'm a long way from anywhere really, and it's one year today until the 100-metre freestyle final in London. The 2012 Olympics. How can I seriously consider being in that race with 18 months' preparation after four years out of the water? I sometimes wonder if I'm really doing the right thing, but only for a moment.

The idea to try again had come from nowhere, like some pesky fly to be swatted away.

I was flopped as best as I could with my long frame in an aisle seat, bored and uncomfortable on a plane two hours out of Chicago. It was early October, 2010. I'd just left a conference and was headed to London to do some BBC studio commentary on the Commonwealth Games in Delhi. The movie was crap and my mind had started to wander, which isn't unusual; I often note down some of the crazy things that cross my mind on flights like these. But this time I didn't need to write anything.

It's not as if I hadn't thought about swimming since I'd retired from competition. Of course I had, but on each occasion I'd dismissed it immediately. There were a lot of reasons why I didn't want to get back into the pool. Looking back, I'm surprised at just how frank I was at the media conference in November 2006 when I announced I was quitting. I knew how big the decision was, not just for me but the expectations of the Australian sporting public. But I had to be true to myself, and what I said then was coming from the heart.

I'd thought a lot about what I wanted to say that day. By then I'd mastered the art of the media conference; answering questions enthusiastically but with only just enough information to be truthful and without giving more than I had to give.

I didn't have all the answers myself, actually. I knew that I had to stop, if only as a final attempt to remove the media cancer from my life. If I stopped swimming then there'd be no reason for them to hound me. Right?

But there was a broader reason, probably more serious. I had to start to look at myself, my life, as something more than swimming. I was a young man who hadn't actually grown up. I was mature, I'd travelled widely and experienced many things, but I hadn't really found out who I was or even what I liked. What would I be if I didn't have swimming as the safety blanket it had become? What would I want to do, who would I meet, what would I think and would anyone like me if I wasn't an Olympic champion? As I said very specifically, I was going out after my fears, and some of them were very dark indeed.

The reason why I didn't instantly dismiss the idea on the plane was because I'd now faced many of those fears and answered some of those life questions. In my mind, swimming was possible again. In fact it was something I now needed as part of a much more balanced life. I continued to mull it over as we crossed the Atlantic.

The next few days with the BBC in London only reinforced my thinking. In between commentary shifts I had a tour of the Olympic pool site and, standing in the half-constructed arena, I could still feel the excitement of being on the pool deck and the thrill of competition. I hadn't watched much swimming in the years since I'd left but in the London studio it was my job to add comments to the coverage, which included the amazing comeback by Geoff Huegill to win gold in the 100-metre butterfly at the age of 31.

As I sat there watching and wondering, I was asked yet again by the host about my own future and what life was like without swimming. I'd been asked these things so many times before that it'd become annoying, but now those same questions were running through my own mind. I had no choice but to fib. I couldn't really talk about my thoughts because they hadn't fully formed.

By the time I got back to Sydney the idea had become something I couldn't push away. I decided to go and see Deidre Anderson, a friend and psychologist at Macquarie University whom I'd consulted before I made the final decision to stop swimming. I wanted to know in my own mind if these thoughts were serious or just a flirtation. I figured that I'd know what to say to Deidre, and that she'd help me come to the conclusion that I really didn't want to do it.

But the opposite happened. About halfway through our conversation I stopped and looked at her.

'I'm going to swim again, aren't I?' I said.

'I think you might. I think you need to do this for yourself.'

'And when I walked into your office last time, you knew I was going to stop swimming, didn't you?'

'Yes, I did.' Deidre seemed to know me as well as I knew myself; better perhaps, because she could see what I couldn't see, or found difficult to admit to myself.

It took a few more visits to work out what I was going to do and why. The next problem was how I was going to dive back into the pool without attracting the very thing that had forced me to stop four years before: the constant glare of publicity and intrusion into my life. I wasn't worried just about the media attention; I didn't want people around me to know either, at least initially, because I didn't really know how far it would go.

It wasn't about swimming a few laps and enjoying myself again. It was a personal challenge, and I only wanted to continue if I thought I could swim as well as I used to. There's a part of me that enjoys the process but there's also a part of me which is very competitive – not so much to beat an opponent as to test myself.

There were only three people who needed to know at this early stage. The first two were my long-time managers, Dave and Michelle Flaskas, who were going to have to accept a big change in my busy schedule of corporate commitments. The third was a coach; someone who could set me a training regime, because I had no idea where to start. I knew I couldn't just dive into the pool and train by trying to swim further or faster each time. I decided to get in touch with the head coach of the Austra-lian swimming team, Leigh Nugent, who was still in Delhi, and texted him to see if it was a good time to call and have a chat.

It wasn't, he wrote back, the team was on its way to the airport to come home. Could it wait until he got back?

Not really, I replied. I was too anxious. He relented and I called.

'Are you by yourself?' I asked. 'I have some news. You might need to sit down to hear it.'

'Yep, fire away.'

I took a deep breath, knowing how big a deal it was that I was about to articulate my thoughts to someone else. 'I'm thinking about swimming again.'

There was a momentary silence as Leigh took it in. 'Shit. I never thought I'd hear you say that.'

'Yeah, me either.' Then I laughed, the tension broken in a moment.

But Leigh was already being practical – and supportive, which is one of the reasons we're so lucky to have him as head coach: 'What do you need from me?'

'The first thing is secrecy. If anyone finds out about this before I'm ready, I can't do it.'

'Understood. No one will find out.'

'And I need some training sessions. I need to know what I have to do.'

Leigh didn't answer immediately. Then he said, 'Ian, how much swimming have you done in the last four years?'

I had to think about it. Then realisation set in. I'd only been in a pool a handful of times since November 2006. How on earth could I be contemplating a serious return to Olympic competition, barely 18 months away? Failure was the most likely outcome. Did I want this so much that I was prepared to fail?

I decided in that moment. Yes.

By the time he'd arrived in Sydney, Leigh had devised an initial training schedule, insisting that I had to commit to swimming six days in a row, even if some of the sessions were at the beach rather than the pool. I'd already decided with Deidre that I'd commit myself to at least three days, no matter how frustrated or crappy I felt. If I got through them then I'd commit to three weeks and then three months. After that I'd be in a better position to decide if my return was serious or just an interesting little experiment which I could abandon without anyone being the wiser.

London was a nice goal to have but I knew when I put the wheels in motion that the timing wasn't very good. I wish I'd felt this way a year earlier, which would have given me much more preparation time. But it just happened. One morning in Chicago I was never going to swim again and the next, flying over the Atlantic, I was thinking the exact opposite.

In hindsight, the decision wasn't about any dissatisfaction with my life. I was enjoying my time away from the pool. I had a beautiful house in Sydney and another in Los Angeles, lots of friends who I cooked for every other day and a steady income from endorsements and investments; I spent time in the garden and made the odd appearance. My life was very comfortable, although the global financial crisis had made an impact on my financial situation. The issue was more that I'd spent several years convincing myself that I needed to be away from swimming; that I didn't need it anymore. I'd reached a point where I was pretty happy without swimming, rather than being miserable with it. Now I was testing myself to see if swimming could be a part of a much broader, but simpler, life.

I didn't quit swimming because I didn't like it anymore. I stopped because I didn't like what it had become for me. I felt like my career had been taken over by others; that I had no control over what I did in the pool. I felt as though I took a lot of the pain along the way and everyone else shared in the success without seeing the damage I was doing to myself to get there. Mostly I felt like a performing seal in the zoo.

I liked racing and I liked training but there was also a line of public scrutiny that had been breached. Surely there were more important things in the world the media could focus on other than what I had for breakfast? I wasn't prepared for those kinds of demands and it had never happened to a swimmer before. Now I was going to have to face it all over again – the photographers at the end of my driveway or peering through swimming pool fences, and journalists asking me the same question about my sexuality over and over again, just because I hadn't given them the answer they wanted to hear.

I got back in the pool for the first time on my 28th birthday – 13 October 2010. I'd spoken to Leigh the night before and he'd set me a fairly easy session. I saw no sense in waiting and my birthday seemed the perfect start. Despite his warning not to turn up early – 'Only serious lap swimmers go early' – I was at Caringbah pool complex, the pool closest to home, stretching just before 7 am.

My first problem was equipment. I had swimmers, of course, but none of the specific training gear like kickboards or pool buoys, which I'd given away over the years. I approached the pool attendant to see what I could borrow.

'We haven't seen you here for quite a while,' he said, smiling. It was a comment more than an inquiry about what I was doing.

Once I was in the water, it was obvious to me just how long I'd been away. Even a week off can make you feel a little uncomfortable, let alone four years. The water seemed to bubble and groan around me when I dived in. I surfaced, stopped and adjusted my goggles, while bits of me I never knew existed jiggled in the gurgling water.

Then I set off up the pool for my first proper lap since November 2006. It felt sluggish rather than slow and the turn at 50 metres just felt wrong. I was low in the water and my arms weren't rotating as they should. I was supposed to be easing my way back in with a comfortable 200 metres but by the 150 metre mark I was struggling, my heart racing. What once was natural had become very difficult. What was I doing?

I touched the wall at the finish and looked up at the timer, an instinctive reaction from years of training and racing. I'd dominated this distance in my career, breaking the world record five times and winning the gold medal at the Athens Olympics in 2004. I'd once covered the distance in 1:44.06. On my 28th birthday, as the sun began to warm the complex, it took me almost an extra minute – not too bad for a weekend swimmer but a mile away from an Olympic performance. And it hurt.

Luckily the rest of the session Leigh had set me was made up of shorter drills, using a kickboard or a pool buoy between my legs to concentrate on form and technique, but by the end of it I was spent – sore, red and sweating. Thinking about it now, I remember how hard it was even to get out of the pool which, by tradition when I trained as a kid with Doug Frost, meant pushing myself up on the pool wall with my arms, then putting a foot – never ever a knee – on the pool deck and standing up. It was drilled into us as children but now it was a strain, my triceps cramping and my foot barely clearing the pool wall as I clambered out.

As I drove home my arms were shaky, my body spent, and yet the sense of achievement I felt was akin to completing a great session in serious training. I could also feel that I still had important elements of my stroke. Without that I might have given up on the spot.

But the endorphin rush only lasted until I got through the front door. Exhaustion set in as I grasped the enormity of what

I was attempting to do. My dogs, Max and Kito, demanded attention but I wasn't interested, gently shooing them away and collapsing on a couch, wrapping self-pity around myself like a blanket. The dogs watched, quizzically, at my feet.

This was going to be tough. For all the natural talent I have, that alone wasn't going to be nearly enough to succeed. Strangely there was comfort in the realisation. Even though I was born with physical attributes that helped me as a swimmer, I've always believed that without my ability to train and focus it would have come to little – no world records and no Olympic titles. As crappy as I felt at that moment, I knew if I was going to continue then it was dedication that was going to get me there. And my dedication was beyond question.

I managed to rise later that day and head to my parents' house for a home-cooked birthday meal with the immediate family. I hid my physical pains pretty well but I must have smelled like chlorine because someone asked me what I'd been doing. I gulped.

'I went for a swim this morning,' I admitted, waiting for someone to drop their fork and ask me what was going on, but everyone kept eating.

My mother broke the silence: 'That's nice, dear.'

Somehow, with Deidre's advice in my head, I got through the next two days, then the next three weeks of swimming. So far so good. But in those early days there was one issue that plagued me – how to begin training without the media finding out. Stealth was required. Over the next three months

I devised a routine which allowed me to train quietly, without the pressure of expectation, and reach a decision about whether I was able to return to elite swimming.

I realised I couldn't just turn up to the pools nearest home like the Caringbah complex, or where I used to train at Sutherland Aquatic Centre. Not regularly, anyway. If I showed up occasionally then it'd probably pass unnoticed but I couldn't go twice a day, as I needed to, and certainly not in the early morning.

Instead, I chose eight pools across Sydney and rotated my training sessions between them. I really wanted to find a private 50-metre pool, partly because I needed a coach to watch what I was doing. It sounds easy enough, but it wasn't. One of the great things about Australia is the egalitarian nature of our swimming facilities – most pools are public, which means that anyone can front up, pay their entry fee and have a swim. But that wasn't going to work if I wanted to stay under the radar.

I was able to train for a while at Macquarie University because of the Christmas–New Year break but I needed somewhere a bit more permanent where I could take a coach. Leigh was coming along to my sessions on occasion, sometimes wearing a beanie as a disguise and sitting by the pool pretending to read a newspaper while he watched me plough up and down. We even met at an ocean pool at Cronulla once. It was a covert operation and harder to manage as time went on and I became more serious.

It was Deidre who found the solution. Waverley College is a private Christian school in Sydney's eastern suburbs and it has a 50-metre pool. I had a meeting with the headmaster and the brothers there, explaining that I needed a little privacy to do some training. The school was amazing. I'm sure they knew what was going on but they said nothing and gave me access to their facilities when others weren't around.

Looking back, I have to chuckle at the whole thing, particularly as I got closer to making the decision that a return was possible. I even devised a contingency plan in which, at the slightest hint of a media leak, I could load a coach, a trainer and a physio onto a plane and leave the country for a secret location, which is ultimately why I'm here in Tenero, as far from the spotlight as possible.

For the most part, though, I saw it as a game; me against them. I hate to express it that way but there's an aspect of the Australian media which is ugly. There's a small but prominent section who are only interested in two things – success or misery – and anything in between is irrelevant.

Of all the pools that I could have been busted at, it was Caringbah, the pool I used least because it's so close to my house. It was a Saturday morning in early January 2011 and I'd already made the decision to aim for the Olympics. At that stage I was swimming about five kilometres at each session but that morning I'd swum just 600 metres, gone to the beach for a surf and then a run. An hour or so later a reporter turned up at my house to tell me I'd been photographed at the pool.

'Are you swimming again?' he asked through the intercom.

'Well, if I was photographed swimming then it's obvious I was swimming,' I said.

'No, that's not what I mean,' he replied. 'Are you making a comeback?'

I asked him to leave, saying I thought it was rude to turn up at my house with his questions.

'Do I take it you're not commenting?' he persisted.

I bristled: 'No, I made a comment. It's just that you didn't like what you heard.'

The reporter retreated, but only as far as the top of my driveway. I could see him standing there through the CCTV cameras, which I'd had to install when I was swimming competitively in order to feel secure in exactly these kinds of situations.

Some might argue there's no harm in taking my photo at a public pool or that, as a public figure, I should expect to be asked questions. I agree, but only to a point. My concern is that parts of the media think they have a right to ask anything, no matter how many times, and a right to get the answers they want to hear. As I see it, the public's 'right to know' is a term bandied about with no context and without consideration of a private citizen's rights.

That's the main reason I'm here in Tenero, training with a group of Swiss swimmers. It'd be impossible to attempt this in my own backyard, with cameras everywhere I went and persistent questions about what I was doing, and how, and why. I tried to train quietly in Los Angeles in 2006 and it ended in tears, so I quit. Hopefully the Swiss Alps will be a barrier too high, even for the Australia media.

two

26 AUGUST 2010

The view from my balcony on the hillside above Tenero is breathtaking – the milky blue waters of Lake Maggiore are shining in the late summer sunshine against their mountain backdrop. It's warm and peaceful at this time of year, but I'm not here for the view.

When I arrived here five months ago, the small town was still waking from its winter hibernation; its streets bleak and all but deserted, most of the restaurants shut and the houses shuttered. I checked into an almost empty hotel to be near the outdoor pool, which had been encased in a big white tent for winter, making the chlorine stifling after long training sessions.

It was only when I found my hillside apartment that
I began to relax. The estate agent flung open the windows
to the balcony and I looked down at the lake. It presented an
entirely new perspective on the beauty of this place. Not only
that, I had space, room to move – I could walk down the street
in relative obscurity, away from the glare of publicity that this
campaign would generate back home.

I'm a person who thrives on routine. It was the backbone
of my life for so long. I like to know what I'm supposed to be
doing for the day, where I'm supposed to be and at what time,
which is why I find living the life of a professional athlete so
comforting. My car is the one exception. To be honest it's a
tip, probably because I carry most of my life around in it –
the boot is always full of damp towels and swimming stuff.
I approach communications with the same kind of chaos.
I'm hopeless with email. For some reason I can't get my head
around it, although I love the immediacy and freedom of SMS.

I chose Gennadi Touretski to be my coach for several reasons,
but mainly because he was the man who steered Russian great
Alexander Popov to four Olympic gold medals. I also considered hiring Dutchman Jacco Verhaeren, the coach of Pieter
van den Hoogenband, who won three Olympic gold medals.
Elite swimming is a very small world. I won the bronze medal
in the 100 metres at the 2004 Athens Olympics behind Pieter,
having qualified for the final by tipping out Alex, which effectively ended his career.

It's difficult to compare my Athens 100-metres swim to the
rest of my career performances, which were in the 200 and 400.
I didn't win the race and I didn't set a world record and yet,
when I consider that I wasn't actually training for the 100 and

probably shouldn't have even been in the field – was an impostor, almost – I suppose it could be considered a surprise performance.

If you add my swim in the anchor leg of the 4 × 100 metres at the Sydney Olympics in 2000, in which I beat Gary Hall Junior and we won gold, then it raises the question of potential. Was I a middle-distance swimmer who occasionally competed in sprints or was I really a sprinter who became a middle-distance swimmer and had the speed trained out of him? That's the question I want to answer and Gennadi can help me. My priority is the 100 metres, because I want to test myself, and then the 200 metres, which is probably my best chance if I get to London. Besides, I don't have enough time to prepare for the 400.

There were other reasons why I chose Gennadi. He happens to be the Swiss national coach, which gives me a base at the Swiss Sports Institute facilities here in Tenero – attractive, again, because they're far from the madding crowd back in Sydney. I also like his no-nonsense pragmatism and ability to see that training can take many forms and differ from one athlete to another. Above all, it's the combination of technique and efficiency which leads to speed.

I'm one of the few swimmers who uses a classic, natural stroke which hasn't been adapted to make the best use of swimsuit technology. I'm certainly a supporter of technology, but not when it's left unchecked. At one point, the suits became so rigid that they allowed swimmers to simply lie on top of the water and just use power. It also meant smaller swimmers could compete, buoyed by the suits, their arms thrashing like windmills. Technique was lost, and without technique I think the sport will struggle to move forward.

Gennadi has also come as close as anyone has in under-standing my feelings for water. He knows there's something innate about what I do in the pool and that I feel unique about what I do when I swim. He gets it, and not many others have. To tell the truth there have been times when I wished I'd never become involved in this world; when I loathed having this natural ability, whether I should have stayed at school and done something else with my life. Thankfully, most days I feel the opposite. I know swimming is some-thing I have to do. I have to be involved in some way with the water or it could become unhealthy for me.

I think it was best summed up recently when I overheard Gennadi telling a group of parents of squad members that all athletes train so they can race. I thought, 'No, it's the other way around for me. I race so that I can train.' That's how I feel about what I do; I can justify doing the training because it's necessary to compete. But I'm happiest just doing the training; following the black line at the bottom of the pool as I search for perfection. I have past results as a benchmark to work out if this new stroke is better. If I can set the bar higher for myself then I can set the bar higher for everyone else.

It's not quite as simple as that, of course. Although I love the process of training – the exploration, the pushing through to new kinds of performance – the only way to judge whether I'm succeeding or not is through competition. I could be the best technical swimmer in the world but that doesn't mean I can swim faster than everyone else – the only way a value can be given to the training sets that Gennadi and I put together is by testing them in a race.

What I fear most is that when I get back into competition in a few months' time I may not get the answer I want.

It's difficult to talk about myself publicly when even I don't have all the answers. I've tried to honestly since I was 12 years old, interviewed with a swag of medals around my neck after the New South Wales titles, not knowing what it all meant.

I was an innocent 15-year-old when I won my first world title and a wide-eyed 17-year-old with the world and all its temptations at my feet when I won Olympic gold. By the age of 20, lost and brow-beaten, I felt like quitting, and came within a whisker of it as a psychologically exhausted 22-year-old. Finally, bitter with the constant pursuit, accusations and innuendo, I retired prematurely at 24, knowing that I could have achieved so much more.

Now I'm a few weeks from my 29th birthday, with many achievements in and out of the pool behind me. But with so much of my life left to live, the unanswered questions are a very big part of why I am swimming again. Although commentators may view this as an attempt to capture past glories, while others have suggested it's for financial reasons, the truth is that it's actually a process of self-discovery.

No matter what happens – and all I have at this stage is hope and faith in myself – the opportunity to swim again is a way of piecing together the jigsaw of my life so I can see the whole picture, rather than a fractured puzzle of what might have been. If I'm truly honest with myself, it's a frightening prospect.

I define myself as a person made up of several parts. The physical is the easiest to explain. I worked bloody hard for many years, pushing my body and mind to, at times, ridiculous limits to achieve what no one else ever had. There were occasions when, in closed rooms out of sight of the cameras, I collapsed and convulsed in pain, trying to shake out the lactic acid build-up in my legs after a major race. I trained in a cast after breaking my ankle, and routinely got out of bed at 4.30 am in the middle of winter, my chest wracked with muck, to swim kilometre after kilometre in a cold pool.

My story isn't unique in this regard; it's similar to that of thousands of other athletes' who spend their lives pursuing their own ultimate performance. The most successful are usually among the most determined, but the most determined don't always succeed. I've often felt embarrassed by the attention focused on me, rather than on some of my fellow competitors, and wished the interest was spread a little more evenly. Sadly it's been one thing I haven't been able to control over the years.

The second part is my media face. Since I was 15 I've tried to control events around me – an impossible task amid the media madness and one I'm not looking forward to resuming when I begin competing again. Those closest to me would say that this urge to control has been to my personal detriment and that trying to protect others around me has only hurt me. They might be right, but I don't regret it. The inclination wasn't a selfish one but a means of survival.

I perfected a mask: a confident smile which made it look as if I were master of the occasion, comfortable with the battery of questions when often the opposite was true. On more than one occasion Dave Flaskas found me sitting by myself outside a media conference room trying to calm my nerves, but on the stage there would be no sign of anxiety. I treated it as a game of chess where I constantly analysed the implications of a question and constructed an answer to ensure it couldn't be misinterpreted or misused, or so I hoped.

I have never lied or misrepresented the truth with the media, but there have been times when I have not told the whole truth. After all, I'm not going to give someone gold just because they're digging in the dirt.

The mask I wear at a public appearance or function is slightly different. This is my professional face: confident on a red carpet, adept at meeting people and engaging in small talk. My interest is sincere but by nature I'm a shy person, content with my own company or a small group of friends. If you take away the gloss, I'm a boy from the south-western suburbs of Sydney. The Thorpes have always been a modest family; it's something I like about myself.

That's why there were never any signs of my success around our family home. I wanted to feel as normal as possible, so Mum and Dad were allowed to have their 'proud parents' room' but were banned from putting up posters and display-ing trophies. I still don't have anything in my own house (the Olympic medals are in a bank vault) because I know what I've done. I don't need a reminder. Besides, there's a part of me that thinks it's garish and ridiculous to have those sorts of things on display.

The private me, seen by very few, is still delighted by childish pranks, building Lego with my nephew, cooking for friends, gardening and walking my dogs. I love the unspoiled beaches of Brazil, the villages and food of Italy and the fashion houses of Europe. I'm fascinated by industrial design and speak basic Japanese and Italian. I always have a book beside my bed, am opinionated politically with an avid interest in social and economic policy, and continue to explore the mysteries of religion.

But there are shadows in my life, a clutter of darkness, angst and misgivings which have confused my path and continue to pose questions more difficult than any inappropriate jibe about my sexuality. The water gives me respite. It's one of the few places I can be completely comfortable with myself; a place where I'm truly happy.

When I was 18, I pleaded with my parents to stop buying newspapers. My argument was that they were supporting an industry which was hurting me, their son. I was angry about the way some sections of the media had begun to invade my private life and I wanted to shield them from the stories and innuendo. It was a very big thing to ask of them, particularly for Dad because it was his connection to the world, but they both eventually agreed.

It was probably an overreaction because, for the most part, I've had a constructive relationship with the media and have enjoyed being involved in it myself in various roles over the years, including commentating and making environmental documentaries. I respect many journalists, some of whom have spent years covering Olympic sport and swimming, because they go some way toward understanding the pressures and demands on athletes.

I understand there's an expectation that high-profile athletes like me should make ourselves available and be willing to reveal more, personally, than would otherwise be expected. It's part of the deal. But this is where I draw a very clear line. There are some journalists who seem to observe no boundary, not even common decency. Asking inappropriate questions is one thing but there's much more to it. For example, photographers who follow cars or set up camp outside swimming pools or private homes; who peer over walls, even follow me on holidays, to get what they think is a dirty picture. There's simply no justification for capturing images of me eating a hamburger because it's supposed to prove I'm fat and unfit, or cropping photographs of me walking into an office with a female friend so that it looks like we're sneaking into a seedy motel.

Right now there's a fierce debate in Britain about media intrusion and privacy. Although it's concentrated on the misuse of technology to hack into phones and bribes paid to police, it's also raised much-needed discussion about the behaviour and expectations of the media. I don't believe they have the right to demand answers from people, even if they earn money from sponsorship and advertising. There must be a valid reason for questions that strike at the heart of privacy – a genuine public interest claim rather than the general argument that 'people want to know'.

They might like to think their coverage reflects public opinion. What they publish can certainly shape the way the public sees things but I dispute that it can be described as a representation. It's an important distinction, not only because of what it actually achieves but what it could aspire to achieve. Wouldn't it be better if the media aimed to educate and inform the public so they can make their own considered judgement, rather than seek to corral, lead and pigeonhole people?

In the lead-up to the Sydney Olympics my experience with the media had been largely positive, but one afternoon, in the heat of competition, it all changed. I'd just swum the semifinal of the 200 metres, which I went on to lose to Dutchman Pieter van den Hoogenband. I'd usually say a few words in a poolside interview, do a swim-down and then go to the main media conference. But on this occasion I wasn't feeling very well and needed to rest, so I skipped the conference and headed back to my room.

Instead of accepting I had a valid reason for not appearing, some journalists reported my no-show as sour grapes at not having been the fastest qualifier. It was absolute rubbish. Some journalists will write something negative just because I haven't done something or answered a question in a way they didn't like. I hate the idea of being expected to buckle to that kind of pressure. It was then that I realised there was a vindictive edge to some sections of the media that was beyond my control. I decided then and there that I would only give over what I was prepared to lose.

I haven't had a single day of media training and I don't think anyone else should, either. Otherwise you become a boring, cookie-cutter athlete. The only way to be is yourself. Do things your own way. Protect yourself and learn to get what you want, not what the media dictates.

three

11 SEPTEMBER 2010

The Verzasca Dam is just outside Tenero, in the mountains on the other side of the lake. It's an arched wall of concrete made famous by the opening scene from the 1995 James Bond movie *GoldenEye*, where Bond (that is, a stuntman) plunges 220 metres down the face in what one poll a few years later voted the greatest movie stunt ever filmed. Since then more than 10,000 people have made a similar bungee jump, including me after a Saturday morning training session a few months ago.

It was a strange way to relax, I suppose, but indicative of my state of mind. At this stage in my training I'm in the mood for some outside stimulation, another challenge – if only briefly.

Athletes revel in the rush of risk. For some it's a fast car (for the record, I appreciate the aesthetics of sports cars more than their speed) and others like the dangers of skiing or skydiving. Me, I love the pressure of live television or public speaking as well as the physical risk of something like bungee jumping.

Your legs feel like lead as you walk toward the edge, your heart is pounding and your instincts are screaming that you're about to die. Meanwhile your head is saying 'calm down' and trying to convince you that it's safe. On top of the Verzasca Dam, my head won out and I plunged straight down the grey concrete wall, my arms outstretched in a dive that I hoped would look graceful, if only to the passing birds. As you plummet there's a mixture of fear and adrenaline coursing through your body. The fall only takes a few seconds and yet it feels much longer, the fear subsiding just as the rope catches and springs you back. The danger is over and the rest of the experience is pure joy.

It's exhilarating, and yet standing on the edge of a dam preparing to plunge is much less frightening than standing on the blocks for an Olympic final. It's the kind of calculated gamble you have to take at elite level to catapult your performance forward but at the risk of potential failure – heart over mind or mind over heart – to see which will win out.

I was the kid who loved the rides at the Easter Show, even though they were scary. I remember being frustrated in my wait to be tall enough to go on the roller-coaster by myself, unlike my father, who was forced to ride with my sister. His grimace showed his discomfort but he did it anyway, one of the early examples of how different he and I are as people but also how we share some of the same characteristics, like the determination to push through discomfort.

There's been a lot of experimentation with my training. I wasn't expecting it when I came to Switzerland and, frankly, I wouldn't have attempted it with any coach other than Gennadi, but I've made a conscious decision to try different things, including changing my stroke, to be better than I was. Some will say I'm mad to tinker with a technique already considered one of the best, and only time will tell.

I realise now that as the first stage of my career progressed I took less and less risks in training, becoming more of a formula athlete for gaining success rather than taking a punt on what I believed in and what I could potentially achieve. It's a key motivator for me. I've always said that I don't race against others as such. I see their times but I don't judge them as benchmarks because that would set limits. I'd rather look at the potential. I swim against myself, to be the fastest and best that I can be, and that doesn't have a limit.

Gennadi and I have a training language which describes what we're trying to achieve. Take the style we call 'Easy Look Good', a lap of the pool using the best technique possible. It is what it suggests – a gentle walk. Depending on how I feel, some days it's fast and some days it's slow, and I learn as much on the slow days as the fast.

The hardest thing for me to do is swim really slowly while maintaining a reasonable stroke. Occasionally I have to do it at training and I find it very difficult because neurologically, my body is screaming out in protest. By the end of the session I feel mentally rather than physically fried. But the reason behind doing it is that if I can technically coordinate my body at a very low speed then it will make it easier to do it at high speed. And that's the ultimate aim. We want to create speed in a very organic way rather than forcing it to happen; training so that over time and through repetition, changes in speed – up or down – happen with a minimum of fuss and with almost no impact on technique. The goal is to swim the same way, whether it's really slow, comfortable or really fast.

We have two speeds during sessions – training speed and racing speed. Gennadi will set me a task to swim at a certain speed without compromising stroke or technique and there are times when I can actually do the work at racing speed. There are also rare occasions when I use a technique we've dubbed 'Swim for Your Life', which is exactly what it sounds like. Gennadi will set me a time in which to swim a certain distance and I have to find a way to do it even if that means sacrificing form, although I don't see much benefit in it because it seems counterproductive that we compromise technique.

Instead, if we're doing a lactic acid session, in which I train to create a build-up of lactic acid in my muscles so I can learn to cope with the agony of a final lap in a race, then I'll swim them butterfly so that I can push myself to the limit and get the training benefit without compromising my freestyle stroke. It also means I'll be fresh the next day to swim freestyle because the strokes use slightly different muscle groups.

What constitutes a life-changing moment? Breaking a world record or winning an Olympic gold medal? For me, neither of these do, because they were things I'd been training to achieve for more than a decade – they were life confirmations more than life changers. I suppose what I really mean is what makes up a moment – a second, a minute, perhaps a day – which alters your perception about life and perhaps even the direction it's taking?

I've had such a day. We all shared it, really – September 11, 2001, which was ten years ago today. The reason it's so personal for me is that, had a few different decisions been made in the hours leading up to the attacks, I might have been inside the south tower of the World Trade Center, on my way up in an elevator to the 110th floor as the two hijacked planes destroyed thousands of lives and turned the world on its head.

I have thought about it since, often at critical moments. It was in my head when I decided to change coaches in 2002, again when I retired from swimming in 2006 and more recently when I decided to come back to the sport. Life is about making decisions, altering direction and taking opportunities. Otherwise it's wasted. Now, a decade later as I sit in my apartment and watch a television news special on the anniversary of that horrifying event, I can still remember the day and those that followed with a clarity I don't have for many of my record-breaking races.

Michelle Flaskas, who often travelled with me overseas to help organise my schedule, and I arrived in New York in the early evening of Monday, 10 September. We'd made the 15-hour flight from Sydney via Los Angeles at the invitation of the Italian fashion house Armani, with which I'd struck up a relationship the year before in 2000 when I'd attended a retrospective of the designer's work at the Guggenheim Museum. On this trip I'd be attending shows at New York Fashion Week and Mr Armani (I never call him Giorgio) would be there himself to host a number of events and open a new store.

It was an exciting time; the Sydney Olympics were well and truly behind me and I'd begun to explore what life had to offer outside swimming. I was a few weeks from my 19th birthday, full of energy and eager to see and do new things, including meeting one of the world's great fashion designers.

Swimming had become a bit draining and I needed a break. New York was the first leg of a six-week trip that would include stops in Japan, Germany, Switzerland, England, Italy and France and then back to LA, a mixture of sponsorship commitments and free time.

It had been an anxious beginning – the day before leaving, we discovered there'd been a mix-up in the bookings and we couldn't get into the downtown hotel we'd planned to stay at, the Tribeca Grand, which is at the southern end of Manhattan, just up the road from the World Trade Center. A last-minute ring around found us a place a few kilometres north, virtually on Times Square in midtown, not far from Central Park. We checked in and spent a few hours stretching our legs, drinking in the amazing atmosphere of the city and working out what we'd do between fashion events over the next few days.

As we ate dinner that night, we ended up having a friendly argument about what to do in the morning. Michelle wanted to go to the top of the Empire State Building, which was close to our hotel, but I was insistent we go to the top of the World Trade Center because the view was so much better during the day with the light falling over the East River. I'd been up there once before and you can see for more than 70 kilometres on a clear day – it's like standing on the roof of the man-made world. I suggested we could do both, given we were staying for a few days, and that the view from the Empire State Building would be better at night because we'd be looking down at the city lights.

Michelle eventually gave in and we finished dinner and hailed a cab. The driver was bragging about how great the weather had been considering it was early autumn, but as he talked it started to pour with rain and the traffic, always bumper to bumper, slowed even more. I didn't mind. Getting stuck in New York traffic at night means you can drink in the city without looking like the tourist that you are, constantly staring up, mouth agape, in awe of the skyline which engulfs you and confirms your insignificance. It's the giveaway, apparently – New Yorkers don't look up.

We decided to go early to the towers the next morning, to try to beat the crowds. Michelle was keen to have a run through the city first as she sometimes did, maybe up through Central Park, but I was in favour of a good sleep-in. We agreed that she'd bang on my door when she got back in case I overslept, and we'd leave in time to be at the head of the queue when the gates opened at 8.30.

But as the Robert Burns poem says, the best-laid plans of mice and men often go awry. I woke at about 6 am, my head full of the excitement of New York. I decided that a run was probably a good idea, too. It's not something swimmers do regularly but a bit of training variety is always good so I headed off downtown, through the wakening streets, still largely empty of the crowds which would soon swarm up from the subways.

I jogged steadily down Seventh Avenue toward Lower Manhattan and the financial district, past the boutiques along

Fashion Avenue, across Broadway, past Carnegie Hall, Madison Square Garden and Penn Station – all familiar names in books and on television and now right here in front of me, one after another. I just kept running, happy to be in the middle of the city at one of the few times of day when there's room to move.

It was an incredible morning, with the clearest of blue skies and only the faintest puff of wind, even there in the concrete canyon of buildings, which makes you feel as if you're in a tunnel. People would later describe the air that morning as crackling. I understand what they meant. There's an energy to New York I haven't felt anywhere else in the world. I continued further and further downtown, eventually reaching the plaza of the World Trade Center. It just seemed to draw me in, this 110-storey landmark above the biggest city of them all. I couldn't wait to get up there. I grabbed a coffee and then, realising I was running late, hailed a taxi back to the hotel, hoping Michelle had finished her own run and would be ready to go.

I had a quick shower, got dressed and then knocked on Michelle's door. It was 8.30 by now, much later than I'd hoped, but if we hurried there was still time to get up the tower before the crowds arrived. A dazed-looking Michelle eventually answered the door. She'd slept through her alarm. I stomped off, asking her to hurry while I waited in my room. Bored and impatient, I switched on the TV just as the news channels began telecasting the first images of the north tower, hit by the first plane at 8.46 am.

I flipped from station to station in disbelief. The Fox channel coverage, like the others, was confused, not even sure at first what had hit the tower, or if it was a bomb. The footage, shot through the trees from below, didn't really show the devastation. It wasn't until the first helicopter shots were shown that people realised the impact of what was happening. Then, at 9.03 am, the second plane hit the south tower – where Michelle and I might have been standing if our plans had been on schedule. The reaction from the commentators was a stunned, 'Oh my God' – spoken quietly, as if they couldn't quite believe what they were seeing.

I rang Michelle on the hotel phone but she was still in the shower and told me to leave her alone while she got ready. She hung up on me before I could blurt out what had happened so I ran to her room. Dripping and wrapped in a towel, she eventually opened the door, and for the next few hours we sat glued to the television, watching the towers burn and bellow smoke like two giant chimneys, before President Bush formally announced what we could see – that terrorists had brought down the biggest symbol of western economic power.

Even so, it just didn't seem real that it was happening *so* close. I rang home at some stage, concerned that my family would be worried. When I told Mum that a plane had flown into the building where we'd planned to be, her response was almost of disinterest. It wasn't until later that I realised why: it was late at night back in Sydney and many people had no idea what had just happened. Mum wouldn't have had the slightest idea that I was talking about a giant passenger jet. In her mind, it was probably a small plane which had hit the side of a very large building and come off second best.

It wasn't until later in the day, when Michelle and I ventured outside to see the damage for ourselves, that reality set in. What I saw was horrifying but compelling; the worst and best of humanity on show. There was ash and noise and confusion in a city where smog and noise and confusion were usually accepted as part of everyday life. In the flow of people streaming north from the devastation there were so many faces – in any other circumstance too many to look at – yet from that day, each one is a lasting memory in my mind. There were people slumped on the footpath, pasted in white ash and weeping, while others were screaming, and many were silent. That day, every single New Yorker looked up – only to see the cloud of dust which was all that remained of the Twin Towers.

New York is usually a brash, harsh place that can be so easily misunderstood by outsiders. It's a place where you can be, feel or try to be anything that you want but where single-mindedness is necessary to achieve those dreams. On this day I saw the city change. I saw the good that shone from tragedy, a huge city of millions come together in the manner of a small country town; people rushing to support one another, responding to a disaster with dignity and love.

Michelle and I stayed for three days, unable to get out because the city was in lock-down. It was an endless loop of wandering the streets, trying to make sense of what had happened. Fashion Week and meeting Mr Armani had been cancelled but it was the last thing on my mind. Our families wanted us to come home but we couldn't even if we wanted to because the airspace above New York remained closed. We also wanted to help if we could. We felt part of something that was enormous, compelling and frightening all at the same time. We tried to give blood at one stage but the queues were too long. In those few days there were 36,000 units of blood donated, such was the response. Only 258 units were needed.

On the third night, Michelle and I went down to Union Square on 14th Street, which had become a central grieving point for thousands. During the day people came to post pictures of their missing loved ones or write messages and pin them to the steel fence which ringed the square, dominated by a statue of the first US president, George Washington. It had been a place of social activism for 150 years and even amid the devastation the notion of free speech was played out. At times arguments sprang up between those who came to preach peace and others who came to vent their anger and desperation.

At night people came to light candles in remembrance and respect and sang songs in an attempt to draw the city together. They chalked messages of peace on the base of the Washington statue. We were there among them one night when a group of four New York firemen walked past. As if on cue, people rose to their feet to give them a standing ovation. It was a very emotional moment. Michelle and I joined the clapping and cheering in appreciation for their courage and selflessness in saving others inside the burning buildings – which, tragically, cost the lives of 350 of their colleagues.

In those days I saw the best that New York had to offer. It wasn't the breathtaking skyline, the history, the excitement or the staggering wealth of Wall Street, but its human spirit. It was impossible for me to understand completely what the people in front of me were going through but I was a witness nonetheless and it left an indelible mark on my own life.

It was a life-changing experience, as if I'd grown up in a single day. I was 18 years old and had seen plenty of the world but only through the sheltered prism of swimming pools, red carpet openings and sponsorship events. I now realised it was a complex place where wonderful things happened but terrible things did, too. The beauty and wonder of an autumn day had changed to ugliness and terror in the blink of an eye.

What about my own lucky escape? I am a believer in fate, and I felt grateful, guilty almost, that events had conspired to keep me away from the very building I'd so desperately wanted to be standing on top of with Michelle. What had seemed important to me – the travel, the buzz of being involved with the fashion world, letting my hair down a bit – now seemed irrelevant. Somehow, life's priorities had become a bit skewiff; too many delays on too many important decisions and not enough attention paid to people who matter.

It's a lesson worth remembering as I relive the horror a decade later. This is a time to knuckle down and concentrate on getting the important things right – in and outside of the pool.

four

20 SEPTEMBER 2011

It's hard to complain about the way things are going at the moment, although I'm sure that won't last. There must be ups and downs ahead because training, like life, is a roller-coaster that must be endured in order to enjoy the thrills. Gennadi and his group of elite Swiss swimmers, who I'm training with, are preparing for the first high altitude camp of the campaign and the work feels good. My only whinge is the decision to put the winter tent back over the pool. We've been training under blue skies for months, a joy that I knew couldn't last. I really don't like the claustrophobic feeling of the winter cover – every morning session is dark and cold and every afternoon is darker and colder. Why have they done it now, when it's still 25 degrees outside? Surely there's no need to rush.

Gennadi and I have been working on a way to increase the speed of my stroke rotation without compromising my technique. We've found that my natural inclination to pull harder beneath the surface is actually counterproductive, not only because it changes my stroke but because it also demands extra effort which, in turn, increases the build-up of lactic acid (created when there isn't enough oxygen for energy), which would be like pulling on the handbrake in a sports car.

The new stroke technique we're developing means the increased rotation speed comes above the water as I throw my arm forward at the top of the stroke, a little like surf swimmers who have to cope with the rolling ocean but with a bit more finesse. Like numerous other aspects of training, the changes feel unnatural at first and it will only be through repetition that I can be sure they'll work under race conditions when the pressure of competition can mean mistakes begin to creep into technique.

What's special about today is that for the first time since I returned to the pool ten months ago, I've laid down a marker – a time – which gives me a sense of where I am. Late in the afternoon, toward the end of a satisfying training session, I decided to swim a 100-metre time trial. Gennadi and I had an agreement that if I felt like stopping mid-session and 'racing' then he would encourage it.

Everything has felt a bit surreal to this point, experimenting with technique and training to tease out potential improvement, but it's all been guesswork until now. I felt good, it was warm and the water was silk. I signalled to Gennadi that it was time and he eagerly grabbed his stopwatch. I don't think I've ever swum a faster 100 metres in training, even in my earlier career. That said, Gennadi is notorious for being a 'fast' timer, which means he tends to anticipate a finish and what he clocks might be slightly out, but even accounting for his enthusiasm my time was a tick over 51 seconds. With a rough calculation of an accepted 2 per cent improvement between training and race day, it means I can probably go under 50 seconds.

The bottom line is that, although the time was reasonable, I need to improve by two seconds in training to be competitive at the elite level. That's a lot but it also means I'm capable of racing faster than I've ever raced. My personal best, when I won bronze in Athens, is 48.56 seconds and I can't help feeling excited that I'm capable of nudging that number again so soon. Perhaps I should be a bit more circumspect. There's a long way to go. Am I right to compare my times to what I achieved at peak training or should I simply be concentrating on the best I can do now?

James Magnussen, the young Aussie who swam 47.63 to win the 100 metres at the World Championships in Shanghai a month ago, is the man to beat but I don't see that as a target. I've never paid too much attention to the performances of others, not because they aren't impressive or that I don't respect them but because I would be setting limits on myself. While many people are awe-struck by others' performances, I look at them, acknowledge them and then concentrate on my own improvement – how can I go faster. People will continue to swim faster and times will be lowered. I never thought about limits when I swam before and I have the same attitude now.

The next thing that will happen in sprinting is that we'll start to define 100-metre competitors as being front-end and back-end swimmers; in other words those who swim the first half faster than the second, and vice versa. I revolutionised the 400 metres as a back-end swimmer and now I'm working on the same philosophy for the 100. James is one of the few elite competitors who's capable of swimming the second 50 metres faster than the first and the reality is that, to even make the Australian team, I have to compete against him and a dozen others who can break 50 seconds.

It's something I don't want to dwell on, and not because I'm afraid of the competition; quite the opposite. The difficulty, physically and psychologically, is that I have to peak twice, first to qualify and then to race in London. If I don't make the first hurdle – the Australian Championships in Adelaide next March, which are doubling as the Olympic team qualifier – then I won't even get the chance to start.

The 105-metres freestyle isn't an Olympic event and yet I've lost count of the number of times people have wistfully told me how close I came to winning the gold medal in the 100 metres at the Athens Olympics – if I just had a few more metres.

It wasn't only my best performance – 48.56 seconds – but probably the most comfortable I've ever been in a 100-metre race, even though it was an Olympic final. The 400 metres on the first day had been enormously stressful because of the intense media scrutiny over Craig Stevens' decision to give up his place for me, and my performance in the 200 metres two days later was determined and controlled, but on this day and in this race I was totally relaxed. It was a race where there was simply no pressure. Yes, I had a chance of medalling but even if I'd finished without a place there was still the satisfaction of having reached the final.

I was among the last to the wall at 50 metres but nailed the turn. Instead of having to thrash my way through the wash I came up well and was set up for a good second lap. From Lane 8 I couldn't see anyone else other than the swimmer next to me but I knew I was coming home very quickly. In hindsight it was probably an advantage to swim in an outside lane and not be caught up in the carnage. I wouldn't have swum the race any differently if I was in a centre lane. In fact, if I had a choice, I'd probably swim in either two or seven, simply because I like clean water and avoid the wash as much as possible.

I touched the wall and turned instinctively to see the board – 48.56 seconds. Not bad, I thought. It was only as an afterthought that I looked to see where I'd finished: third. I'd won a bronze medal in a race that was a bonus rather than an expectation.

The only reason why I swam 100-metre events, at least initially, was to keep my speed sharp for the 200 and to swim the relays, which is what I enjoyed doing. It was only when I suddenly began winning events in 2001 and 2002 that I decided to take it more seriously. It also coincided with the period when I began to seriously question my future.

My coach, Doug Frost, had never devised a plan for me to swim the 100 metres. Neither did I learn to dive or turn for that event, which has almost no margin for error, let alone train specifically to develop raw speed. These are some of the reasons I'm confident I can now swim significantly faster than ever before, particularly if I can match better pool skills with the new stroke developed with Gennadi's help.

I've looked back at the 100-metre races I swam and it's clear that, unlike the 200 and 400s, I lacked a strategy beyond going as fast as possible, which was probably the only tactic I could have used, given my training was slanted toward the middle distance events. I felt as if I needed 60 metres just to get going.

The 100 metres is a race that requires the elimination of all mistakes and my training is much more specific now – and so are my tactics. The dive, for example, becomes a critical element of the race, particularly for me because my size and weight are an advantage if I can get it right. The entry point has to be fairly flat – roughly 30 degrees – to pierce the water like a spear, making as small a hole as possible. It's something I was never taught to do; instead, my dive had a distinct, feline-esque curve which may have looked nice but wasted precious power. Now I stand a lot taller, with my weight better distributed, and dive out further.

Once I hit the water I have to remain tight to make the most of the force. It feels like I'm doing nothing, which is counterintuitive, but if I count to two before making any movement I can streamline further underwater, which is much faster than swimming.

My first kick goes up rather than down, so as not to disrupt the streamline position and to deliver a small propulsion while directing me back to the surface at about 13 metres. By comparison I used to kick hard from the dive and surface at about 10 or 11 metres. One of the commentators during the Athens final made the remark that my dive was awful and I didn't streamline. He was right.

At this point in the race I want to find a speed that is fast but comfortable because there's no sense in over-extending down the first lap and leaving nothing for the way home. It's where the new stroke comes into play, something I have to learn to trust in a race situation, even though it feels so different. As I approach the wall at the halfway mark I need to begin to increase power and then use the spike in speed which comes from the turn.

One of the biggest changes to the sport in my absence has been the rethink about what makes a good turn. Before, the theory was that taller swimmers had an advantage because they could turn earlier, touching the wall with both feet while on their side and then rotating up to the surface.

Now we're taught to flip onto our backs so we are facing the surface as we kick, feet slightly higher than the shoulders to angle down and beneath the wash created by the surge of swimmers arriving at the wall together. The idea is to be in a tight body position on the wall in order to maximise the power of the turn itself.

After the turn I travel another 11 or 12 metres under water, trying to time my surfacing to get over the top of the second wash which comes down the pool from the swimmers' feet, then use it like the face of a wave at the beach. Breathing is also important, particularly at this point in the race when I need oxygen to fuel the charge home. I haven't worked out yet how many breaths I want to take in the 100 metres in London. In theory, it would be as few breaths as possible while remaining comfortable, but that never happens. It's not going to be comfortable.

The number of breaths varies widely among elite athletes

but generally they want to get out fast so they take a few breaths on the way out and then have to survive oxygen depletion on the way home. When I swam into third place at Athens I took between 16 and 18 breaths, which is on the high side of normal.

I'd like to cut that back to just 10 breaths for London – four breaths in the first 50 metres and six coming back, because I don't want to be too depleted with 30 metres to go. At that point my brain is telling me that I'm going faster and my stroke is longer when the opposite is true. In the end, it'll be the man who slows down the least who will win the race.

Even though the dive and the turn are really important to manage, in my mind the only place you can lose a tight race is at the finish. I don't touch the wall to stop myself at the end of the race but to stop the clock, and if that means breaking a finger then so be it.

The speed of the last stroke is actually quite fast as you rotate and stretch. I don't always finish with my left hand – in fact, I've been finishing on my right lately and I have no idea why. One of the things I learned as a youngster was how to turn and finish on either arm, so that's come in handy. It's the same with the turn. Even though the first stroke is always with my right arm when I surface after the dive, it's chance rather than design that decides which side I will turn on at the wall each time.

Some swimmers train to swim robotically – the same number of strokes, the same pace and the same turns – but I prefer to get feedback from the water, even in a race as short as the 100 metres, so I can adapt to the way I'm feeling at the time.

We change each day; we learn. None of us swim the same every time we get up on the starting blocks.

five

6 OCTOBER 2011

A couple of nights ago I spent half an hour spinning my car in circles in a darkened Swiss car park. It wasn't madness, hoonery or boredom but a desperate attempt to get used to driving in the icy European winter, which is almost upon us.

It might have looked amusing but it wasn't that funny actually. I'd been driving through the mountains to a small ski resort at Livigno, a mountain-top village just across the Swiss border into northern Italy where the squad was attending a high altitude camp.

There'd been an overnight snap which had dumped half a metre of snow across the Alps. The hills above Tenero were covered in white as I left the next morning. Then it snowed again and by the time I'd passed through the motorway tunnel at the Swiss city of Davos where it crosses into Italy, the road was blanketed in white. It looked like Christmas – well, the kind of Christmas you see on picture postcards, anyway. At first I was captivated by the beautiful view (how typically Australian) but the danger was quickly obvious. I had no chains and I'd never heard of the difference between summer and winter tyres.

I pulled over and called some Swiss friends to ask what I should do. It was a steep climb to the resort where we'd be training, which sits almost 2000 metres above sea level, and I didn't want to take any more risks, particularly as Livigno's name is derived from its German origins which, roughly translated, means avalanche. Practise, they advised. Get to a safe place and get used to slipping around. The car park was the best place I could find. After 30 minutes or so I continued on my way, a bit more comfortable in my foreign surroundings.

The journey home a few days later was much easier, partly because the cold snap had been just that. The roads were clear and the layer of white temporary, at least for now – a bit like the altitude training itself.

The benefit of this type of training is that it teaches you about how the body oxygenates itself and, specifically, how to deal with the anxiety-driven breath that you take when you are running out of oxygen. Swimming at high altitude mimics that kind of breathing. I need to learn how to breathe less when I race because each breath you take tends to slow you down. Like many other aspects of racing, it's a matter of tiny margins, but they all add up to a total performance. I want to be comfortable taking fewer breaths and getting the best out of them.

It's actually the hardest thing for me to do because it's the opposite of what I was used to as a middle-distance swimmer, when my routine was to take breaths with almost every stroke. To starve my body of oxygen is really difficult but as a part of my training Gennadi asks me to complete a set of laps in fewer breaths than I'd intend to during a race, to convince my body that it *is* possible, and not to panic.

It's called hypoxic training. I might have to swim 25 metres at high intensity but with few breaths and then complete the lap with a much more comfortable five-stroke breath. I might also complete an entire 50-metre lap without breathing at all.

In essence it's the biggest challenge; to convince myself that I can swim without taking a breath and not be anxious that I'm going to drown. Instead of turning my head to take the breath, which is easy, I take another few strokes to improve the performance. It's a battle of the mind as much as it is of the body.

There's another benefit to altitude training; a tiny window of opportunity that hits you after two or three days of work: you feel amazing. It doesn't last long, but it's the moment when you can lift your performance to a new level. There is a skill in recognising it and using it to almost leapfrog forward in your training – a physiological moment when you feel better in the water; feel as if you can do more. If you can grasp it, the body remembers whether you're at altitude or not, and it means you can do it again and again.

There's also something fresh about driving to the top of a mountain – it gives you a clarity of mind that transcends sport and enables you to rationalise things better. I tend to do a lot of walking while I'm up there, to enhance that sense of wellbeing, and it stays with you when you come back home, a new focus that allows you to get back into routine training and concentrate on what more needs to be done. You also need to back off the work a little to allow your body to recover – but crucially it's the moment when you can make that leap forward in performance. It's a balancing act.

To be honest, though, despite all this talk of clarity and wellbeing, I've felt pretty sluggish since I got back to Tenero. It hasn't been a bad week as such, but everything feels a bit harder to get through. Most of the time I'm very process-driven; focusing on the task at hand and getting the best out of it, but I wouldn't be human if I didn't cast my mind forward from time to time. I just have to fight the sense of being over-whelmed.

I can't help worrying about what might happen if I feel this way in a few weeks when I swim publicly again for the first time in Singapore. I don't want to feel this way when I'm there and the chances are that I won't. In the interim I'll console myself with the idea that I can't expect to feel good all the time. In fact during training you're not supposed to feel good most of the time.

I really have no idea about what I'm expecting when I'm there. All I can think is that it will be my first competitive swim after a long break. It's the World Cup short-course swimming comp, which starts in Singapore and follows on in Beijing and then Tokyo. I should have a better answer than that but I guess I'm waiting to see what happens as much as anyone else, not least because it's a short-course meet (swum in a 25-metre pool), which I've always detested. I did my best to avoid these sorts of competitions in the past. I couldn't see the value in swimming for the sake of it in a pool which took only a handful of strokes to cross before you turned, meaning you had no chance of finding a rhythm. Still, I'm stuck with it. A victim of my own decision.

I'm planning to swim the 100-metres individual medley on the first day of competition and then the 100-metres butterfly on the second day. I'm doing those events in all three cities and have also entered the 100-metres freestyle in Tokyo, which poses the really big question – do I swim or not? That decision will be made by Gennadi, not me.

I can get away with swimming the medley because most people will see it as a fun event, when in fact it's one of the most taxing races you can swim because of the effort to change strokes mid-race. It hurts a lot, but I like it. My expectations there are low; it will just be about getting into the pool and racing. It might be terrible, because I haven't specifically trained for it, but I might surprise myself.

The 100 fly is different. I think I should be competitive for that so it's a serious hit-out, to qualify for a final and then race against other competitors who are better than me at this event. I want the feeling and the taste of competition again.

Of late, all the preparation for competition has been throwing me back to childhood memories, maybe because it was a simpler time. I grew up in a normal house, the youngest child of a normal family with normal values and modest aspirations. I often think that our street would have looked comfortable as a set for *Neighbours*, as Aussie a cliché as you can get:

rough-cut wooden telegraph poles and a criss-cross of power lines softened by eucalypt and peppermint trees, backyard cricket, cubbies in the bush and tadpoles down at the creek. Everything but the Holden – our car was a Toyota Camry.

It's not a critical description; I remember it in the most positive of ways because it's been my bedrock in a world that at times doesn't seem real. It's no accident that many of Australia's sporting icons have come from similar backgrounds, where nothing is taken for granted and families make sacrifices to foster success. It's not just financial impost but simple things like the grinding task of getting up early six days a week, doing pick-ups and drop-offs and trekking to countless events to offer support.

These are the early experiences that leave an indelible mark; where the basics of the sport are ingrained through endless repetition, the grandstands are half empty and the towels have to be washed and dried overnight. For all the moments of glory, like standing on an Olympic podium with the weight of an Olympic medal around my neck, I'll always remember the plywood crates shoved together to make a dais down at the local pool and the brushed silver medallions that were engraved at the local hardware store.

Christmas best sums up my family, the biggest celebration because it signified everything we cherished – hot weather, holidays and family. And lots of presents. The size or cost didn't matter, as long as there was a sea of wrapping paper covering the lounge room floor. Even as young children we were allowed to stay up late on Christmas Eve, sometimes past midnight, to put out ginger beer and biscuits for Santa and to arrange the presents under the tree. Then it was back to bed to sleep until a decent hour in the morning. I guess it was Mum and Dad's way of ensuring we slept past dawn.

Present-opening the next morning was a structured affair. One person at a time opened a gift while the others watched politely, my sister Christina and I fidgeting with eager hands until it was our turn. Rather than an orgy of ripping and tearing, each present had to be opened carefully, cards from relatives read out aloud in an appropriate tone and without shaking the envelope first to see if there was any money inside. This was a time to be grateful for what we received.

My father was the driving force behind our Christmas cheer. It wasn't about materialism but a reflection of his own childhood. His father, Cecil – or Cec as he was known – grew up around Armidale in northern New South Wales and was a farmer until rheumatic fever changed his life and fortune. In 1946, and at the age of 22, unable to farm because of his heart condition, he left the land with his young wife, Gwen McLeod, a local farmer's daughter, and headed to Sydney to find work. It's strange when I think of what might have been and what might not, thanks to the quirk of fate.

My gran is still driven by the hand of fate. To her, Sydney has been an ugly place of hard work and disappointment. I asked her recently how long it had been since she had made a trip to central Sydney from the family home in suburban Padstow. 'Must be 30 years,' she replied.

Grandpa Cec found work as a crane operator in the warehouse district of St Peters, where he would stay for the next four decades. Settled financially, they now wanted a family. Ken Thorpe, my dad, was born in 1949 and was the second of Gwen and Cec's seven children (their first died in childbirth). His early years were spent moving around different rented accommodation, until the mid 1950s, when Cec and Gwen took their growing family and moved to Padstow, into one of the government-built homes which fed the city's need for expansion and push west toward the Blue Mountains.

Despite the cheap housing, it was always a struggle for Cec to provide for such a large family on a single income. Not that they were any different from the families around them: God-fearing and hard-working in an era when lives were set early, rooted for good and spent accepting what you had and not what you didn't. No one went without but there were few luxuries in life, even at Christmas, when a single gift each was all they could usually afford, hence my dad's desire to provide a Christmas bounty each year for his own family.

Dad has always had a reputation for not showing much emotion. When the cameras panned to the crowd after one of my races he would be standing and clapping with everyone else but without the clamour of those around him. At times it seemed as if he could barely raise a smile, but perceptions can be misleading. My father is the kind of guy who sits back and watches with quiet satisfaction at the impact he's made; whether it's his son winning a gold medal or his kids excitedly opening the presents he'd been able to provide through hard work.

But as it is for most people, it's the intangible contributions of our parents which ensure our achievements are possible. The biggest impact my own mum and dad made wasn't the Christmas presents, of course, but their time and their interest in the lives of me and my sister.

Aunt Cheryl was the reason my parents met. Dad's youngest sister played netball with a vivacious and friendly girl called

Margaret Hathaway and decided that her teammate might be the right girl for her oldest brother, who was still at home and a bit on the shy side. In May 1977, she orchestrated a blind date at a restaurant near Botany Bay. By the end of the night, apparently my mother had decided that the quiet bloke opposite was the right man for her. They were engaged six weeks later and married in January the following year after a seven-month engagement, their lives so organised that the block of land had already been bought and the footings for the house dug two days after the wedding.

Although they grew up in the same area, the Hathaways and the Thorpes were from opposite sides of the industrial fence. While Cec and Gwen Thorpe had six kids and were strictly blue collar, Jim and Gertrude Hathaway had two children – Mum and her younger brother – and were decidedly white collar. Poppy worked for Sunbeam as a fitter and turner but was really an inventor who helped design shearing equipment, while Nan opened a shoe store in East Hills which became one of the city's first factory outlets. And while the Thorpes were enthusiastic Baptists with enough moral elbow room for Cec to have the occasional beer and a flutter with his mates, the Hathaways were strict Congregational Christians and ran a house in which no one swore and alcohol and other vices such as tobacco never crossed the threshold.

Despite their differences, the core values of the two families were largely the same. My dad and his father-in-law, in particular, always got on very well – even to the extent that Dad copied the design of the Hathaways' home simply because he believed Jim knew what he was doing. He even used the same builder. As far as Dad was concerned, the design was tried and tested, so why change?

When it came to children, Mum and Dad decided to split the difference between their two families. I'm told four was the ideal number but it changed on 13 October 1982 when I was born. Christina, who'd arrived a couple of years earlier, had been a nice normal size, but not me. I was close to 4.5 kilograms – 10 pounds in the old scale – and Mum's blood pressure went through the roof. Helped along by her doctor's advice, she and Dad had a change of heart – two kids were enough.

Whenever I describe my childhood I always hesitate to use the term 'ordinary', in case it's misconstrued as a declaration of some sort of inadequacy, a kid from the wrong side of the tracks. It's the same when I tell people we were an average family who made the most of limited finances. It's not a suggestion of hardship, but of commonsense and diligence, because I never felt that it defined me or limited my opportunities. The world was what I made it.

Even the place where I grew up – a suburb called Milperra in Sydney's west – might have negative connotations because of an infamous shootout between rival bikie gangs that took place there. I was two years old at the time and had no idea about it until years later when I was asked about it by a French journalist. If I'd been in a defensive mood I would have pointed out that it actually happened in the next-door suburb of Revesby, although the Revesby Massacre doesn't have quite the same ring. I guess that's the media for you.

Our family life was ordinary in every positive sense of the word. My parents are conservative by nature, which makes their backing of my sporting career with all its inherent insecurities even more remarkable. My father in particular was always anxious about money, insisting on paying off their house in just 12 months – Dad working three jobs and Mum working two – before they had children.

Home life was the same: plain but intrinsically good and decent. Christina and I went to the local public school – Milperra Primary – which was barely 500 metres from our front door. It was established after the Great War for the children of returning servicemen and, like the caravan park at Forster where we would go for our annual holidays, the surrounding streets – Pozieres, Bullecourt, Amiens and Lone Pine – echoed their roots. My mother had taught at the school until the year Christina started kindy, when she negotiated a transfer to avoid the probability that one day she would end up teaching one of her kids.

Mum wanted to remain our mother and not our teacher. It went hand in hand with the sense of right and wrong, effort and reward that were instilled into our household. Religion didn't play a significant role in our family beyond regular attendance at church, although the core values were front and centre in our daily lives.

It's hardly a surprise that Mum, as a primary school teacher, believed the public education system should be supported, and later, even when sporting scholarships began to flood in, my parents insisted that I attended the local school, East Hills Boys Technology High School in nearby Panania. There's another thing about school teachers: they find it very hard to drop the act, even at home. Mum still talks to me like a teacher at times and I have to remind her to stop before it does my head in.

Home was a split-level two-storey house with a formal lounge, a dining room and an open plan kitchen, with a second living room and a laundry at the back. The three bedrooms were upstairs. The only part which didn't make sense was a huge concrete slab in the backyard. I could never work out why it was there and it was certainly never used. Eventually Dad dug it up and put in an above-ground swimming pool.

It was a big yard – at least in my eyes – completely flat with nothing but a washing line, and later, a trampoline. There was hardly a plant to be seen, the only exception being a couple of citrus trees which went, too, when Dad decided to clear the area for a cricket pitch, hoping it would magically summon some inner talent which might be lurking inside his young son. He gave up eventually when he accepted that it wasn't my thing, but it took a while before he was convinced. That's when we got the swimming pool. In hindsight, it's funny, because I don't think I ever beat him in that pool. He can't swim, it's true, but he used to race me from one side to the other by running on the bottom of the pool. Looking back, it's still one of my fondest memories.

Our street was a long, straight road on a slight slope. Our house was about halfway down, which was perfect for racing bikes from one end to the other. Thankfully it was a time and place of very little traffic. My sister and I both had friends in surroundings streets, and my mates and I would play in the nearby creek and sometimes head down past the Riverlands Golf Club to the Georges River, which wound its way inland from Botany Bay. We built cubby houses in any available spot, even under the trampoline, and when the pool went in we held mini-triathlons.

Even when swimming began to consume our lives, my parents insisted on maintaining a normality and family aspect to our lives. It was my sister Christina who was the star of the family. She was in the New South Wales squad by the age of 12 and already dreaming of the 1996 Olympic Games in Atlanta.

Weekday afternoons were spent with our maternal grand-parents, doing homework after school and before training, and Sundays meant a roast dinner with the paternal clan. When the swimming season ended around the Easter holidays we'd always go away on a family holiday, usually squeezed into a caravan towed up to the mid north coast.

The Forster–Tuncurry Caravan Park is nestled on the foreshore of one of the Great Lakes about four hours north of Sydney. To a kid, the place was huge and smelled of space and freedom with its long clipped lawns, flocks of pelicans and the still waters of Ohmas Bay, the surf breaking in the distance. The park also had a couple of small swimming pools, where I first learned to splash around. In hindsight, it was an important introduction to water and swimming – the pool was a place of enjoyment and fun. Sometimes, in later years, we'd go further north and venture into Queensland to places like Dreamworld and Seaworld, but my heart always lay in that caravan park.

I was a Lego kid. My dream job was to be the guy who built the huge displays for the annual exhibition at Darling Harbour. My Lego-centricity was well known in the family. Invariably a relative would give me some Lego kit and, desperate to build whatever was inside, in a matter of hours I'd have finished it, dismantled it and already started on an alternative design.

When I think about it, it really sums me up as a child. I loved playing outside with my friends but I was equally happy inside, in my own company, something which has never really changed. I still have all my Lego collected in several plastic tubs stored at my house and I often buy it as presents for my nephew and other kids, probably because I know they'll relent and let me build it for them.

s i x

18 OCTOBER 2011

I t was my 29th birthday last Thursday. I had hoped to feel fantastic – swimming well, times tumbling and excited by the prospect of what lies ahead over the next eight or nine months. Instead, I was as crook as a dog and feeling pretty low. Could I have ever had a worse birthday?

The only saving grace was that Mum is here, although it wasn't the celebration either of us expected. Rather than sharing a nice Italian meal down by the lake I asked her to make me chicken soup. It's crazy but she's travelled halfway around the world to play nursemaid, even inching her way down the steep, winding hill in my car to buy the ingredients, never having driven in Europe before. Chicken soup is a childhood thing – a comfort rather than a cure – which says there is someone who cares. Lemonade is the other taste I remember from my childhood, administered when Christina and I were sick and vomiting; like some sort of sugary mouth rinse. I tried to find it once here in Switzerland when I had a bout of food poisoning but ended up having to make do with some sort of raspberry drink. It didn't work and the resulting hurl over the dining table in vibrant red wasn't pretty!

So my birthday was spent on the couch watching movies, sipping on soup and opening a few presents. I didn't even feel like tucking into the Darrell Lea licorice or the macadamia chocolates which I adore and usually get as a birthday treat.

I'm not sure what happened but I'm not the only one on the squad to get sick after returning from the altitude camp. Maybe it was the change in temperature, from a quite humid 26 degrees by the lake to 11 degrees in the mountains. Elite athletes live on the edge physically, our immune systems teetering even during heavy training, so any drastic change can hit us for a six. I knew something was wrong. I could sense it during a training session; that I shouldn't push myself because I was getting sick. But of course I couldn't resist, ignoring my instincts and finishing the session with some sprint-work. I swam well, probably the fastest since I arrived here, but regretted it the next day when I couldn't get out of bed. I ended up missing two more days of valuable training.

I shouldn't feel so sorry for myself really. It's not as if this kind of thing hasn't happened in the past. I've often trained through illness, some of it my own making. Preparation is rarely perfect and, right now, I don't have time to be sick. To make matters worse, we're swimming under the circus tent

– the balloon as we call it – because winter is on its way. I don't have a view of the mountains anymore and inside the tent it smells and feels as if there should be people running around in lab coats testing for anti-viruses and global pandemics. But I have to make it work.

Besides, there's been an unexpected bonus. Even 48 hours away from the pool during training has an impact and it's usually negative, but in this case there's been a positive spin. It's reconfirmed that I should trust my natural talent a little more. I might have won bronze in the 100-metres freestyle in Athens but until recently I've harboured niggling doubts about making the transition from a middle-distance swimmer to a sprinter.

But as soon as I slipped back into the water I could feel a change in my stroke, a relaxation that hadn't been there before. For months Gennadi has been pushing me to slow everything down, to become comfortable with the refined stroke so it would work reliably at high speed. There's something Zen about the whole idea – it's 'Gennadi science'. He trains you for speed by making you swim slow. And for the first time I think it might be working.

The accepted philosophy about the 100 metres is simple: you get out there and go as fast as possible. But I've come to realise that it might not be the best strategy; that it might be more complicated than a flat-out sprint, and now that I've developed some natural speed in my stroke I can start playing around with combinations.

For example, there's a point in every freestyle stroke called recovery, where the hand is poised in the air, just before you reach forward to plunge it back into the water. The movement is a bit like tossing a ball underarm but in reverse. It's a passive part of the stroke where you aren't propelling yourself and, by relaxing, I can create a micro-second of rest. It doesn't seem like much but in this game every gain in efficiency – no matter how tiny – can add up to a much better performance.

The biggest issue in Singapore will be anxiety – trying to counter the fears and excitement of racing again after five years. I have nerves like everyone else but in general I'm not a nervous person, particularly when it comes to competition, because my training results have always been a great predictor of what I will do in a race – at least, in the past. My pre-race routine has always been designed around harnessing the anxiety to work to my advantage when the gun goes off. But this situation is very different. I'm used to being ready to race, physically and psychologically. This time I'm not ready, on either score. I'm going to have to see how I feel on the day – a case of suck it and see. I hope I don't vomit.

It's the first race that really counts. I'll be very nervous but if I can get past the medley without too much embarrassment then I'll be fine. I have to look at it not so much as a race to win but as a marker, to see where I am at this point in the process. I may well come away feeling that I've wasted my time for the last 12 months. I don't feel like I have but I can't help but have that sort of negative thought – what am I doing? Why am I doing this again? – popping into my head.

The truth is, I've really enjoyed the process so far and even if I swim poorly I'll continue to swim because I love doing it. And now I've started, it's something I have to finish.

The strange thing is that people have been talking about the butterfly as much as the freestyle. It's something I hadn't really considered before. I haven't been a competitive butter-flier since my junior days. But people around me are starting to ask about it as a possible qualification for the Olympic team. Perhaps they're just musings about what might be. Expectations again. It'd be a tough ask considering the depth of talent in the Australian team at the moment but I don't want to rule out anything.

At this stage the focus has been on the 100-metres free-style. The stroke changes have been complicated and now it's a matter of time and repetition. The silver lining is that the distance I've been doing in training each week – more than 60 kilometres – is setting me up well aerobically for the 200 metres. Gennadi and I have started to talk about tweaking the training schedule when I get back from Asia to begin specific preparation for the 200.

Although the 400 metres would be regarded as my signature event, I've probably had more serious battles in the 200 metres over the years. For a start, I didn't win all the time. In the early days Michael Klim always made it tough by using his front-end speed to make me chase him, and Grant Hackett beat me once and chased me often. Then there was Pieter van den Hoogenband, who beat me at the 2000 Sydney Olympics when the world – and me for that matter – expected I would win.

The race has been special to me because it's a true sprint that requires tactics and patience to swim well. Looking at my split times over the years, it took me a while to come to terms with how to structure the pace so I could make the most of my kick in the last 50 metres. Not all races end up this way of course, but this is the way I believe the 200 metres should be swum, at least for me:

The first 50 metres has to be a comfortable, easy speed which is fast but not overwhelming. At times I've been surprised at just how quickly I've been able to swim it, compared to a 100-metre race where you put in a lot more effort for a marginally faster split.

The second 50 is the most important part of the race, being able to take that sense of easiness from the first lap to build into the race. It has to feel like it's easy because if you're already trying to force yourself to swim faster, you're not going to take that speed into the back half of the race. You can play around with it by going out a little easier but in terms of efficiency that's the best way to get through the first 100.

When I turn into the third 50 I should be feeling as though I need to increase speed, when in reality I'm only maintaining speed. The increase should be gradual, coming out of the turn and into the first part of the lap as if you're warming to a really solid performance. The last 15 or 20 metres of the lap is where I want to feel as if I'm winding up for the final lap. That's where my legs come in. Contrary to the opinions of many commentators over the years who seem to think that I have consciously brought in the six-beat kick, it actually starts as a consequence of me working harder with my arms.

You need to carry speed into the final turn because it's too difficult to generate afterwards. As I come out off it, I feel as if I'm in full speed for the last 50 metres of the race. My kick is responsive to my stroke. I can't have one without the other, even in training. There are certain speeds at which I don't have to kick hard. Then, when the intensity of my stroke changes, so does my kick. There is a balance between the two.

What I try to do as I fatigue down the last lap is make sure the stroke feels stronger. Although it's actually shortening, I have to make it feel as if it's long, and my kick responds to that feeling. And even though you've been feeling the pain since the third 50 – when the lactic acid explodes in your body – in the first half of the last lap you still feel as if you have some control of your body. But the last 20 metres is largely mental: about 11 full seconds of willing yourself through the pain.

So how have my better-known swims compared to this plan?

2000 Olympics, Sydney

After the fireworks of the opening night when I won the 400 metres in world record time and anchored our amazing win in the 4 × 100 metres relay, the day of the 200 was a complete contrast.

Pieter van den Hoogenband had been foxing about his form in the lead-up to the Games and exploded in the semifinals that day to break the world record, which I almost matched in my semifinal immediately afterwards. And of course there was the ill-informed speculation about my health after that race, the media accusing me of sulking about losing my time to Pieter, simply because I hadn't fronted the media conference. They couldn't have got it more wrong, I wasn't well and needed to rest, but I would never use it as an excuse for the race that followed.

In the race itself I knew Pieter would almost certainly be ahead at the first turn. I wasn't going to chase him. It's a great lesson in this race that there are different swimmers competing and to chase a sprint specialist when I was essentially a middle-distance swimmer who also sprinted would have been a big mistake. It also shows the value of swimming your own race, which I have always advocated.

My race plan remained the same, easing through the second 50 in order to be neck and neck with Pieter. So far so good. Then, I remember going through the turn into the third 50 and realising that something wasn't quite right. By the time I was halfway down the lap I should have been increasing the effort but it felt like something wasn't quite there. Something was amiss. We were tied at the turn.

I pushed off the wall for the last 50 but when I surfaced, instead of finding the stroke I needed there was nothing left in the tank. There wasn't anything I could do then, other than hope Pieter was feeling a whole lot worse than me. If I'd been in that same position in any other race I'd probably have come out a full bodylength in front of Pieter but on that night he swam away from me and I finished almost half a second behind.

2001 World Championships, Fukuoka

By the time I was 19 I'd won three Olympic gold medals and set a handful of world records, but despite the accolades I often still felt as though I was just a kid who could swim fast. The meet at Fukuoka changed all that. There I felt like a fully fledged adult swimmer who not only belonged but was dominant in his sport. I was strong, I owned the arena, I knew what was going to happen.

For this race, most commentators and journalists were convinced that I was motivated by a desire for revenge against Pieter van den Hoogenband for beating me in Sydney. They were wrong. I'd accepted the Sydney result within moments of touching the wall. This was a year later and a new challenge, and I had a quiet knowledge that I was going to swim well. It wouldn't have mattered who was in the race.

The only question was whether I could swim faster than ever before. There was no reason why I couldn't. A few months earlier at the Australian titles in Hobart, which had doubled as the qualifier for Fukuoka, I'd broken Pieter's world record, even though I'd swum a heavy program – including the 800 metres for the first time in competition the night before I swam the 200-metre final.

Despite my sense of calm and expectation, or perhaps because of it, I ended up swimming the Fukuoka race a little differently than I'd planned, going out a little slower, particularly through the middle part of the race. Halfway down the third lap I remember the swim feeling effortless, and even though Pieter was within an arm's length I had so much left that I would win comfortably. My last 50 was actually quicker than the second and third laps. It was the moment I knew I'd found the perfect way to swim the 200.

2004 Olympics, Athens

For the so-called race of the century in Athens I was wrapped up in a different set of emotions. I pretty much knew I was going to win the race, not because of supreme form, as I'd felt in Fukuoka, but because I'd just won the 400 metres despite all the dramas of being disaqualified at the Olympic trials for a false start and the pressure I'd felt to come good on Craig Stevens' offer of his place so that I could swim. It was the most pressure and expectation I'd ever felt in my life, but now that the race was over, the burden had been lifted and I could just get on with swimming. I felt like a million bucks and I took that energy to the race.

Most of the time I can't recall the detail of races but for some reason I clearly remember sitting in the marshalling area with Pieter, Michael Phelps and Grant Hackett. Everyone was quite relaxed – even Michael, who is known not to be relaxed pre-race, had music blaring through his headphones – but at the moment we were called and stood to walk out onto the pool deck we all went as pale as ghosts. I think we all realised the significance of the moment, emphasised as we emerged into the arena to be confronted not only by a crowd buzzing on the edge of their seats but the brightest orange setting sun, which hung like a giant glowing lantern at the far end of the pool. This moment was special.

I didn't know if my swim was going to develop as a race against the clock or a tactical battle against Pieter and Michael, but I did know that I felt free to respond to whatever happened in the pool and to trust my stroke. If I had to critique anything about the race it would be that I went out a bit too fast, but I couldn't help it; it was a natural reaction to the race rather than an intentional tactic. I just went with my instincts.

I can remember coming out of the turn after 100 metres, taking the lead from Pieter and still feeling very comfortable, which was in contrast to the race in Sydney four years earlier. I knew then that I was in complete control and could ramp it up for the final lap. At the last turn I could see I had him beaten. The replays show that he got close but I had switched off with 20 metres to swim. I couldn't even see what Michael was doing. All I knew was that he was behind Pieter.

The memories are so clear but it all seems long ago and so far removed from where I am now – off-colour and feeling glum as the weather begins to turn in preparation for a European winter. It reinforces the fact that there's a long way to go.

seven

25 OCTOBER 2011

I'm back at high altitude in Livigno. If there was ever a place where I could get away from the public glare but still be able to train seriously it would be in a medieval village founded by shepherds at the top of a mountain.

We've backed off training a bit and I feel pretty good; the flu symptoms which ruined my birthday are gone. For the last two days I've felt like a million dollars, actually – training for three short, precise sessions a day then being really active. I'm finding pockets of time to go for walks, gym sessions and even some serious downtime, although I don't want to disconnect from all the work I've done just because I've lightened my load.

I'm leaving for Singapore in a few days and my thoughts have been unavoidably occupied by imagining what it's going to feel like when I get there – the media attention, publicity demands and expectation, not to mention my own nervous thrill at being back in competition almost six years after my last competitive swim at the 2006 Commonwealth Games trials.

I don't really know what to expect with the media but at least I'll see them coming. There'll be pressure, but I won't feel like a fugitive, constantly looking over my shoulder at who might be following me, like in the months before I quit in 2006 when I ended up having to drive different cars each day. I accept that there is media interest in elite sport but it was the intensity and the demands about my private life that I found physically and psychologically debilitating, and the reason I was living and training overseas – in Los Angeles – just like now.

My return to competition in Singapore is still in the realm of the unbelievable. Physically I feel ready to race but it's quite strange because my mind isn't there yet. I'll probably feel differently after I've done a media conference when I'm there – reality slapping me in the face.

I don't even know if I'm going to shave down for the competition. I'll probably do it just to feel as if I'm in mode again. There's no particular need – I could probably swim with stubble and it wouldn't slow me down that much – but it makes you feel electric, silken, as if nothing can touch you. It feels as if you're sliding through the water like mercury. I've known some swimmers who won't shave parts of their forearms because it's just too sensitive.

I'm always most nervous about the start of a race. For me, the competition begins not on the blocks but in the marshalling area behind the pool deck. Others like to shut off and focus, sticking in earphones and listening to their iPods, but I like to stay relaxed, maybe even have a chat with my opponents because I want to walk out and engage with the crowd waiting to watch the contest. I want to feel like a gladiator owning the coliseum; that it's my arena and I take ownership of that space. It gives me a sense of control – you win the crowd, you win the race. I take it all in and hold it as energy that I want to use in the race.

Then there's the moment when the whistle is blown, signalling for competitors to stand up on the blocks. It's my last rush – a shock to the nervous system, my heart beating faster. I'm literally on the brink of it all being too much; that I can't actually handle the rush of adrenaline. Instead, I channel it as a surge of energy as the gun fires.

That's how I used to do it, anyway. What will happen in Singapore when I haven't raced for so long? Will I succumb to nerves?

I hope not.

My father knows all about anxiety. Its crushing impact, brought on by the fear of not living up to expectation, was one of the reasons he prematurely cut short his own promising cricketing career – one that I wasn't even aware of as a child, such was his modesty. As a kid, Ken Thorpe practised his batting endlessly in his backyard and it paid off when he debuted in the first grade team for Bankstown District Cricket Club in their 1967–68 season when he was only 17 years old. A potential star was born but a year later he quit, the combination of crippling anxiety and the relentless demands of his father – my grandfather.

Cec Thorpe's own sporting dreams to be a top-class cricketer had been dashed by the same illness which had forced him to move from Armidale to Sydney all those years before. But in his bitterness he made the mistake of trying to drive his son to achieve, to the point where Dad couldn't take it and quit almost before he had started. He returned to the game seven years later and topped the Sydney first grade averages in 1975–76, ahead of Test players like Bob Simpson and Neil Harvey. But he was overlooked for state selection and, with it, any chance of the ultimate achievement – the baggy green cap.

There's some resonance of Dad's story in my own experience, at least in the sense that I had to walk away from the sport I loved before I was ready, simply because of an off-field aspect which destroyed my enjoyment. Of course, I've been lucky compared to Dad. I'd achieved a lot before I felt forced to walk away and, like him, I also harboured desires to finish, and not allow myself to succumb to the expectations or limitations of others – yet another reason why I'm doing this.

If Dad has any regrets he hasn't revealed them, although it's clear that his own bad experiences with his father impacted enormously on the way he treated and managed the expectations of his own children. It's difficult to speak ill of my grandfather, other than to say he was coloured by his own regret and made big mistakes with his eldest son, who recalled once that he hated being dismissed from the pitch, not just because it ended an innings but because it began a confrontation with Cec, who would badger him about the mistake. On at least one occasion Cec even demanded that he write an essay about why he had been dismissed to a bad shot.

Perhaps I should thank Cec, because one of the strengths of my childhood was the way Mum and Dad encouraged and managed our careers. The only driving they did was in the family Camry, a constant ferry not just to swimming but to the other sports Christina and I played – soccer and Little Athletics for me and netball, tennis and gymnastics for her – before the demands of the pool took over. They insisted only that we persisted and didn't give in easily, as children often do; that success wasn't about winning but doing our best; and that we enjoyed ourselves.

They're philosophies that have stayed with me. Persistence is what is getting me through, the self-belief that it's only a matter of time and that if I work hard enough then I will succeed. I've always subscribed to the idea that performance is about how I swim and not about the other competitors. Whenever I got out of the pool – even after breaking a world record – I would tell the media that I was just trying to swim as fast as I could; that winning was an important but secondary consideration. I was once quoted this way: 'For myself, losing isn't coming second. It's getting out of the water knowing you could have done better. For myself, I've won every race I've been in.'

I've also always believed that the starting point for swimming is kids splashing and having fun in the water. You have to enjoy what you're doing in order to succeed. It was one of the reasons why I walked away in 2006 – I'd lost the enjoyment – and the reason that I am training now. I love the life of a swimmer.

Like Cec, Dad harboured great ambitions for his son in the game they both loved, but the cricket gene pool was empty by the time it reached me. It simply wasn't my game, although Dad kept his dream alive when I was young with the cricket pitch in our backyard and neighbourhood games. But he accepted that I was a swimmer, even though he couldn't swim himself, traumatised by a childhood incident when he was thrown in the deep end of a pool by his teacher and told to swim. Although I couldn't take advantage of Dad's coaching skills, there were other kids in the area who benefited, among them the Waugh brothers, Steve and Mark, who grew up playing for Bankstown before their fabulous Test careers.

Dad's manner as a mentor was as spare as his character. There were very few occasions when praise went beyond general encouragement and even then it was mostly indirect. The first time I remember hearing him speaking with any enthusiasm about my skills was during a phone conversation with one of his friends when I was about 12. He was trying to explain how extraordinary he thought one of my performances had been, and I remember feeling embarrassed – not only because of what he was saying but because I was eavesdropping!

Christina and I always got positive feedback from Dad but it was always balanced by the message that our success might be fleeting, like it is for most junior swimmers, and that there was much more to life. Yet the conversation I overheard suggested that my performance meant something else, and that it might lead to other, much bigger things. It was the first time I understood that I might be more than just a talented young swimmer.

The only other time I remember this kind of conversation was a few years later, in 1999. I was 16 and had already won a world title, set world records and was expected to win Olympic gold, but Cec, my grandfather, still struggled to understand the relevance of a sport that wasn't his beloved cricket and the impact I was having on it. He was 77 and too old to change.

He knew I trained hard and had won titles but didn't quite get the fact that I was changing the face of swimming. Dad was talking to him on the phone and, even though I could only hear one side of the conversation, it was clear he was trying to put my performances into perspective and decided the only way was to use a cricketing analogy. Dad thought for a moment and then, very hesitantly, compared what I was doing to the performances of Sir Donald Bradman. Cec died soon after, a happy man.

Of course, I'm not forgetting Mum in all of this. I share characteristics of both my parents but I'm possibly more like my mum than my dad. Dave Flaskas reckons I'm a contradiction in personality – a laid back control freak – which is probably the mix of Dad's penchant for perfection and Mum's unstressed thoughtfulness.

In childhood, Christina was always the one outside in the backyard with Dad throwing, catching and running, whereas I often preferred my own company in some indoors activity, usually building things with my beloved Lego, or helping Mum with the cooking. I'm naturally quiet and patient and can get down from time to time, which I've had to manage over the years, but I also have a temper which is slow to boil and even slower to cool. Mum understands me best which is probably why she is my conduit to the world. She wasn't without her own sporting ability, having been an A-grade netballer and a promising swimmer herself, although she didn't feel the need to pursue either beyond enjoying her natural talent.

It can't be easy having a child – or in my parents' case, two children – who express an interest in pursuing sport professionally. I'm sure most parents, especially those like my own mum and dad, whose own lives are underpinned by social conservatism, would much rather their kids knuckle down and study hard to find good solid careers.

There was never any compromise when it came to schoolwork, of course. While Dad drove us to and from training we'd often be reciting our times tables or face snap spelling tests. I was lucky because schoolwork came easily to me and any leniency I was shown was only because my grades stayed high despite the tough after-hours swimming schedule.

The key, though, was that Mum and Dad never let us forget that things might not work out in swimming. Even as I thrived in competition in my teens and seemed to have the world at my feet, they still talked about Plan B – what would happen if I stopped swimming.

As it turned out I didn't need a Plan B until much later and then it proved to be the biggest challenge of my life. Perhaps I'll be looking for a Plan C when this is all over.

eight

4 NOVEMBER 2011

The deed is done. I've swum my first competitive race in more than five years and survived without making a fool of myself. The sanctuary and isolation of the training pool has gone. Here in Singapore I'm well and truly back in the heat of competition and the media – the pool of expectation.

Even though I was treating that race – the medley – as dispassionately as I could, I felt like a kid on his first day at school; packed and ready far too early, jittery and lost in a place I didn't really know. I hesitate to say that I wanted my mum but there I was, about to swim a heat of a race that meant almost nothing in a 25-metre pool – a course I have always shunned – and a long way from home. I'd never felt more alone, even in an environment where I was the centre of attention. I was putting myself on the line, physically and psychologically, driven only by my desire to participate and get it out of the way.

I squeezed into my racing togs, stretched and tied my goggles until it felt like my temples would burst (I always worry they'll fall off) and dived in to do a warm-up at least 10 minutes too early. The times taken for me by a team trainer meant nothing and I trudged off to the marshalling area with nothing else to do but wait.

This is where I normally expect the nerves to kick in – as I begin to prepare myself mentally for the race ahead, usually by chatting with those around me. The problem was I didn't know any of my competitors. Not only have I rarely swum short-course competition – and frankly hate it – but my absence had delivered a whole new batch of competitors. There were eight of us sitting behind a curtain.

To ease the tension, I began playing a silly game in my head where I named each competitor according to where they came from. There was a guy from Austria who I dubbed Arnold and another from South Africa who became Nelson. We sat around talking about nothing in particular until the marshals came and attached our sponsor bibs.

Then, suddenly, it was time to race. I was shocked at how quickly it'd come around. I walked out to the pool deck, glanced around and realised there was no way I could wave to or acknowledge the spectators, something I normally would have done to help ease away the anxiety of the moment. There was only a tiny knot of them, mainly school students whose screams only emphasised the emptiness of the place, and they were gathered in the stands behind the sea of media, most of whom wouldn't have been there if it wasn't for my appearance. It was a long way from the kind of Olympic-style atmosphere I'm used to but the media attention was as unrelenting as usual: Did I expect to win? What if I lost? Was I foxing? They see everything in black and white when the answer is always a shade of grey.

I probably looked a little apprehensive on the screen as I turned my back on the phalanx of cameras and stripped down to my swimmers, almost forgetting to adjust the kick-board at the back of the blocks, which are akin to running blocks used by track athletes in sprint races and yet another thing which has changed in my absence from the pool.

I stood on the blocks, bent down and waited for the customary adrenaline surge; the sudden shot of anxiety which, if I can harness it, is actually beneficial to performance and something I have been good at using to my advantage in the past. It literally puts me on the cusp of a fight or flight response. I have always embraced that rush – never tried to suppress it – in order to use it as a firing pin when the starter's gun goes off. This time it had the reverse impact and nerves got the better of me which, I hope, doesn't become a problem.

I remember diving in and perhaps the first few strokes of butterfly, then nothing else except a vague sense that my back-stroke leg was a bit rusty. The next thing I knew was that I'd touched the finish and, instinctively, looked up to a time – 56.74 seconds. It seemed as meaningless to me as the race itself. I had no idea whether it was good or bad, given that I hadn't trained for the event let alone swum it in competition. Then again, perhaps it was my best time: the last time I'd swum it was probably at about the age of 11. I'd also made the final in my first race, which was good.

The final that night was even stranger. I forgot to breathe in the first 25 metres butterfly leg, took the smallest mini-breath at the wall as I turned to backstroke, then travelled 15 metres under water before I got my first real gulp of air. I was still admonishing myself as I turned for the breaststroke leg, which is my least favourite, and then copped everyone's wash, which made me hate every stroke down the third leg. By the time I'd turned for the freestyle I was over it. Yet somehow I improved my time by half a second.

I'm not sure if I should be surprised at the media attention. It was bound to happen, I suppose, and so far the interest has been polite and not too judgemental. I'm not sure what they were expecting but if it was victory in an event I've hardly ever swum, in a pool I hate and after barely a year of training, and against short-course specialists, then they would be disap-pointed.

I'm expecting that the coverage will, as usual, be simplis-tic. There's no room for nuance in the 6 pm news, not that it bothers me. Perhaps if they think I'm going to flop then they'll leave me in peace.

It puts a complaint by one Australian official that I'm hogging the limelight at the expense of up-and-coming swimmers in the ludicrous light it should be seen in. If I wasn't here then the cameras wouldn't be here either, and the young swimmers would have even less chance of some recognition. It's a double-edged sword for me. I don't want the attention but I realise that the interest in me, however perverse, is actually good for the sport I love. If the media has flocked to Singapore for an inconsequential meet then imagine what it will be like in Adelaide next March for the Olympic trials.

For someone who sees himself as a natural swimmer, my beginnings in the sport were anything but. For a start, when I began learn-to-swim classes at the age of six I was almost forced to give them up because of a diagnosis of bronchial pneumonia. In the end it proved to be something less serious but still a major issue for a swimmer – I was allergic to chlorine.

The reason I began to compete was equally strange – boredom. From age five I was dragged along by Mum and Dad to watch Christina play sport. I didn't mind because there was usually plenty of room to run around in, particularly when she was playing netball or doing gymnastics. But when she broke her wrist she took up swimming, which for me was like being trapped in a prison. I was enclosed in a space bounded by wire fences and dominated by the pool, which of course was being used and therefore out of bounds. There was no space to move.

From memory, the last straw was watching Christina compete at the Sydney metropolitan championships at Blacktown in 1980. She had really shown some talent by then but being a spectator in the stands really sucked. The only way out was to be in. I can imagine it must have been tough for Christina a few years later as she watched my career blossom. She trained just as hard as I did and had a golden opportunity to go to the 1996 Atlanta Games as a middle distance and relay swimmer but had one of those races in the trials and missed the team. It just shows the difference that pressure can make, and it's something I'll have to keep in mind for the trials in Adelaide.

It'd be natural for her to have some misgivings about my success given her own disappointments but, if she has, they've never been expressed to me. Christina has always done the big sister thing and been incredibly protective of me and my success.

In the end, I asked Mum if I could join the local club that Christina belonged to at Padstow, close to where we lived at Revesby, and ended up swimming a 50-metre event at Revesby pool in an open competition soon afterwards. I can still remember Mum sitting in the stands with some of the other kids. I was swimming in the outside lane and I could hear them cheering me on. From memory, I finished fourth. It left a mark.

Growing up in Sydney's often sweltering south-west meant that swimming clubs were popular with kids and more than a few Olympic careers have been forged here, like the 1500-metre swimmer Graham Windeatt, who won silver at the 1972 Munich Games, and John and Ilsa Konrads, who won medals at the 1960 Rome Games. Encouraged by that first race, I began lessons with a friend of mine from school – half an hour once a week – which then progressed to club meets. I'd been doing Little Athletics at the time but after one club race I gave that up and decided swimming was what I liked. It just felt right. From then on I swam every Friday night at Padstow and trained most Saturday mornings at the Revesby pool.

I have no real idea what attracted me to swimming other than I enjoyed playing in the water, which I think is the best way any child can come to it. Even my training was play. I would imagine that my body was a giant ship with all these people, the crew, who were making the ship run. Inside my goggles was the control room. If I had a drink, I was refuelling. When things got difficult it meant making parts of the ship work harder; for instance getting my legs going. The way I've always responded to pain is to kick harder, and even as a young kid I knew that making myself work better meant making the ship go faster. I don't use that analogy anymore but many of the same things apply. When I begin to hurt, I don't back off – I hurt myself more.

But my introduction to swimming certainly wasn't plain sailing. Because of my allergy to chlorine I suffered sinus trouble, which sometimes led to chest problems and kept me out of the water for up to a week or more. I was also prone to migraines. But I didn't care. My joy at simply being in the water was turning into something more: I felt good about myself, even if I was coughing and spluttering and my nose was running like a tap at the end of a race, and whether I won or not. I progressed quickly through local, regional and then state events. By the age of nine, barely three years after taking my first lessons, I won my first state title. That's where the story changed and swimming became serious.

A lot of people like to take credit for my success – some far more than they should – but there are others who deserve credit but have been too modest to accept it. Chris Myers and Jenni Ashpole, two of my first coaches, are among the latter.

I was a little scared of the water when I first began swim training under Jenni. I'd come from Little Athletics, where I could run fast and jump high simply because I was much bigger than the other kids, and now I had entered a world which initially caused me migraines and a runny nose. It was her patience which encouraged me and my fear quickly turned to joy.

Chris took over as coach around my 10th birthday. I spent three years under his wing before I went to the senior coach Doug Frost, and it was during this time that the important basics of my stroke were put in place. I still chuckle at Chris's coaching method, instilling the need to keep our elbows bent and hands tucked beneath our armpits as we completed the rotation above the water – 'Tuck, tuck, tuck, tuck, tuck' he'd say, his head bent in position, waddling backwards like a penguin along the edge of the pool. Those basics were the cornerstone of my success and the love of the sport which has brought me back.

Interestingly there was a time, probably in 1993, when I almost became a student of Gennadi Touretski. The decision was more about Christina, whose swimming talent had emerged in her mid teens. Mum and Dad were tossing up what to do about her career. The natural flow was to stick with the local Padstow pool coach, which was Doug Frost, who was also the New South Wales state coach, but there was an opportunity to go to Canberra and train under Gennadi, who had been drafted by the Australian Institute of Sport to train Olympic contenders the year before. I remember sitting around the dining table as a family, discussing what to do, and my parents' decision that leaving our home to live in Canberra was simply not going to happen. The Doug Frost swim school it would be. The die was cast.

Recently, I've thought quite often about what might have happened if we'd moved to Canberra. I'm not at all dismissing

Right My first baby portrait showed an eager young man looking forward to life.

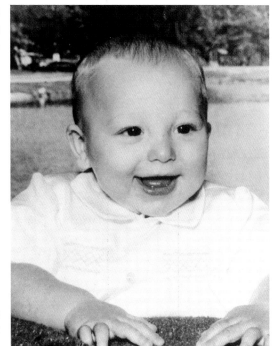

Below The beginnings of an Aussie childhood, on the front steps of our Milperra home.

I had an affinity for water at an early age.

I've improved my entry since this was taken. Note the old Hills Hoist in
the background.

Top right My first swimming medal. I look pretty pleased with myself, but I had no idea about what lay ahead. *Middle right* Genetics were on my side in my early swimming days. I didn't need a dais position to tower over my competitors. *Below* I may have looked the part but I was never going to be a cricketer.

Below Me and my big sister – with always, a protective arm around me. Christina and I have always been close, sharing blood and swimming dreams.

My first taste of public attention, in Perth 1998.

I love the background sign here. This is the other side of elite swimming:
early morning training.

Above My family at the Pan Pacific championships in Sydney, 1999. Mum and Dad always looked relaxed at swim meets. Here, Christina is phoning the news that I'd just set my first world record, breaking Kieren Perkins' long-standing 400-metre time.

Left Mum has always been my main confidante, even though I look as if I don't want the attention.

Above Opening night at the Sydney Olympic Games, 2000 – Chris Fydler, Ashley Callus, Michael Klim and I couldn't contain our glee at beating the Americans in the 100-metres relay, although my swimming was better than my air-guitar technique.

Opposite If my grin was any wider my face would split. My first individual gold medal at the Sydney Games.

Left I wasn't smiling two days later, beaten by Pieter van den Hoogenband in the final of the 200 metres. But despite my disappointment I was really happy for my friend.

At the 2001 world titles in Japan. We might have looked a team but the relationship between me and my coach Doug was, shall we say, frosty, when this photo was taken.

The beginning of a special relationship. Tracey Menzies understood me better as a person and the main reason I was able to keep swimming and compete at a second Olympics.

my results or the enormous influence that coaches like Doug and others had in my life but I believe Gennadi and I could have been a dangerous partnership, and I mean that in a good way. We could have done something really special.

Behind my success there are two stories. I was naturally talented with a strangely flexible body and, yes, big feet, but again, I didn't win five Olympic gold medals just because I was genetically gifted. I don't know of any other swimmer who swam more kilometres in training over the years, which was both the foundation for my performances and ultimately a frustration which contributed to my decision to leave the sport.

Looking back, to me there seems to have been a generation of coaches in Australia whose goal was to train their swimmers to breaking point, until they could go no further, then aim to get past that barrier and find the next and the next and the next. But I refused to be broken. It was a point of principle with me that I accomplished everything asked of me at every session. No matter what was thrown at me I'd complete it as expected, or better.

Doug and I clashed frequently. It was inevitable, I suppose, given that we were very different people. As much as Gennadi understands me, Doug did not. He had his way of doing things and I was his pupil. There was simply no room for discussion and eventually it had to come to a head.

But for all our problems, I have to give credit to Doug in a few areas. He was always organised, often an entire season in advance and certainly day by day. I would always know what was expected of me, either seared into my brain or written onto the ever-present board beside the pool. The mistake, I think, was the day he told me to call him Doug rather than

Mr Frost. It changed the dynamic of the relationship, away from one of respect and authority.

I was reminded recently about a pool deck interview I did in 2001. It was in Hobart during the selection trials for the World Championships in Fukuoka and I had just won the 800 metres – an event I had never swum before in competition – and set a world record. I was asked by former teammate Nicole Stevenson, who was reporting for one of the TV stations, 'The obvious question is: distance swimmer or sprinter? How did that feel?'

The question caught me by surprise. I said, 'It didn't feel too good. I'd prefer to be a sprinter but that's not happening at the moment either. I'm just trying to find out where I fit in the scheme of things.'

I don't remember much else of the interview but that's certainly the way I felt; constantly being put in a box that just didn't fit. There were times when my training schedule seemed to be designed to make me the best distance swimmer in the world and yet I wasn't allowed to swim the 1500 metres. It made no sense to me. As a result I felt as if I was faking my way in the sprint events. This is one of the main driving forces behind my return to swimming. It turns out that I am a really good sprinter.

But my frustrations with Doug's coaching style began much earlier in July 2000, at a high altitude camp in Colorado just three months before the Sydney Olympics, and one session in particular. I was almost 18 and it triggered the decision-making process that would eventually lead me to leave him after a decade of coaching.

It was customary for Doug to throw a series of tests at us to see where we were in our training, and they were scrawled on a blackboard by the side of the pool so we knew what was expected of us. On this occasion I had warmed up over two kilometres before swimming a timed 3000 metres, which I did in a little over 30 minutes, the fastest anyone had ever swum it in training. For some reason Doug hadn't put anything on the board at this stage but the squad knew the drill and expected a few sprint sets to end the session.

When I next looked up, I saw he had chalked up probably the hardest set we ever did in training – 30 × 100 metre sprints based on heart rate. At that moment I realised I had lost confidence in my coach but I wasn't going to let it get to me and admit failure. I just got on and did it as best I could.

But I wasn't going to let it go. Such is the fine line with elite athletes that I believed what he'd just done was a potential threat to our training regime and put the Olympics at risk.

I challenged him as we left the pool: 'Doug, we've done two main sets in one session which means I can't train properly for four days. What did we achieve?'

'Don't be a smart-arse with me,' he snapped back.

He started to give me the old line about putting in the hard yards to get anywhere and it was at that moment I realised I had outgrown him and his methods. Although the split didn't happen for another two years, I knew then that it was time to move on.

I don't believe the negatives were deliberate on Doug's part; the way he coached was all he knew. His style was to flog swimmers in the belief that it was the way to get the best out of them but I think that approach was wrong for me. In many respects, the technique is fine for age-group swimmers and there is no doubt you get results. There is a place for his style and a case to say that young swimmers, with their heads full of the notion of being the next superstar, need to slog through the hard work in order to realise that dedication is the tool that will make the difference. In hindsight, though, I think some of the training I endured was overly harsh. Thankfully, coaching has changed a lot since then.

I had made the decision to leave Doug after the Manchester Commonwealth Games finished in early August 2002 and had started to discuss with friends – privately – what I would do and which coach I might go to. Unfortunately, though, word got around that I was dumping him and I had to act quickly during the Pan Pacific championships, which followed a month later in Yokohama, Japan, to make it official.

I remember being told that a Sunday newspaper was about to run a story about my decision to leave. I had just stepped off the podium after Australia had won the 4 × 100 metre relay and knew I had to tell Doug before the story broke. He needed to know from me and no one else. When I fronted up, it was clear he'd heard something and was expecting me to reassure him that everything was fine. Instead, I had to tell him there would be stories in the papers the next day about me leaving, and they were true. I had to make changes if I was going to keep swimming and, clearly, nothing was going to change in our relationship. It was over.

Doug looked at me stony-faced. I don't remember what he said, if anything. There wasn't much either of us could say at that moment. But the next morning he came to see me on pool deck. I didn't really know what to expect given that my decision must have hit him very hard. But instead of anger, I got an olive branch: 'Ian, I've thought about it and if you want I'm happy to coach you through the rest of the meet, to take your times during warm-up and anything else you need.'

I was taken aback but very grateful. It was an amazing gesture and it made all the difference, because the animosity had been building for years and it could have ended sourly. Instead, we ended things in a dignified manner and I continue to admire him for that.

When I told my parents that I had split with Doug and wanted his assistant Tracey Menzies to take over, I'd expected some argument. Instead, they expressed surprise that I'd stayed with Doug for so long and agreed that Tracey was the obvious choice, particularly given that she had been fulfilling the role for the previous two years anyway, as Doug and I drifted further and further apart. I'd been virtually training myself while Tracey kept my times.

Her appointment was met in a very cruel manner by elements within the Australian coaching community who couldn't accept that a woman could coach at the elite level, let alone be in charge of Australia's best swimmer. I can say categorically that Australia would have won two less gold medals at Athens if Tracey hadn't agreed to coach me.

My relationship with Gennadi is different for many reasons. It was forged between two adults, not an adult and a child. Gennadi also has a more relaxed attitude; he's interested in learning and evolving, not instructions and direction. He doesn't tell me what he thinks of a training session but invites me to explain what I felt and then adds his own observations.

Most importantly, Gennadi isn't afraid to experiment with something new. And that's what excites me.

nine

10 NOVEMBER 2011

I've had my first moment of doubt. Lying on a massage table isn't the recommended place to make career assessments but that's where the stray thought snuck through. I'd just failed to qualify for the butterfly final here in Beijing, the second of the World Cup events, and I couldn't hide my disappointment from myself. Putting on a brave face in front of the cameras is one thing but lying on a table being pummelled by a trainer and feeling like crap tends to lay bare your innermost feelings.

I hadn't expected this when I left Switzerland. I'd held out some hope that I'd surprise myself; that the butterfly, for example, might offer an extra string to my bow for Olympic qualification. Instead, I can't even make a final, unable to shake the sense of anxiety on the blocks. What was once a strength – harnessing my nerves – is now a weakness I have to overcome.

Swimming endless laps in the training pool is a joyful cocoon of tranquillity but the glare of competition is exactly that – an uncompromising dose of cold, hard reality. When I got here I told myself not to expect too much but somehow I got seduced by the possibility of immediate success. Lying there on the massage table I found myself asking, 'Is this really what I want?' Wouldn't life be easier without the pressure to justify my decisions, reflecting on who I was and enjoying the privacy of who I am now? My hesitation was momentary, though. Of course this is what I want.

Thankfully my roommate, Victorian butterflyer Andrew Lauterstein, put the situation into some context for me. 'I know how hard it is after taking a break for a few months. Anyone who starts swimming again after four years and can finish a race is doing pretty well,' he told me after the swim. His words came at the right time. I allowed myself the luxury of feeling misunderstood for a moment and then replaced it with a sharp reminder that I needed a backbone and to get on with it. Andrew and I did some extra work in the pool to make up for gorging ourselves on Peking duck. That's about as exciting as it gets when you're in competition. There's no time to explore the culture of the city you're visiting.

I swam the 100 metres freestyle here as well. It wasn't planned. I had it pencilled in for Tokyo this weekend, only ever as a maybe. But Leigh Nugent, in his role as the Australian team coach, reckoned looking at it like that was a mistake. One night by the pool after a training session he told me,

'Why not put a late entry in here in Beijing? Get the first one out of the way. You have to swim it somewhere and it might as well be here. Nobody will be expecting it so you might get away with only a few people watching you.'

It made sense to me. The truth is, I was itching to see what I could do in the 100 under race conditions, even if it was short course, which doesn't allow you to settle into your stroke. I thought it might be a good way of alleviating some of the emotional expectation I'd placed on myself about the return to freestyle by virtually sneaking into a race and getting on with it before anyone else knew.

I remember the first 25 metres of the race, which I thought were quite good, but after that it fell away. I just don't think my head was ready. My turns are normally fine and yet every time I touched the wall at the end of a lap it felt like I turned myself off and lost speed. It turned out to be a disappointing nothing – 50.21 seconds.

Then came the silver lining. The tradition is that everyone in the Australian team goes to the pool to watch the finals, whether they've made them or not. It feels like a punishment but that's part of being in a team. And that's what I am here – part of a team. I might be training alone but Swimming Australia is contributing financially to my coaching, training and costs like scientific services, which are so important to preparation. Likewise, Gennadi is my coach but the Australian team coach, Leigh Nugent, has a big voice in what I'm doing, not only at this meet but looking toward the London Olympics.

The tradition in the Aussie team is that those who haven't qualified must do a training session in the evening – a longer version of the warm-up that we would have been doing to race – before making way for our teammates preparing for the finals. Gennadi and I had spoken in Singapore about how best to use these sessions if I missed out on a final, and we decided that I should make use of some of the adrenaline and the remains of the lactic acid build-up still in my system to have another hit-out – halfway between racing and training – and that meant another timed 100, but in a 50-metre pool, which served as the warm-up pool for this short-course meet.

I stopped at the end of a lap, stood and signalled to Leigh that I was ready. If I'd got out of the pool and dived from the blocks then those watching would have paid attention, so I did a push start instead. It felt so different being able to stretch out in a longer pool and as I touched and looked up to Leigh I knew the time would be good. Allowing a half-second deduction for the push-off start, I had just swum 49.8 seconds – more than a second better than the September training swim in Tenero.

I only missed one final in my 'early' career – the 400-metre trial to qualify for the Australian team going to the 2004 Athens Olympics. The disaster of the morning of 28 March 2004 was that my disqualification on the blocks happened at probably the most routine event of my Athens campaign. Ironically, it happened not amid the pressure of the final itself but in a morning heat and my first swim of the trials, the result of which should have meant little in the scheme of things. All I had to do was turn up and swim reasonably to get a lane in the centre of the pool for the final.

Instead I heard a noise in the crowd in the almost empty stands at Homebush Stadium and reacted as if the gun had gone off. I realised my mistake in the same split second it was made, and tried to grab the bars on the side of the blocks. But gravity had already taken over and I toppled into the pool. The photographs, which can still be found on the internet, show those gut-wrenching moments as if in slow motion, ending with my feet disappearing like the stern of a sinking ship.

I remember getting out of the pool, walking around to the blocks, ignoring the other swimmers and standing up again, as if nothing had happened. There was stunned silence around me. I don't think anyone else could really believe what had happened and what it meant. I didn't know what else to do – the situation was so surreal. Then an official came over and told me to step down. The words hit me like a tank. I tried to offer an explanation but I knew I had to go so I walked away without another word, my shoulders slumped and my head down. Then reality set in – I'd just blown it.

Initially I felt cheated. The one-start rule had been brought in to stop swimmers from manipulating false starts to their advantage, not to penalise genuine mistakes which would have no bearing on a fair race, especially when the race is for qualification to be selected on a team. Two other Australian swimmers, Phil Rogers and Petria Thomas, had previously been granted exemptions after false starts because of background noise. The difference in my case was that the sound couldn't be picked up on television replays and yet, two other credible people – Craig Golding, a veteran photographer, and Grant Hackett's coach, Denis Cotterell – said they had also heard it.

Surely that was enough to prove I was telling the truth. After all, there was no other explanation for what had happened. Why would I manipulate a start in the heat of an event in which I'd set the eight fastest times in history? I know it sounds arrogant but I could have fallen into the pool and still won comfortably. I have no objection to tough rules but they should be administered with common sense, not inflexibility. Despite the disappointment, I quickly came to terms with the idea that I wasn't going to swim the 400 metres in Athens. That night I sat in the stands and watched the final to see Grant Hackett win and Craig Stevens take the second spot and qualify for the Olympics. I was genuinely pleased for Craig because he was a good friend and training partner.

Two days later, even before I had qualified for the team in other events, I fronted a media conference and said I recognised what had happened and wanted to move on: 'I've accepted that I'm not swimming in it, and that's the way I've got to look at it. I don't see an alternative for how I could swim it.'

I meant it. People around me were trying to find ways for me to swim but I didn't want to deal with maybes. It was difficult enough to accept what had happened and concentrate on the 200 and 100 metres, and I certainly wasn't going to ask Craig to stand aside. Neither did I suggest the idea. The hypothetical question – if I would swim if Craig stood aside – was put to me by a journalist, so I answered honestly: 'I'd have to consider it. It depends under what circumstances. It's probably not going to happen. It's not the right thing for me to think about it. I dealt with it when it was happening. I've accepted that, and now everyone else has to as well.'

What else could I have said, given that I desperately wanted to defend my Olympic title?

Yet if I could have imagined the intensity of the media furore which followed as Craig went through the angst of deciding whether to swim or give me a second chance, I would have refused the swim there and then. I had no idea that the response would be so vitriolic; that I'd be accused of trying to pressure Craig. In hindsight it was the beginning of the end for me, although I didn't realise it at the time.

It was Tracey Menzies – like Chris Myers, an assistant coach to Doug – who made the difference. I've thought back many times to my decision to ask Tracey to coach me when I split with Doug in 2002 and I can say emphatically that she was the right coach for me at the time, and kept me in the sport during a period in which I could have walked away.

I think we helped each other, actually. Coaching me was a career opportunity for her and I needed someone who could understand me as an individual and have faith that I would deliver when it counted. She provided that flexibility, while facing a mountain of unfair criticism by men who believed that she wasn't up to the job. As the debate about the 400 raged, I began to doubt myself and Tracey convinced me to steel myself; that the experience should be character-building rather than soul-destroying.

I was torn between an obvious desire to swim the 400 and the realisation that to dwell on my misfortune had the potential to ruin my chances in the 200 and the 100. I had to steel myself to the reality of the situation and simply get on with training. Besides, I'd always wondered about my sprint capabilities and whether Doug's coaching had been tilted too far toward the middle distances. This could be the opportunity to test my theory.

I took a few days off from my training schedule and drove down to the south coast, where I met Craig, who was still deciding what to do. We had a quiet lunch at a pub in the town of Huskisson – two mates caught between the excitement of being selected for an Olympic Games and the quandary of choice. Craig hadn't expected to qualify for the 400 (and had little realistic prospect of a medal) and now had a program which included the 200-metre relay, as well as the 400- and 1500-metre individual races, which would be a stretch for any elite swimmer.

I was facing the opposite situation – years of aerobic preparation and thousands of laps now a waste. And yet the discussion that day over calamari barely touched the controversy. I just wanted him to know that he had my support, no matter what his decision was going to be. I wasn't even certain at that stage that I would take the swim if it was offered. I wanted to be assured that Craig was making a decision that made sense for him and not just because he felt pressured.

As history shows, Craig gave up his spot for me, although the battle wasn't over. Just a week before the Games, at a training camp in Germany, I almost quit and would have if, again, it hadn't been for Tracey. I couldn't control how I felt about the pressure created by the controversy. I remember trying to explain it to her, saying something like, 'I'm doing this for my country but I don't love what the country does to me. I don't think I can go through the criticism, the tall poppy thing; it's just not worthwhile for me in my life.'

Tracey looked at me without flinching, her tone steely despite what was on the line: 'You have to make the decision for yourself. I don't care if you swim, but make the decision now, because it's now or never.'

Giving me ownership of something that I felt had been completely out of my control gave me the conviction to go ahead with it. The psychology of the decision was as important as the physical task – something I would have to face myself when I came to race. It would be the worst race of my life and yet one of my greatest achievements.

My state of mind on the first night of competition at the Athens Games was completely different to the same evening four years earlier. Perhaps it was just youthful naivety but in Sydney I had been devoid of nerves – dazzled by the lights and attention, unaware really of the true pressure of an Olympic meet and oh-so calm.

This time it was the opposite. I was still the race favourite for the 400 metres but the 'unbeatable' tag now gone because of the events of the previous few months. And instead of expectation I was carrying a new and much heavier burden – responsibility. Four years earlier, the Sydney Olympics hadn't been easy either, with a pitched battle between the Australian Olympic Committee and Adidas over the marketing of the full body swimsuit I was wearing, and allegations that I was using performance-enhancing drugs – not to mention a broken ankle! – but those issues were about overcoming personal obstacles, not about other people.

When I got out of the pool after the morning's heat I knew that, in order to win gold, I was going to need to beat my own mental barriers as well as my opponents. It felt as if I had the weight of a dozen people on my shoulders – Craig Stevens, obviously, but also the people around me like Tracey and Dave and Michelle Flaskas, who had also borne the brunt of the media backlash. Then there was my own family. Even Dad had made the trip despite his fear of flying.

Dave Flaskas says he loves watching me compete in the 400 more than in any other distance because I can swim it so many different ways. Some of the races I've swum have been simply about going fast but if tactics are required then I can go out hard to burn off the opposition early; I can negative split – swim the second half of the race faster than the first – to come home over the top of anyone else; or I can keep control by covering and responding to my competitors. But this time it was different. This time it was a slog where I had to trust my training, keep my head clear and just hang on at the end.

Still, it was my race to lose and Grant Hackett's to win, and he had issued the challenge psychologically in the days leading up to the race when his coach, Denis Cotterell, revealed they had changed Grant's preparation so that he'd be fresher for the 400. One newspaper headline read 'Hackett can smell blood in the water' and though I had a policy of not reading news-papers, I was certainly aware of what was going on.

But Grant got his tactics wrong. It was all set up for him but he didn't trust himself enough to take the race out hard and really test me. Instead, he let me dictate the pace, and we were more than one second outside the world record time within the first 100 metres, which suited me more than Grant, but also brought swimmers like Massi Rosolino and Klete Keller into the race. By the halfway mark I was two seconds behind my world record but feeling much more comfortable because I knew Grant was trying to swim over the top of me, which would be tough given the slow pace had left me with plenty of reserve.

I tried to put some distance between us in the third quarter and managed to get a body length on Grant with 75 metres to go, which is usually where I can kick away, but that's where the race changed. Suddenly I had nothing left, the clutter of the past five months crowding my mind and sapping my energy. Grant turned only half a body length behind and sensed he could catch me. I knew it too. He had never done it before but this was his opportunity. With 10 metres to swim he was almost on my shoulder but somehow I found the strength to hold him off. I stretched for the wall with my left hand. If I missed I would lose. I didn't and won – by just 0.26 seconds.

The only way to describe my emotion at that moment is raw. I turned to the wall, expecting that all my pent-up emotion was going to explode into tears, but nothing came, just gulps. Grant and I embraced and I waved to my family in the crowd, still on the verge of crying, and yet no tears came. I got out of the pool and high-fived teammates, including Craig, then moved on to do the post-race interview with Grant alongside. The journalist said I looked exhausted and emotional. He was right but I held it together.

But after that I fell apart. I don't know who saw it, and I wouldn't have cared at the time, but the person who copped the flak was Tracey. I screamed at her, the pent-up emotion of the past few months bubbling over: 'You will never make me swim this race ever again. I will not do it and I will not swim a race anyone expects me to swim.' I was an absolute prick, screaming at the person who'd help me hold myself together. She just looked at me calmly: 'That race is over, you can move on. It's finished now, you don't ever have to do it again.'

Two days later I was a different athlete – confident, in control, elated by swimming again. It was incredible, and without Tracey I would never have won my fourth and fifth gold medals.

ten

12 NOVEMBER 2011

I'm at Narita Airport in Tokyo, packed and ready to fly back to Europe to resume training. Sitting on the plane will give me time to reflect on the past week, if only to try to put things into some sort of perspective in this game of numbers. I've swum seven races at three meets in three cities over eight days. I made just one final and finished seventh. But there has been some improvement.

This morning I swam 49.45 for the 100 metres freestyle – not fast by any means but better than last week in Beijing and less than a second behind the reigning Olympic champion, Frenchman Alain Bernard, although I missed out on the final again. It wasn't the time that was pleasing so much as the way

I swam and my attitude to the race. I just let it happen, and funnily enough it seemed to work. The less I tried the better I swam.

Before that swim I was pissed off with my form in Asia. It wasn't that the performances were terrible but that they didn't reflect the quality of my training. I felt like a stunned mullet in Singapore and Beijing, unsure of why I was there in many respects and unable to get myself into competition mode. It was almost as if the event itself wasn't big enough. It sounds conceited but it's not what I mean; rather it's a reflection of how and where I've raced in the past and the reality of where I am now.

I can't pretend the experience has been a success – it's tougher than I'd imagined, actually – but neither was it a disaster. It had to happen; I had to feel what it was like to compete again, even if it was in a 25-metre pool against race-hardened competitors. My preference would have been to swim at a smaller long-course meet but there was nothing available. In the end Gennadi and I thought it was more important to start racing than to wait for the right competition. And he was right.

When I put the training marker down back in September I swam just over 51 seconds. When I did the secret stand-up in Beijing my time was 49.8, which is a big improvement. I skip over it sometimes because I tend to look at where I want to be rather than where I've come from, but it's given me a big boost.

If I look forward to the next competition, the Italian winter championships (a long-course meet) at Riccione next month, then I'd be hoping to swim something like 49.5. I'd be happy with that but it'll depend on everything going to plan. Then I go back to Australia in January to compete in the Victorian championships, where I'll want to be under 49 seconds. Everything seems so close now – the Olympic trials in March are only four months away. I should be able to do it; I've done the training. Now it's just a matter of putting it together.

The other aspect of all this has been dealing with the media interest. The almost constant demand for interviews and press conferences is exhausting, mentally and physically, the worst possible preparation for competition, but something I accept that I have to do. I've swum publicly now; the bubble has been burst. I'm hoping the interest will die down a bit, at least until the Victorian championships.

The thing that frustrates me again and again is the fact that so many journalists have no idea what they're talking about. I'm constantly astounded by the questions, even from people who say they know me well, because it appears they simply don't have a clue about the process and what's actually happening. I'm not trying to convince people that my performances are any better than they are. They were average results – and I'm content with that. This is real for me, not a movie script.

Perhaps I expect too much. It's impossible for most, especially the media, to understand the complexities of training your mind and body to do something beyond normal limits. It's a world of unknowns, ifs and maybes – shades of grey which journalists in particular want to squeeze into black and white boxes. But it's maddening: because I'm a five-time Olympic champion and I've set a dozen or more world records I'm supposed to be superhuman. Anything less is incomprehensible, as if somehow I'm letting myself, and more importantly them, down.

Of all the commitments I have outside the pool, whether it's meeting sponsors, public speaking, endorsements or posing for photographs, the hardest is satisfying the media. I hate sitting there all day doing interview after interview, repeating the same answers to the same questions, like I did yesterday. If I don't come across as enthusiastic enough it can be interpreted as meaning that I don't care or I'm not cooperating. But the real problem is that I have to be so guarded in what I say, because experience tells me that if I allow any room for interpretation then what I say will be contorted and that makes my life harder. Being guarded and enthusiastic at the same time isn't natural; it takes a lot of energy and becomes a performance more draining than swimming laps.

I remember sitting through an interview in Japan once and felt myself nodding off to sleep. It was at the end of several days of these sorts of commitments and I was exhausted, I could hardly keep my eyes open. And yet it didn't matter. As long as I answered the questions in English it was okay – they'd do the translation and edit around my slumber. I was simply the machine to deliver the message.

Sitting here waiting for my flight reminds me of when I flew in to Japan with the Australian swim team in 2001 for the World Championships. As the doors slid open and closed to allow passengers through Customs and into the airport terminal proper, we could hear the unmistakable sound of teenage girls screaming in anticipation of the mere sight of the celebrity they'd queued to glimpse – in this case, me.

We were in Fukuoka, the capital of Japan's southern-most island, Kyushu. It was July, high summer in the northern hemisphere, and the middle of Japan's rainy season, exacerbating its already humid summer temperatures, which can climb into the early 30s. It was big difference to the cold, stormy winter we'd left behind in Australia.

Even as we collected our bags we could hear the large crowd outside. My freestyle relay teammate Ashley Callus must have glimpsed the throng through the doors and could see the placards, some with my name scrawled in English. Ashley asked casually: 'Does anyone know you here? Are you popular in Japan?'

It was a difficult question to answer. I was 18 years old, had been a world champion since the age of 15 and by then had won three Olympic Gold medals. I was used to fame in the sense of being recognised and asked for an autograph most places I went. The Australian team travelled the world for competition and we generally found that our popularity depended on the popularity of the sport itself in each country. That suggested that Japan, with two silver and two bronze medals in the pool from the Sydney Games the year before, would show perhaps a modicum of interest in our arrival.

But Japan is different. Japan is crazy. I'd been here a few months before with Dave Flaskas to sign some sponsorship deals and there'd been lines of fans waiting for me as if I was an arriving rock star. I'd seen huge billboards of me in the heart of the Ginza shopping district of Tokyo, advertising products in a language I couldn't understand. It was like looking at a cartoon of myself, something which wasn't quite real. I'd also been on Japanese television, not just doing interviews but on reality game shows. As bizarre as it seems, at the time my life was changing so fast and I was embracing so many new and incredible things that it didn't seem strange that there'd be screaming teenagers.

'Yeah, a little,' I said to Ashley, as the doors swung back to reveal a crowd of people, in places 20 deep, held back by ropes and police with furrowed brows. They were mostly young girls and boys waving signs and calling out my name, which sounds a little like 'Soarpo' when yelled in a Japanese accent. Others were calling out 'Maguro', which is Japanese for bluefin tuna and how they characterised my movement through the water.

I watched in amusement as the rest of the team freaked out, unable to comprehend what was happening. To be honest, I enjoyed their reaction far more than the adulation, which was a little unnerving. As we finally made our way through the crowd and got on the bus, Ashley, who was gobsmacked, grunted: 'A *little* popular? Why didn't you tell me? Wow.'

He was right. Japan is wow, but the feeling is mutual. The country, its people and customs have been a very important part of my life for a long time now, as my current passport indicates. I've been filling it since 2008 and it has 11 Japanese arrival stamps scattered through its pages.

I was just 14 years old when I made my first visit. It was 1997 and I was there as a member of the Australian team competing in the Pan Pacs, which were also at Fukuoka. But my relationship with Japan didn't get off to the best start. On the flight over I thought I'd try the Japanese dish on the menu and proceeded to smother the green paste, offered on the side, all over the seaweed noodles. It was wasabi, of course, and my mouth exploded as I swallowed the first big mouthful. My response was to search for water but there was none so

I grabbed someone's bottle of orange juice which, adding insult to injury, contained an additive that I'm allergic to, so I ended up spraying it all into a sick bag.

Thankfully, it was my one bad experience and I must have left an impression on the Japanese because in the lead-up to the Sydney Olympics three years later I was swamped with fan mail from Japan, mainly boxes and boxes of folded paper cranes. I had no idea at the time but they were sent as good luck – the finer the origami, the more powerful the wish. One crane, which I still have, was so small that it had been folded and creased using a needle.

The interest took me and my manager Dave Flaskas by surprise. I was avoiding media interviews during the Games but we decided that I should make myself available for a few Japanese requests, if only to satisfy our curiosity about where it might lead in terms of sponsorships. The response was amazing and by the time we returned to Fukuoka a year later there was near hysteria, as we witnessed at the airport.

I've never been able to understand why I'm so popular in Japan. For a start, the Japanese don't have the usual widespread fascination with sportspeople, singers or movie stars that the majority of the developed world does. Instead, they're highly selective and become obsessed with a small number of celebrities, which makes my popularity even more difficult to fathom, given I'm a foreigner in a relatively minor sport, at least outside an Olympic year.

I've asked marketing people if they can decipher the puzzle but they all have different answers, including my being humble or respectful, being good-looking, being Australian; or because of my swimming prowess or my interest in Japanese food and culture. Even my apparently calm manner before a race has been given as a reason, perhaps because it sits with the Japanese sense of what we would call being Zen. I'm sure this is all true but in the end, my instinct says that they sensed there was something different about me; not just what I was doing in the pool but also outside of it – an X-factor, perhaps, and one which can't really be defined outside of Japan. After all, I actually won an award one year for the way I smiled.

Another theory is that my popularity began because the Japanese saw me as *kawaii*, or cute and adorable, when I came onto the scene as a teenager before the Sydney Games, which then became *kakkoii*, or stylish and cool, when I swam in the 2001 World Championships in Fukuoka. Whatever the reason, I seem to have become part of pop culture in Japan and even after I stopped swimming I was still ranked third among foreign celebrities – behind soccer star David Beckham and golfer Tiger Woods.

My own fascination and respect for Japan and its people is easier to explain. I fell in love with the culture, particularly the way it marries history and tradition with modern life. My experiences in the city of Kyoto, about an hour west of Tokyo, are good examples of what I mean. Kyoto is a flourishing, modern city of 1.5 million people and yet it remains the heart of ancient Japanese culture and tradition. It was the nation's capital for more than 1000 years until the mid 19th century, with over 2000 Buddhist temples and Shinto shrines in its boundaries.

I've stayed there several times in a traditional guest house, or *ryokan*; a place where the wooden sliding doors are never locked, you sleep on traditional rice straw tatami floors and are woken each morning by an elderly woman who, like a human alarm clock, first speaks softly in your ear in Japanese. If you don't respond she gradually raises the volume of her voice, even gently tapping you until you wake up. It was a bit unsettling the first time to be woken by a stranger kneeling by your bed, but I got used to it pretty quickly. The room was her responsibility and she would even serve your meal if you decided to eat in your room.

For all the civility of the *ryokan* you can still get locked out, though. I remember going out one night, trying to find something to eat after a particularly hard training session. It was a few minutes after midnight when I got back to the gates, only to find them closed. I avoided a night in the streets of Kyoto thanks to an observant hotel worker who accepted that I was an inattentive westerner rather than a security threat.

I was fascinated to find out that, over the centuries, shoguns, the all-powerful military dictators, had stayed in that very *ryokan* with its intricate traditional ceremonies and delicate, manicured gardens. It fed my appetite at an intellectual level, as did the Philosopher's Walk, a 200-year-old pathway in the north of the city which cuts through the surrounding mountains and meanders alongside a canal beneath a canopy of cherry trees, which were in blossom when I walked it.

Time just seems to disappear as you stop to see temples and shrines along the route. There are half a dozen of Japan's most significant religious buildings along the way, too, such as the Ginkakuji temple where ancient traditions such as the tea ceremony, flower arrangement, garden design and masked theatre were developed back in the 14th century. At the other end of the walk is the Nanzenji temple, which was built by a

13th century emperor, and the Eikando temple, which dates back more than a thousand years.

These rich historical traditions aren't dusty exhibits in a museum. They remain at the heart of the shifting contemporary demands of this tiny country in which the carefully structured culture of Kyoto knits seamlessly with the futuristic glitz and shimmer of Tokyo, and young men strutting in punk gear, crazy hair and make-up stop to bow as an old lady crosses the street, before reverting again to being the coolest people on the planet.

There is a genuine respect here for the past. If you accidentally bump into a stranger in London you would both keep walking with a stiff upper lip, as if the collision hadn't happened at all, and in New York you'd turn around and swear at each other. But in Tokyo you each bow and go on your way. That's the difference. Everything is finely balanced, even relationships. I've learned to speak Japanese to a passable degree but I was warned once not to show how much I understood or could speak, simply because it would diminish the aura of being a foreigner who was respectful and interested.

Clever use of space is another interesting feature of Japanese culture, along with reverence for nature. In Australia we take it for granted and you can see trees whenever you look out of a window, even in the suburbs of a major city. In Japan, space is at a premium and every bit is treasured in everything from house and garden design to flower arrangement. Even a single flower and twig in a vase by the window of a hotel room is about bringing nature into a tiny space.

These attitudes resonate with me and many of my own life experiences. My parents both worked when I was growing up which meant my sister and I often spent afternoons after school with our maternal grandparents, who lived around the corner. And every Sunday we had lunch with our paternal grandparents – 12 noon on the dot.

Their influence was huge, not unlike the Japanese tradition where grandparents play an important role in the family. Many of the things I enjoy outside swimming, like cooking and gardening, are activities and skills I learned from my grandparents. They have time to share their experience and even two generations later, most of it is valid and valuable. I grew up in a time of plenty, when many necessities were taken for granted. The debate over our environment has really made me appreciate my grandparents' insistence on thriftiness, not just with money but services like water and electricity – they were brought up in an era when these things were scarce and they learned to appreciate and protect what they had.

Not everything about Japan is serious, of course. I love the wacky aspect of the country, too, like the city of Nara, where the deer have been taught to bow for food, and their television programs, which just defy description. It appeals to my sense of silliness, which people don't often get to see. After seeing the deer in Nara I taught one of my dogs, Max, how to kiss my feet. My other dog, Kito, dives into the swimming pool on command.

One of my favourite experiences in Japan was during a promotional visit when I was invited onto a reality game show – a cross between *MasterChef* and that old 1980s show *It's a Knockout* – for which I had to give the producers a list of two meals I particularly liked and a third that I hated, without revealing which was which. Maybe I should have lied but I *was* in Japan and it didn't occur to me to be cleverly dishonest. I chose peppermint ice cream and a classic Italian dish, veal saltimbocca, as my two favourites, and scrambled eggs, which I hate.

The idea, which was never clearly explained to me before I went on air, was that I would be pitted against another contestant and we would have to eat part of our nominated three dishes while trying to conceal our feelings about each one – good and bad. The winner was the person who could correctly pick the other's hated dish. My competitor was a Japanese woman who chose a banana, a fermented bean dish and a third meal which now escapes me. I decided to eat everything as quickly as possible, particularly the eggs, so that she couldn't read my face and see that the eggs were making me gag.

When she asked me (through an interpreter) why I liked eggs, I told her it was because they were so easy to prepare in the morning before training. I then managed to eat a little more, helped by a smothering of tomato sauce, without vomiting. The tactic seemed to work, although I needn't have bothered because she'd decided I didn't like the ice cream, simply because I'd used a small spoon to eat it with. In fact, I'd chosen the small spoon for dessert in order to savour the taste!

I decided that her hated dish was the fermented bean slush, mixed with egg yolk and soy sauce, which looked disgusting and smelled foul. She certainly didn't look like she enjoyed it. It was a breakfast dish, apparently, but she didn't seem to know much about its preparation. Then I got my own back by making her taste it a couple of times just for effect. But I was wrong – she hated the banana but had hidden her distaste by nibbling very politely.

The way I feel about Japanese food actually sums up the country for me as a whole. I'm a person who by nature likes extremes. I don't like the boring middle ground. Food-wise, that means I'm either in the mood for the big, rustic flavours of an Italian dish or the delicate, finely balanced perfection of a Japanese feast. Although I love Australian barbecues I find myself cringing at the way meat is often just slapped onto the hot plate. Our day-to-day food is definitely improving but there are so many better ways of doing things.

When I go out to dinner with my Japanese friends I will want to know what ingredients are in everything I eat, not because I'm wary but because I'm interested and staggered by the inventiveness and flavours. But like many things here, some of the ingredients simply can't be translated – a fungus from a tree or a vegetable which reminds you of spinach, but isn't. I find it all so visually stunning, too, that I'm forced to eat neatly, as if I might spoil the artistry of the presentation if I just hoe in or don't put something back in its place on the tray when I've taken a bite.

I think I've tasted almost everything there is to try. The only time I was slightly unsettled was when I was watching sashimi being cut from live seafood. Talk about fresh. The lobster was the worst because their eyes still move after death, as if they're watching you eating them. It shows how disconnected we've become from the source of our food. Everything in Japanese cuisine is so clean, fresh and perfectly balanced. I love blowfish, for example – a perfectly clean-tasting, slightly sweet flesh that has a unique texture – or the underside of a fish that has a slightly gelatinous quality.

But I'm leaving all that behind me, about to board a plane and fly back to Switzerland and the training pool. Not that I'm complaining about the cuisine in a town which sits close to the Italian border.

eleven

25 NOVEMBER 2011

It's 10 am, there are clear skies and it's 15 degrees on the balcony of my Tenero apartment. Not bad when you consider the average maximum temperature in Switzerland for this time of year is just 10 degrees, plunging to overnight lows of close to zero. I might be missing home but there are definitely bonuses here, apart from the privacy for which this country is so well known. Morning training is the biggest plus. Back in Sydney I'd be up at 4.17 am (an extra two minutes adds up to 12 hours' extra sleep a year) and in the pool at 5 am, but nobody moves here, even slowly, much before 9. It doesn't mean you work less, just a little later.

My training routine has been pretty much set for months

now, the only difference pre and post the Asia World Cup meets is a couple of new training sets and the upping of the speed of the work as we move into preparation specifically for the 200 metres. Most mornings start with 30 minutes of core strength work before 90 minutes in the pool, the only exception being Thursdays when I have a weights session in the gym. I swim again most afternoons, sometimes mixed with weights and even a tennis lesson on Saturdays. Sunday is a day of rest.

Although the pool training is familiar and comforting, the core and gym work are pretty new to me, not because they haven't been an important part of training but because in the past I was, well, lazy. It didn't seem as relevant as my work in the pool. Back then I could break world records and win gold medals without having the strongest core in the world. I don't have that luxury this time around.

I'm still not obsessed by it, as others might be. I remain convinced that there's a textbook way to train but that there's also room for the individual. (There's that word again – individual.) I don't want to do exercises for the sake of it but I realise that I need to do more abdominal work to engage my core in a functional way – a real movement which is related to swimming. Besides, the work also helps me stay injury-free outside training.

The same applies to gym work. It hasn't been a significant part of training in the past, mainly because after ten two-hour plus training sessions in the pool each week the last thing you feel like is gym work, particularly when recovery is so important. Something has to give and for me it was always the weights room. I don't regret it, but this time it becomes more relevant because of the changes I've made to the way I swim, the biggest of which is the muscles I use in the stroke. It used to be driven by my triceps but now the muscles under my arm and across my lats and into the deltoids tend to dominate.

At the moment I'm doing three weight sessions a week, the heaviest on Tuesdays and Saturdays, which are based on power and speed. I don't do standard push and pull-type exercises, such as curls or bench presses, but more dynamic, coordinated movements in which I extend and even rotate, almost throwing the weight as if mimicking the movements of swimming. The Thursday session is a little lighter; that's when I do what I call goofy exercises – because they would look a little strange if someone was watching – which are more specific to particular aspects of my stroke.

The key is to get the balance right. For example, I concentrate on my back rather than my chest but have to counter that work by doing a chest fly exercise to avoid developing a forward roll in my shoulders. I also have to pay more attention to my upper body and glutes simply because my legs are so dominant. It's almost as if I have to do three or four upper body exercises to even out the impact of one leg exercise, otherwise I can actually feel the imbalance when I'm in the water, which isn't good.

What really counts is the shape of my body. What I'm trying to achieve is what might be called the Superhero physique; a big upper body to power the stroke and a tiny waist and strong glutes with big legs to drive the start, kick and turns without dragging at the back. My weight is less of an issue. I monitor it but not to the point of being obsessive. I was 102 kilograms when I raced in Singapore and the same when I got back here last week. When I race in London I would expect to be a little heavier, perhaps 106 or even 107 kilos, because of the weight work I've been doing and the fact that I'm concentrating on the sprints rather than the 400 metres. By comparison, I was 105 kilos at Athens, which made me the heaviest swimmer ever, and just 95 kilos at Sydney.

Training is a complex beast, as it is with any elite sport. It's not just a matter of diving into the pool and repeatedly swimming as fast as you can. In fact, what we work on most of the time is teaching the body to be more efficient – as Gennadi keeps saying, slowing down to speed up.

I swim between five and six kilometres in most sessions, which involve sets of various distances which concentrate on a mixture of efficiency, heart rates, stroke rates and even breathing. The main set on a Monday morning, for example, is about three kilometres (60 laps) in which I focus on maintaining a long, efficient stroke rather than power at a low heart rate. The main afternoon set is almost the same but swum at a slightly higher heart rate, and a faster stroke rate and time. I also do some shorter, speed-based sets.

There are several ways to train. First, Gennadi and I decide on the number of strokes for each lap. Then I swim the distance at a prescribed heart rate or to a specific time. The goal over a period of weeks is to maintain the heart rate and reduce the time, or maintain the time and reduce the heart rate.

I also aim to reduce the stroke rate. I've got it down to 24 per lap, which is about as low as I want it to get. I could reduce it by another four strokes but the danger is that I'd get to the point where I'm gliding rather than swimming efficiently. Reducing the stroke is a refinement rather than a major breakthrough in performance; it's not intended so much for the wow factor but because it will help me to swim longer without increasing lactate levels.

Training isn't also just about direct improvement. It's about repeatedly experiencing something in the water so that during a race, when I'm going faster than in training, my body delivers the same length of stroke and my hand goes into the water at the same point. As strange as it is, there are exercises where we are pulled through the pool while swimming at speeds that we can never achieve, just so the body can learn to accept that it can act in a certain manner at high speeds.

It's the same with breathing and why we train at high altitude; a psychological tussle to convince or even trick our bodies into believing that we can achieve things it has never done. I've seen graphs which map the deterioration of speed by swimmers during 100 metre sprints and it demonstrates that the person with the greatest ability to slow the rate of speed loss is the person who is likely to swim best and win the race. It sounds simple, but it's quite difficult when you try to put it into practice, to the point where it's important even to convince yourself that you are accelerating in the second half; to capture the sensation of acceleration and delay slowing down.

If I had another year before the Olympics I would be so relaxed at the moment. The only issue for me is the time I need to achieve the results necessary just to be a contender. When I started this comeback it wasn't about the possibility of winning at the London Olympics; it was about unfinished business. London is definitely a great motivator but I've come to realise that it's going to go beyond July 2012. I have no doubts about what I'm doing, how I'm doing it or what the end result will be. I will swim as well or even faster than I did in the first phase of my career. What I don't know is when it'll happen.

I've never felt normal; not because I have big feet or swim better than most but because I think differently to other people. Many times in my life there's been a darkness; a sense of isolation which is almost sinister. It's like I can't relate to others, or they can't understand me.

Even when I was little I was a black sheep; a kid whose mind wandered constantly. When I concentrated on what I was doing I could block out everything else – like a curtain of oblivion – which undoubtedly helped me later in competition. Fearing I was deaf, my parents tested my hearing because I'd sit for hours by myself building things with Lego, seemingly ignoring what was going on around me.

At primary school I was told how brilliant I was, which I found uncomfortable because it meant I didn't fit in with the other kids. It's great to encourage children to have a positive sense of themselves but this, although well-meaning, was excessive. To this day I have serious doubts about singling young kids out with psychological testing and streaming them through so-called gifted and talented programs in primary school. Does this mean that the other children aren't special? Praise shouldn't just be about academic or sporting achievement but for things like behaviour and effort as well.

The same applies to sport. The acknowledgement shouldn't just be for the people, like me, who win medals but for the others who have trained just as hard and performed as best they can. I remember the communication board at the front of my primary school which one day trumpeted the message: 'Ian Thorpe has won six gold medals at the national championships. We are all very proud'. I understand why they did it but it made me cringe with embarrassment. I was being set up as different from the other kids, most of whom were really excited by my achievement and wanted to see my medals, although there were a few who sneered and thought I was getting above myself. That's life, I suppose.

The one area where I wanted to be noticed as an individual was in my school reports, but they all began the same way: 'Ian is a cooperative and well-behaved student. He excelled in . . . ' It was a little bit too perfect, too glossy and shiny.

That changed when I got to high school, at least initially. The environment at East Hills High was more stimulating and teachers − at least the good ones − saw students as individuals. I loved the mental challenge of debating and found myself sitting at the table musing on how easy it would be to switch sides and argue our opponents' case. I had an art teacher who encouraged me not because of an artistic skill but because of my thought process and interpretation. It made me feel understood. By coincidence, Tracey Menzies − someone who made such a difference to my career because she understood me as a person − also taught at the school.

I loved being given the freedom to explore intellectually. One of my favourite memories was being given an assignment on nutrition when I was 13. I decided to study the impact of poor nutrition on mice so I bought a dozen or so from a local pet shop and fed half of them on the recommended food and the others on a diet of Twisties and green cordial. I then ran them through two similar mazes I'd built out of my Lego and timed each run. Much to my horror, the mice eating Twisties and drinking cordial set the fastest times. I switched their diets and tried them again. Same result. Then I changed their tracks but the mice on the rubbish food still won. In desperation, I built a completely new maze in case they had memorised it, all to no avail. I ended up giving a report on the effect of sugar and hyperactivity!

By Year 9 my swimming was really interfering with my education. My school report recorded that of the 200 school days for the year I was absent for 102, and yet I still managed to top my year thanks to teachers who could see that I was desperate to learn despite the distractions of training and competition. My geography teacher, realising I was bored, gave me Year 11 and 12 workbooks to accelerate my work.

I was happy socially, with a couple of close neighbourhood mates from my primary school days – who I still keep in touch with – and a playground acceptance that meant I was in the cool group at high school . . . well, on the fringes of it, at least. I couldn't quite understand that though, because I considered myself a nerd, happier in the library at lunchtime than playing handball in the playground. I wanted to be a neurologist or an architect, which were the sort of aspirations Mum and Dad encouraged so I had a future after swimming.

My physical size and sporting prowess weren't really an issue. It was just accepted that I was a good swimmer (and pretty average at any sport outside the pool) and was away from school a lot of the time. If I won medals at a competition the other kids would want to see them but, beyond that, it wasn't mentioned. We didn't talk about my other life in the playground.

What was really difficult for me at high school was the way I was treated by some of the teachers. As I became more successful in the pool and began to be offered sponsorships and won prize-money, it seemed there were a handful of adults who didn't like the fact that a kid was earning more than they did. To me there appeared to be a clear desire by some to bring me down in the classroom to make themselves feel better – my first experience of the tall poppy syndrome. One teacher made me count bricks in a pylon because I was talking in class one day, and then refused to accept my answer, which I had calculated mathematically, and kept me in detention. Another consistently marked me down in one of my favourite subjects, possibly because my swimming schedule meant extra work had to be prepared for me.

By the end of 1997, my Year 10 school year, faced with the increasing pressure of juggling study with training and competition, I'd had enough. Instead, I finished my School Certificate from home, going to the school once a week to collect course-work and then studying by myself between training schedules.

I've always been a big reader and the answers were all there in my books and my travels around the world. It definitely stimulated me in ways other than going through the motions at high school would have. As my former classmates studied geography and culture at school, I was seeing it for myself. I even completed two of my final class exams – Maths and

English – on a flight to Rio de Janeiro for a World Cup meet. The Australian team coach Don Talbot was the time keeper.

That would be the end of formal schooling for me. Too much was happening and I couldn't see how it was possible to train for the Sydney Olympics, now two years away, and do myself justice in the HSC. I wanted to drop out of school until I had finished my swimming career, which had accelerated since I'd won the world title in the 400 metres and, in doing so, become an early favourite to win Olympic gold. The plan would be to return to school as a mature age student and continue my education. But what would my parents say?

They were split. My father was having none of it. As far as he was concerned, education came before sport, even for an Olympic gold medal. I could understand his feelings, because he hadn't finished high school. As bright as he was, he had to leave school early to begin work and contribute financially to the family; something he'd always regretted and would fight to ensure didn't happen to his own children. My mother was more relaxed about it, even though she was a primary school teacher. She knew that I could always come back to complete my education, but there was only one chance to be an Olympic champion and I should follow that dream.

I've never asked my parents about their conversations but they eventually consented to my plan. I suspect Dad knew it was a battle he had to let me win. After all, they'd already lost their son to the world, which is what my father told Michelle Flaskas the night I won the world title, knowing they would have to share me with the public, media, marketing people and managers. They didn't want to lose me to the family as well.

In 2008, a decade after leaving school, I began studying psychology and linguistics at Macquarie University. My acceptance was based on my School Certificate results and because I had a reasonable excuse for not studying in the years afterwards. I'm close to finishing my degrees but had to defer when I decided to return to swimming and I don't know when I'll get back to it.

I was a gifted student in many ways but school just didn't work for me. I've realised that I prefer learning from life experience. I'm always reading and always interested in the events and affairs around me, whether it's politics or culture, art or religion. I don't just want to know what others think but prefer to assess and weigh things up for myself. I don't fall into one camp – Freud or Jung, for example. I agree with and find fault with both.

Sometimes I wonder what might have happened if I hadn't been a swimmer. It's a serious question for me because of the huge highs and massive lows that have gone hand-in-hand with my career. Most likely I would have finished high school, gone on to university and found a decent job, but my life would have been vastly different to the surreal world I inhabit now. Would people have responded the same way to me if I wasn't a swimmer? Would I have ended up liking the same things, like exploring culture, food and fashion? And would I have been as interested and involved in the world?

There are times that I wish I'd never swum and hanker for that other, unknown life – the one I gave up to pursue an Olympic dream. Thankfully those moments are rare, because I'd hate to live with regret. But I was always the kid who asked 'Why?' The problem is that the answer always brings another question. Sometimes you just have to stop yourself from wondering and accept things for what they are.

twelve

2 DECEMBER 2011

As much as I talk about instinct and being a natural swimmer, I acknowledge that there are many technical aspects to swimming which aren't readily noticed and contribute enormously to the final performance. I'm no exception and have spent the last couple of days after training having my new stroke filmed for biomechanical analysis and to test the science behind it – to see whether I'm improving and what might have to be tweaked.

I haven't seen any of the data yet but it looks promising and I've clearly improved in certain areas since the last analysis three months ago. The recovery, where my arm is out of the water and reaching forward, is longer, and the catch, where

I cradle a handful of water to haul myself along, is deeper. My body position on the waterline is also much better, higher and flatter, and there's no dip in my lower back and hips, which can really slow you down toward the end of a race. Perhaps all the core work I've been doing has paid off.

I had wondered, initially at least, if being older would make any difference and whether my body would hold up to the physical rigour of heavy training. It has so far and in some respects, my extra age has its advantages, particularly in the quest to redefine my stroke. I'm not sure I could have physically carried the new stroke when I was 24. I certainly couldn't have done it as a teenager. I simply didn't have the upper body strength that I have now at 29, nor the physicality to put my body into the position I need to make the stroke work.

Now, as my hand enters the water, my elbow comes over the top, putting all the weight of the stroke on the lateral muscles in my back and allowing me to pull a lot of water, deep and beneath my body. By comparison, the first movement used to be to hyper-extend my hand forward as it entered the water, which meant it was flatter and I didn't catch as much water at the front end of the stroke. The trick is to keep the movement as relaxed as possible, as if it's effortless rather than a deliberate pull through the water. The question is whether I can reproduce the action under race conditions. So far I've struggled.

It still feels uncomfortable but that's to be expected with something new. I'm exaggerating the change, trying to push things further as I begin specific 200-metre training, which focuses more on lactic acid tolerance. The intensity of the training comes down slightly but the number of lap and set repeats goes up.

I'm also battling an injury, which isn't unusual for someone training as hard as I am at the moment, although it's an injury I've never had before – strained muscles around the collarbone. It began a couple of months ago actually, probably caused by the huge gulps of air we have to take while training underwater, and was then exacerbated by the high altitude training.

The problem is that these muscles are connected so closely with breathing, but the real bother isn't the discomfort but the fascial tissue that I seem to have tightened, which in turn has irritated the muscles across my neck and into the shoulder. I get a searing pain from time to time, which isn't pleasant, but I have to battle through. I managed to get through all the meets in Asia with it, but I doubt it affected my performance all that much.

I've had a lot of work done – massage mainly – and thought the problem had cleared but it flared up again last week. So far it hasn't impeded my training but if it continues then it could become a serious issue, not only because of the pain but because if I start nursing the injury my body will become unbalanced and the chances of a secondary injury will increase substantially.

It's all part of the balancing act when training at this level. In the past we'd tend to push through most injuries like this because that's the way things were done, I think to our detriment. Now we have more science to back up our instinct, which is telling me that I have to get this thing fixed. If nothing else, it's an irritant; a distraction which I don't need.

Not all distractions are bad. As athletes, we search for them continually as ways to spend our downtime during heavy training. We test, stress and push our bodies to the limit but then need time to rest and recover so we can do it all over again and press a little further.

It was during one of these periods that my interest in aesthetics was sparked. Over the years the media has talked about me as a lover of fashion and although it's true, it's a lot simpler than that – I just love beautiful things. It doesn't matter if it's design or the environment, things with a simple or interesting beauty. When I flew – and I flew a lot – I'd be fascinated by what I could see out of the window no matter where I was, whether it was over a raw Australian landscape or the patchwork quilt of Europe, the coastal majesty of Rio de Janeiro or seeing the Chrysler Building for the first time as I flew into New York.

I do remember the first outfit that caught my attention, though. It was 1998 and I was 15 years old – already a world champion but still a boy – when I saw something in a magazine. I wanted to buy it immediately. I was part of the Australian team at a training camp in Singapore, preparing for the Commonwealth Games in Kuala Lumpur, and I was rooming with Victorian backstroker Adrian Radley at the Sea View Hotel, which had long since lost the reason for its name as the city expanded and blocked the view of the ocean.

With time to kill between sessions, I was leafing through a copy of GQ when I saw it: a three-quarter length jacket, teamed with casual pants. The combination really appealed to me. I'd never heard of the brand either – Emporio Armani – but was determined to find and buy the outfit when I got home the next week. Sadly (and it still annoys me) I missed out because the season had changed and the Sydney stores had moved on to the winter collections.

But it was a spark, and as teenagers tend to be, I was completely oblivious to fashion one day and obsessed the next. Until then my life had revolved around training and functional attire – swimmers, T-shirts and tracksuits mainly – so the notion of dressing up was new and struck a chord with me. Also, given that I was one of the youngest swimmers for a large part of my early international career, I tended to be around older people, not just coaches and officials but teammates, too, so I began to watch what they were doing. I remember shopping for clothes for the first time because a group of us were going to a theatre function in Melbourne. The world was changing for me. I was growing up.

It had begun a few months earlier, in the days after I won the 400-metre world title in Perth by overhauling Grant Hackett in the last few metres. In hindsight, the race changed my world in many ways, probably the least of which was the title itself.

The race was a lesson about instinct which would colour the rest of my career and private life. I'd entered it with few expectations, perhaps hoping to finish in the top three, but there was satisfaction enough just competing in the final of a world title. Doug Frost sent me out with specific instructions, to shadow the fastest qualifier and world number one, the Italian Emiliano Brembilla, who was alongside me. The other two contenders were Brembilla's teammate Massi Rosolino, and mine, Grant Hackett.

Grant went out like a bullet and led by two or three body lengths for most of the race, while I did as I was told and swam on the shoulder of Brembilla, although I knew I was going too slow. It was uncomfortable; my body was screaming out to go faster. As we passed the 250-metre mark I gave in to my instinct and picked up speed, not really after Grant so much as wanting to finish the race the best way I could. To everyone else it looked like I had timed my run perfectly as I caught Grant, passed him in the last metre and touched to win the race by a fingernail. But it had nothing to do with tactics.

I knew then that I had to trust myself, to concentrate on swimming my own race and complete the event as fast as *I* could, rather than simply race to beat someone else. I've given coaches headaches over the years because I wouldn't always swim to a race plan and preferred to swim based on how I felt in the water. There's a lot to be said for instinct in general life, too; trusting yourself and not always waiting for confirmation from evidence. There have been times over the years when I've followed instinct against advice and other times when I haven't trusted myself enough. In hindsight, I should have.

I bought my first house on instinct. Even as I walked down the driveway I knew it was the house for me. I'd been looking for a year and knew what I wanted. Everyone thought I should wait and reflect but I thought differently. When I went back later and looked at the criteria, it had ticked all the boxes.

There was another change that hot January evening in 1998 as I stood, giggling nervously during the post-race interview. Not only did my race plan change mid-swim, but from that moment, so did my life. It may have only been one result in a single race but I knew that Mum and Dad's Plan B had just gone out the window. I had a future in swimming.

Looking back, I am shocked at the speed of my transition from successful junior swimmer to world champion. The video of a poolside interview of me at age 12 after winning a slew of medals at a New South Wales age titles competition shows a shy boy, quite uncomfortable with being successful; perhaps amazed at what he could do. I felt awkward talking about it because I wasn't sure what I should be saying, or how I should feel about success. I certainly had no idea it would become my life.

The interview in Perth three years later shows a shy teenager, again giggling nervously at his unexpected achievement and what it might all mean. Until that moment I'd never considered my success in the pool could carry on into adulthood but my world had now changed forever, and not just in the water.

I had become the youngest world champion at the age of 15. It seemed that everybody in the media wanted to talk to me, that sponsors wanted me to talk to them, and dozens of companies wanted to pay for me to talk on their behalf, but who could I talk to about what had happened? I was so young that I struggled to find peers – no one else was doing what I was doing. I was just a kid. It was exciting but it was also lonely.

The only person I could relate to at the time was Grant Hackett, the closest I had to someone who had gone through a similar experience. His mum once told me that the saddest thing about Grant's success was watching him walk down the main shopping mall in the Gold Coast with his head down, just so he wouldn't be recognised. Perversely, my reaction was, 'Oh good, someone else has had the same experience.'

But there were lessons from the past. Even though I was the youngest-ever world champion, I wasn't the first 15-year-old to win a world title. Stephen Holland broke the world record when he won the 1500 metre crown in 1973 and Tracey Wickham won the 400 and 800 metres at the 1978 championships, but both retired from the sport by the age of 18. Shane Gould was an Olympic champion and world record-holder at 15 but retired at 16, and Hayley Lewis also struggled after becoming a Commonwealth Games champion at 15.

Looking back now, I wonder if that success at such a young age was worth the pressure it brought. Back then I had no real choice in the matter, until I decided at age 24 to give it all away. This time I'm doing it on my own terms.

thirteen

13 DECEMBER 2011

I can sense it's almost Christmas. Perhaps it's the absence of snow and unseasonal warmth up here in the Swiss Alps, which has reminded me of the joys of an Australian summer. Whatever the reason, I can almost smell the jasmine and hear the surf at Cronulla.

I'm more excited than homesick. This self-imposed exile has been hard at times, the space and isolation comforting for pragmatic reasons, but the absence of the familiar – friends and family, even simple belongings – is almost claustrophobic. My surroundings here suit the task I've set for myself perfectly but they lack the comforts of home. The only bit of colour in my apartment is a painting I did myself, inspired by Australian Aboriginal artists, hoping to cure the blandness of the white walls.

But I'm used to it now; it's the means to an end – an environment in which I have become comfortable but will almost certainly leave when this phase of my journey back to swimming ends. Although most of the time I am alone with my thoughts, close friends have been and gone, and Mum was here. In a week I'll be winging my way home for Christmas and then the Victorian championships in January.

But first it's the city of Riccione and the Italian Winter Open championships, and what I hope will be an event to ease my nerves and forge the pathway into qualification for the Australian Olympic trials, which are now just thirteen weeks away. It's important to post reasonable times in Italy because the best heats in Adelaide are seeded, and Riccione will count. The fastest qualifier is placed in Lane Four in the last heat, the second fastest in Lane Four of the second-last heat and the third fastest in Lane Four of the third-last heat. The next qualifiers are then ranked in the same way to fill in fields for the heats – the fourth-fastest in Lane Five alongside the fastest, and so on. It's crucial to ensure you get into one of those heats so you can draw better lanes when the competition hots up in the semifinal.

Despite my difficulties in Asia I'm feeling comfortable. I've settled back into training well and the early work on the 200 is encouraging. Dare I say it, I'm even a little wary of posting a time that's too quick at this competition because it's lot easier if I swim poorly, at least from a public perspective. I don't want the continuing distraction of having to discuss my prospects all the time. That's why I came to Europe. I don't have an answer to how well I'll swim and I won't really know until I dive into the pool in London in July next year.

I certainly didn't hold anything back in Singapore, Beijing or Tokyo. If I'd had more cards to play I probably would have, but the main issue for me was how overwhelming and unfamiliar it felt to be racing again. People – the media, that is – just don't get the impact of conditions like those. The fact is that I was racing against elite, race-hardened short-course swimmers. It's not an excuse but the reality, even for my own expectations.

The first 100-metre freestyle in Beijing, a race I hadn't planned to enter, was critical to the way I felt about my progress and my race strategy. If I'd dived in and felt comfortable then I might have taken the option of not swimming as well as I could have; maybe swimming the first 75 metres at speed and then allowing myself to back off a little in the last 25. It probably wouldn't have affected the outcome of the race but it would have given me some breathing space and allowed me to keep a sense of what might be to myself. But that's not what happened.

I feel differently about this weekend's event, mostly because it's in what I'd call a proper long-course pool – an Olympic pool. It's what I'm trained to swim in so I'm hoping it will be a little more relaxed. I'm even driving to the meet straight from Tenero, so it'll feel different to getting on a plane and travelling to the other side of the world, which is what I'd be doing if I was training in Australia.

I also have to keep reminding myself that for these events I'm not tapering, which is the period of rest before any big competition. I don't have the time to back off from the heavy training schedule; there aren't many options between now and the trials. Gennadi wants me race ready at any time, which is imperfect but like everything else, takes time.

Perhaps I'll feel a little better after the 200 metres on Saturday!

Another thing the media don't get is the impact of their relentless questions about my personal life. I was 16 years old when a journalist first asked me about my sexuality. I was sitting in a car in the city talking to a reporter who was compiling a newspaper profile about me.

There were ten questions designed for a Q & A style presentation – short and sharp with no room for anything but black and white responses. When the journalist got to the last question she hesitated, clearly uncomfortable: 'Are you gay?'

She realised immediately that the question had rattled me and hurriedly explained that 'everyone' had been asking about it, apparently since I'd won the world title as a 15-year-old, and that her boss had demanded that she ask me. She felt that her job was on the line; as if that justified the inquisition.

It wasn't just the question which took me by surprise but that it had come from a journalist who I knew well personally and trusted. She'd even made jam as a Christmas present for my family. Then she suggested that being asked by a friend was better than being asked by a stranger as further justification for intruding with the most intimate of questions.

It didn't seem to register with her that I was just a kid, still going through the confusion of puberty and being pushed to label myself before even I had worked it out. At the time I was a self-conscious teenager who only saw a big nose whenever he looked in the mirror and had been told he'd eventually grow into it. As far as I knew I'd never met a gay person.

Why would anyone ask that kind of question of an adult, let alone someone of my age who was in all likelihood still a virgin and learning about relationships and sexuality? What possible relevance did my sexuality have to do with being an athlete? Would anyone ask me about my political or religious beliefs or how much money I had in the bank?

I answered anyway: No.

Almost 14 years later, the question is still being asked, even though it's as inappropriate now as it was back then, put to me like some amateurish, grubby grope. It just never seems to go away. Sometimes I think I'd have had an easier time of it if I'd just thrown my hands up and said, 'Yes, I'm gay', albeit falsely, that first time. Perhaps it would never have come up again. The media simply won't accept the answer that I've given repeatedly. It seems to me that, not only do they think they have a right to ask, they also feel they have a right to the answer they want to hear.

I mostly laugh it off. I mean, what else can I do? There's no point in blazing away and threatening to sue newspapers and television stations because it'd just serve to inflame the situation and create a second problem rather than solving the first.

Of course, I'm not at all offended at the notion of being called gay. I thought it was hilarious the night the US female impersonator RuPaul got out of a lift at an Armani function in New York, looked me up and down and declared dramatically that he'd died and gone to heaven. I've been checked out by men at all kinds of events and functions and I've accepted that I've become a bit of an icon for the gay community. It's flattering, I guess.

My problem, other than the audacity of the question itself, is the simplicity of the box in which I'm being placed. It's like the term 'metrosexual', which is a concocted description that purports to represent, or 'explain' someone like me who happens to enjoy the aesthetics of fashion or dabbles in jewellery, things not normally associated with a red-blooded male. I find the notion banal, and it cheapens what sexuality is for young people. It's a serious issue.

The subject of how young people cope with the exploration of their sexuality is actually a very worthwhile conversation to have, if it's treated intelligently. I know what it's like to grow up and be told what your sexuality is, then realising that it's not the full reality and having to deal with it. I was accused of being gay before I knew who I was. It must be terrifying for gay people to have to come out and tell their family and friends for the first time. To have to explain and justify who you are when a large part of society still says that being homosexual is wrong is a horrible position to be in for any young person.

I sometimes watch TV shows like the one hosted by Ellen DeGeneres, who raises the issue of gay suicide quite often. I find it astounding that parents would be prepared to disown their children because they're gay. Why should a child be blamed for something that's the result of genetics? My own belief is that people are born straight or gay or somewhere in between. Where, how and with whom you grow up are not going to change the genetics, unlike issues like addiction to alcohol and gambling which can be influenced by both genetic predispositions and environmental influences.

For the record, I am not gay and all my sexual experiences have been straight. I'm attracted to women, I love children and aspire to have a family one day. I walk and talk my own way and my manner is my own; it's not an act. I'm not prepared to be disengenuous toward myself or anybody I meet by acting like someone I'm not. But I can also understand what prompts these questions, because I'm not the sort of man who overtly beats his chest in a ritual of masculinity while declaring that he only finds women attractive. I'm not so naive to say that I can't see the aesthetics in a good looking man. I think we can all appreciate beautiful women and beautiful men. I guess that makes me 99 per cent straight.

Let me explain this a little further (I don't want to get too academic here, although it is tempting to slip into psychology essay-writing mode, which is a test of anyone's attention span!). In 1948 the American biologist Alfred Kinsey and two colleagues published what became known as the Kinsey Scale, a human sexuality rating scale, which concluded that human beings do not fit neatly into exclusive heterosexual or homosexual categories but rather along a continuum between the two.

In his book *Sexual Behaviour in the Human Male*, Kinsey reported that 46 per cent of the male subjects interviewed had 'reacted' sexually to persons of both sexes in the course of their adult lives. He wrote: 'Males do not represent two discrete populations, heterosexual and homosexual. The world is not to be divided into sheep and goats . . . The living world is a continuum in each and every one of its aspects.'

I struggle to believe that any 'heterosexual' male, who is being entirely honest, could deny recognising some men as being attractive and some unattractive. Of course, this wouldn't make him gay.

I'm also not like others who might regard sex as the most important aspect of a relationship. It's just not me, and the issue was no less complicated than when I was a teenager. When I become friends with someone I don't base it on their sex. All my relationships are based on the individual and how we connect.

The question of relationships is far more difficult for me than simply what or who I find attractive. The truth is that I've spent most of my adult life trying to avoid relationships, not just because of my demanding lifestyle as an athlete but because I have a complicated personality and it isn't easy to find someone who fits comfortably with me or me with them. There are other, deeper issues at play as well, but if people get too close to me – friends and more intimate relationships – I often end up pushing them away.

One of my relationships in particular is a good case in point. I was crazy about her but I was also a young man who was shy, unsure of himself and had grown up to treat women with a very traditional kind of respect. When I look back on it now I think the affair probably wasn't a great idea. I had a temptress and it was fun but it was never going to work. I learned that lesson.

I don't talk about my other relationships and broadcast roll-calls of the women I've dated because I don't need to justify my sexuality by saying what I've done or who I've been with and when. In fact, I'd prefer that people continue to question my sexuality rather than demand that I produce evidence in support of who I am. Doing that would only legitimise the mean aspect of the media and the parts of our society which need gossip so they can suppress how they feel about themselves.

I accept that there's nothing else I can say or do. There'll always be people who are sceptical; people who want me to be gay, and others who'll try and use it against me. It should have been over and done with a long time ago but people have remained obsessed with it and need to find an explanation which suits their perspective. I suspect there's also a bit of tall poppy syndrome in this, too.

I know I'm different to most athletes. Not just physically, but in my attitudes to the sport, how I think about it and what drives me. I understand that desire to know why I'm different, but what I don't understand is why people want to chip away and expose one of the few areas of my life that hasn't been on public view.

I have nothing to hide, although I fiercely guard my right to privacy and that of those around me. The worst moment was in 2009 when the media targeted my friendship with Daniel Mendes, a Brazilian swimmer who lived at my house in Sydney for a few years while he studied at the University of Wollongong. One newspaper followed us to Brazil, where I was a guest of Daniel's family on holidays, taking photos of us on a beach to imply that there was something more to our relationship when it simply wasn't true. I had to explain the situation and apologise to his family for bringing them into my bizarre life. I've also had to deal with it recently, here in Switzerland, when allegations were aired on a blog site about a male friend I've made. The situation couldn't have been further from the truth – in fact he and I went out a little while ago to buy a diamond engagement ring for his Australian girlfriend.

There has never been a discussion about all of this with my family. It might be a bit strange but I have always gone to great lengths to make sure they're not bothered by what's going on in my life. I think the reason my parents have never raised it is because they've seen me having to deal with it and defend who I am, and they don't want to cause me any more angst. That said, my sister Christina, who is pregnant with her second child, joked recently: 'Are you with someone? A girlfriend? . . . Boyfriend?' It was the first time I'd been asked about relationships by a family member, even if it was my sister being a smart-arse to get a rise out of me. My answer was simply that I hadn't been in a relationship for quite a while.

But it's not the only difficult issue I've avoided discussing with the people I'm closest to.

fourteen

19 DECEMBER 2011

'Hi Mum, swam like a dog.'
I can't remember ever having described a performance like that but, in a strange way, it felt good to text my mother after the 100 metres at Riccione.

It was cleansing, I suppose; getting the disappointment out of my system, refusing to dwell and hoping to move on quickly. I'd been expecting to swim comfortably under 50 seconds and earn a decent qualifying place for the Olympic trials. Instead, I almost fell into the water and thrashed my way to 50.84 seconds, finishing sixteenth fastest.

I could excuse the performances in the Asian short-course meets to some extent but five weeks on from Tokyo, this was a more realistic analysis of where I am in my preparation; I swam in a proper-sized pool against real opponents, fresh from the European championships, even though the time trial format was unusual. I'd driven down from Tenero with Gennadi the day before, a four-hour drive which turned into almost six because we had to turn around when we realised he'd left his bag behind — not that I could blame it for my performance.

As usual Gennadi said little after the race, asking me how I felt, acknowledging my disappointment and then turning his attention to the next training session. He's always been like this — 'I'm happy if you're happy,' he says — assessing the possible outcomes ahead to such an extent that the result, whatever it is, has already been considered and placed into context.

The media had also made an assessment of my swim; less generous of course and much more black and white. There's no room for complexity in print; you're either a hero or a failure. It doesn't surprise me they would regard this performance — failure they wrote — as the moment they could write off my return as fanciful. I should have viewed headlines such as 'Thorpe's comeback is fast sinking' as a blessing really, lowering expectations; but the ignorance is grating and the understanding simplistic and dismissive of what it takes to achieve anything in elite sport. And what's with all the swimming and water analogies? Why is every analogy that mentions struggling about water?

I'm as frustrated as anyone, my own expectations unfulfilled and yet I know the answer lies in persistence and patience. The results will come; I just don't know when and if I have the time before the trials — or the Games. It was always a gamble but, to use an expression straight from a tabloid reporter's phrasebook, I remain buoyant.

I'm battling the changes I've made to my stroke for a start. Imagine a golfer returning to the PGA tour, not only having been fishing for a few years but with a new swing. It's going to take time to get used to the pressures of competition, let alone being comfortable with the mechanics of the new stroke under pressure.

That's how it feels in the water. The changes Gennadi and I have made make sense but they're new and still unreliable, especially under race conditions. I'm struggling to relax enough to slow the race down and make the stroke work for me, which is a blade-like movement with long, strong strokes. I haven't come close to doing it in competition so I end up thrashing around and only feeling as if I'm going fast.

Not all the problems are physical. I'm also battling serious pre-race nerves. Anxiety is something I used to handle well, even harnessing the shot of adrenaline just before the gun fired. Instead, it's become debilitating. As I stood on the blocks next to two-time world champion Filippo Magnini I could feel the bile rising in my stomach.

It had nothing to do with him and everything to do with me. Looking at the photos of me taken on the day I can see it in my face and posture. I wasn't in command as I once would have been in that situation. Instead, my head is down and I almost look embarrassed to be there. But that might well have been my reaction to the generosity of the crowd's reception as I entered the pool deck, the announcer detailing my Olympic and world championship medals, which only highlighted the mountain I'm trying to scale.

To be honest, I'm not sure how to handle it. Will I ever be able to meet expectations when my performance levels are down and the anticipation of my return is so huge? How can I get the balance right? The more I have to justify my performances, talk about my frustrations and explain the complexity of the process, the more the pressure builds on my next race and so the expectation intensifies – and with it the anxiety. It's like a never-ending circle. I just hope the more I race, the better I'll feel, which seems to be the case now that I've got my other event out of the way.

'1:51.5' was the text I sent to Mum after swimming the 200. It had a different tone and she picked up on it immediately: 'Better?' she wrote back. 'Yes,' I responded. The words were few but my relief was enormous, particularly as one of the guys who finished behind me was Massi Rosolino, who won bronze in the 200 metres behind Pieter van den Hoogenband and me at the Sydney Olympics. He's kept swimming over the years and is keen to make the Italian 4 × 200 metre relay team for London.

Some would have viewed the swim as another disappointment, but it was the time and the way I swam the race which were important, not the result. As some journalists apparently pointed out, it may have been seven seconds off my best, but what was gratifying for me was that it was well within the time Leigh Nugent had wanted to see me swimming at this stage in my preparation.

It actually felt more like a training swim than a race; there was a certain level of control and relaxation, as opposed to my hectic dash in the 100. The length of the race was probably much more suited to the benefits of the countless laps I've swum in training over the past year and allowed me to settle into my stroke. I spoke to Leigh later and he seemed pleased with my progress, and understood that this is a process which takes time. I really don't think I could have attempted this if it wasn't for him.

One of the reasons Gennadi has insisted on keeping training sessions long and slow is to embed the changes made to my stroke so I can rely on it under pressure. We train my heart rate so I can perform when it balloons over 200 beats per minute, we train my breathing so I can cut back oxygen intake in the last 50 metres and avoid slowing the momentum, and we train the stroke mechanics so it doesn't shorten and slow as I turn for home.

It isn't reliable at the moment, especially in the 100. The stroke is supposed to be a very long, strong and highly-rotated movement, and I haven't got the self confidence yet to relax and trust it under race conditions. I'm confident though, like everything else, it's just a matter of time. But it's becoming a very frustrating wait. The one good thing about it is that being the perfectionist that I am I can vent my frustrations by pushing myself harder in training – a tool to turn a negative into a positive.

It's impossible to avoid the negatives in elite sport. One of the worst moments of my career was an evening spent around the kitchen table at Mum and Dad's house. It was February 2000 and Olympic fever was beginning to take hold across Sydney. Preparations were entering their final phase, souvenirs were filling supermarket shelves and tickets were arriving in mail boxes. And just as the city's residents were beginning to imagine the reality of the lottery they'd won in Monaco eight years before, so too were the athletes as they began to imagine being on the starting blocks and what it might feel like to win or at least perform at their best. Excitement was in the air.

Yet the feeling inside our home wasn't one of anticipation but of apprehension. My parents had sat me down for what they called a 'serious chat', which sounded ominous and got worse. They'd prepared a list of hypothetical accusations which might be levelled at me or the family in the lead-up to the Games. Dad started reading from the list, which included some quite bizarre claims, such as my mother had been a prostitute and that I was abused as a child. The list went on and on and on and on.

I was shocked and confused, and stopped Dad mid-claim. 'Have they said all of these things about us?' I asked.

'No,' he replied. 'We just want to be prepared for anything.'

The lead-up to the Games for me and my family in our hometown should have been an amazing experience but it was hijacked by fear and loathing, the result of an accusation seemingly from out of nowhere that I was a drug cheat. It was the biggest insult anyone could throw at me because it questioned my core values as a person. No one – not even my coaches and my family – could really understand what I had gone through to produce the performances that were beginning to change the face of swimming, yet here was a mindless, puerile allegation that threatened to derail the hard work and dreams of a 17-year-old boy.

Anything after that, everything the media threw at me was easy, even the gay rumours which would increase in their intensity soon after. The thought still makes me burn.

It had happened a few weeks before, as the Australian swim team was touring Europe for three World Cup meets. The first competition was in Sheffield in the UK, where I won a hat-trick of races in the 100, 200 and 400 metres. Apparently there'd been a discussion on the pool deck between the German swimming coach Manfred Thiesmann and a journalist, which centred on newspaper reports about the use of synthetic human growth hormone by athletes. As I walked past, unaware of the conversation, the journalist pointed to me and asked Thiesmann what he thought about me.

'A lot of people suspect that he dopes,' Thiesmann was reported to have said, going on to say that he'd been sitting on the coaches' bench in Sydney when I broke my own 200-metre short course record:

Almost everyone was asking 'How is it possible?' There's a lot of scepticism about him, but we can't prove it so you can't blame him … Thorpe is not only passing them [Italian swimmer Giorgio Lamberti's times] – he's passing them by seconds. He is a world apart, like the sun and the moon. I acknowledge that he has the best physique for a swimmer – his hands, his feet, his shoulders, his narrow waist, his muscles are very soft – but I am still suspicious.

The story was picked up in the British media, and though Thiesmann tried to back away from his comments soon after by insisting he had raised doubts and not allegations, it had exploded into a full-scale controversy by the time I flew into Berlin a few days later.

In the meantime, the editor-in-chief of swimming's journal of record, *Swimming World,* Phillip Whitten, had dismissed the idea, writing:

> There is absolutely no reason to suspect Ian Thorpe is doping. Detailed underwater stroke analysis shows he has extraordinary technique. In addition, he exhibits none of the physical signs of drug use. His physical attributes, natural talent, excellent coaching and superior technique account entirely for his superb performances.

I fronted a media conference to reject the assertions but it felt – and it wouldn't be for the last time – that responding to outrageous allegations only fuelled the media fire rather than put it out. I was innocent but, in effect, had to prove I was clean even though there was no test that could detect synthetic human growth hormone, or EPO as it's known.

Despite the fuss, I swam a personal best time the next night in the 100 metres and followed it up an hour later by winning the 400 metres. In between events, I was told I'd have to give a blood test, which I'd become very used to and almost welcomed.

It was only when I was in the drug-testing room watching the officials divide the blood into two containers – A and B samples – that I realised something was amiss. The containers are supposed to be tamper proof, sealed with our signatures and sent off to labs for analysis, but the German authorities were still using containers which could be steamed open.

I refused to consent to the samples being taken away, particularly given the circumstances, and asked US back-stroker Lenny Krayzelburg, who was also being tested, if he'd support my stance. I'll forever be grateful to Lenny for standing by me as we sat in that little room at the bottom of the giant concrete swimming complex in Berlin. Even though the US and Australia are fierce competitors in the pool, we're united as colleagues out of the water.

It'd take more than three hours to resolve the standoff. Our head coach Don Talbot and the US coach Jonty Skinner had both supported our concerns, even though the German officials and a FINA official insisted nothing was wrong. Finally, local police agreed to take charge of the samples and even though it was far from perfect, Lenny and I begrudgingly signed our consent and handed them over.

The experience was pretty traumatic and Don knew it. I swam the heats of the 200 metres the next morning but he could tell I was upset and as we sat in the stands above the pool, he offered to allow me to pull out of the final, which was that night. It was the first time he'd ever considered allowing a swimmer to do such a thing but it was clear to him that I'd been badly affected.

I disagree with some of the things that Don has done over the years but on this occasion he understood the situation perfectly. I hadn't actually considered withdrawing from the race but Don thought that I might be. He read my mood before I'd reached that point and gave me the imprimatur to mull it over.

Instead, it spurred me on. I realised that this was a moment that I had to confront rather than avoid, no matter how good the reason to walk away. And I knew that unless I did, I couldn't be sure that I had the mental strength to perform under the pressure of the Olympic Games.

I would swim, I told Don, provided he'd turn a blind eye and allow me to wear one of the swimsuits I was testing. It was unbranded and, though – strictly speaking – not permitted while representing Australia, I wanted to perform at my best and make a statement. I wanted to silence everyone, to stick my middle finger up at all of them.

As I left I walked past the German team. I had no idea which one was Theismann but I guessed he would be one of the older administrators. I'm not a confrontational person by nature but I wanted to let them all know that I was angry about what had been said and that I was innocent, so I deliberately stopped and looked, searching each of their faces. One, a silver-haired man with a square jaw, caught my eye. He had what I would call a small, apprehensive smile on his face, which confirmed not only who he was but that he didn't want to engage with me. The message had been sent.

That night I broke my own short course world record by more than a second. It was one of the few times I used external factors to create a performance and I still regard the swim as one of my best ever, satisfying in a different way to any Olympic medal or world record because it meant I was standing up for who I was and that I had the capacity to perform no matter what happened.

The crowd sensed it, too. As I stepped up onto the dais to accept my medal, the Swedish team stood up and applauded. It spread around the stadium like a Mexican wave as swimmers from other countries joined in the applause. I was astonished at the reaction – but it showed what the swimming world thought of Thiesmann and his comments.

It wasn't finished. After the medals were presented I shook the hands of the place-getters. The second-place swimmer, Hungarian Béla Szabados, congratulated me and added that he wished he hadn't made the final. I asked the obvious question: 'Why would you want to miss the final?'

He smiled: 'So I could watch you swim.'

I had one last surprise. The Berlin officials had offered a car – a bright yellow Jeep Cherokee – to the swimmer judged to have put in the best performance, and I had won. Dave Flaskas reckoned I should drive it into Lane Four and leave it at the bottom of the pool, but as much as I'd have liked to follow his advice, I decided instead to sell the car and give the proceeds to UNICEF.

I thought that was the end of the issue but it wasn't. Six months later, in early July, the German team had another crack at me. This time it was the team captain, Chris-Carol Bremer – a doctor who might perhaps have known better – who gave an interview to the newspaper *Die Welt* (*The World*) which included the following (translated) exchange:

Die Welt: Is it just the fast times that make the Australians suspicious?

Bremer: We must focus attention on the physical characteristics of times. If we are dealing with HGH, as the Australians are accused of, then one of the symptoms in adult athletes of gigantism. That means hands or feet are unnaturally large.

Die Welt: World record-holder Ian Thorpe has size
51 shoes.

Bremer: I am not commenting on this. People should just
know what physical characteristics leave some doping
methods. And let them make their own judgement.

The comments were repeated in a Melbourne newspaper
a few days later, prompting Dave Flaskas to respond with
this memorable quote – 'Ian may well have big feet but the
Germans have big mouths.' As funny as it was, the allegation
was serious and forced my father to speak publicly for one of
the few times in my career, pointing out that big hands and
feet were simply genetic and that he and my mother have
big feet and hands, as does my sister.

Bremer backtracked a few days later, accusing the newspaper of taking his comments out of context and offering this:
'I did not specifically accuse Thorpe of doping, but he is the
best and there will always be people who suspect him.'

Dave Flaskas responded again: 'Every time Ian is accused he
swims a world record. We are therefore looking forward to the
next accusation before the Olympic 400-metre final.'

As it turned out I didn't need another incentive. When
I returned to Australia my mind was firmly on the Olympics.
The first night's competition in Sydney, when I won gold in
the 400 and the 4 × 100 metre relay, was probably the best of
my career.

fifteen

8 JANUARY 2012

My comeback is at the crossroads. I'm at my sister Christina's house, where I've been staying since arriving in Sydney a few days before Christmas, and I've just spent a day at the Prince of Wales Hospital undergoing a series of tests. It sounds like a dramatic development and it is, but not for obvious reasons.

Ever since the Italian Open at Riccione I've been concerned about my level of anxiety, which peaks in the moments just before racing. As I dive into the pool it feels as if I'm short of breath – like I'm literally drowning, my heart racing as if I've already finished a 1500 metre event. It settles down the further I get into the race but by then the damage has been done, my stroke and rhythm thrown into disarray.

I dismissed it in Asia as a natural response to the first few competitive outings but my performance in Italy was a real worry. It's the one thing that's holding me back because there's no physical reason why I'm not swimming better, and I'm sick and tired of people reminding me.

It's not uncommon for swimmers, and particularly those who swim longer distances, to develop lung problems a little like asthma in the latter stages of their careers, probably brought on by the constant exposure to pool chemicals like chlorine. I wondered if that was the cause of my problems and, rather than continue to wrestle silently with the issue, decided to have a full medical to either confirm or dismiss the issue before it got critical – to face up and move on.

To those around me it must have been quite unnerving for me to go into hospital at this stage, and I got a bit worried myself when the doctor told me he wanted me to have not one but several tests while I was there. Typically, he wouldn't say why, which meant I was crapping myself for a couple of days until the results came back.

The answer, which came this afternoon, is good and bad. My lungs are clear, which is good, but that means the problem is in my head, which is bad, and I don't know how to root it out. Now I'm anxious about being anxious, which makes no sense. I've tried to deal with it alone over the last few months but I realise that I need an independent point of view, as much as it goes against the grain – someone who can give me some practical ways of dealing with anxiety.

It's the one downer on a trip home that has so far been a terrific break at the end of a very trying year. The most refreshing aspect has been the public support I've felt. Maybe it's the time of year – holidays and great weather – but the response has been one of encouragement and not a question of how I might perform: 'I'm just happy to see you back in the pool' is a common reaction I get in the street. It's a far cry from the white noise of the media, which continues to talk about failure.

Christmas was a great reminder of my childhood, opening presents on the lounge room floor at home and going to church before lunch at my paternal grandmother's, the house full of noisy cousins and where I could sit and help my nephew and nieces build the Lego toys I'd bought them. Dinner was at Mum and Dad's house where, for once, I was relieved of cooking duties and was able to sit and just enjoy the moment.

Boxing Day was an all-day barbecue at a boathouse on Port Hacking, canoeing and fishing with a few members of the Swiss squad who came over with me and Gennadi. It's nice being part of a training group again and making new friends. Between cooking steaks, most of my time was spent helping the guys take undersized bream off fish hooks so they could be tossed back. I sent them into the city to watch the New Year's Eve fireworks and spent the evening having dinner with a couple of friends. I was asleep before the clocked ticked over to 2012, the heavy training taking its toll. It has also been a tough reality check for me. Being in Australia, surrounded by family and friends, should have been a time to be happy. Instead I felt down, realising just how isolated I have become in Switzerland. I wasn't questioning my comeback but acknowledging the psychological rollercoaster I was riding.

I've been combining time in the pool with a couple of beach outings, including a day at Cronulla scaling sandhills and open water swimming. I've also been working at the Australian Institute of Sport in Canberra, where their high technology pool has helped me improve my starts. I've been able to plot my weight distribution, rotation and even the angle and splash of the dive as well as how long to delay my kick to ensure I don't lose speed at the beginning. I worked on my turns there, too, although it wasn't technology which provided the answer but a technique using an empty water bottle placed on the edge of the pool. If I turned properly from the wall, the splash would knock the bottle off the ledge but if I didn't, the splash would disperse sideways and miss the bottle. I've realised there's a significant flaw in the drill, though – every time you make a great turn you have to go and get the water bottle to set up again!

Then came the health scare, more a build-up from my earlier experiences in Asia than a sudden worry. Anxiety has never been a problem before; if anything adrenaline has been my friend on the starting blocks. Now it threatens to derail everything. There's no other explanation for the times I'm swimming. I had expected to be swimming somewhere close to 49 seconds by now for the 100 but I can't see that happening in Melbourne next weekend for the Victorian championships. Then again, I may get some relief from the medical clearance and some professional help to get this anxiety monster out of my head.

I owe it to myself.

For all my individual victories, records and medals, the most euphoric moment for me was the victory over the Americans in the 4 × 100 metre relay at the Sydney Olympics. The moment was pure joy mingled with surprise and the noise inside the stadium was like nothing I've heard before or since. It wasn't about beating the opposition, as good as it was, but achieving the improbable as a team.

It was also about mateship, that Australian term which means more than sharing an idea or a friendship but putting yourself on the line physically for another person. Swimming might be considered an individual sport by most people but it's very much a team game as far as I'm concerned, from training day in, day out with a group of colleagues, to being part of a club, a state or a national squad, like my camaraderie with the Swiss squad – and being on a relay team.

If you look at my 100-metre results, it's quite bizarre that I've been able to produce performances in relay races that I haven't been capable of reproducing in my individual events. I think it says a lot about us as individuals that we can pull something extra out of the hat in a team situation.

I think my love of relays stems from having been the youngest person on the Australian team for a significant period in my career. I received so much encouragement and help from the older members of the squad that it gave me a sense of belonging to something much bigger than just *my* races. The performances and results were *our* performances and results. We were all in this together.

Relays are a reflection of the depth of swimming talent in a single nation and Australia's success over the years, particularly given our small population, is not only proof of the excellence of its swimming programs but also our attitudes to competition.

We didn't appear to stand a chance in the 4 × 100 relay in Sydney, even though we'd beaten the Americans at the Pan Pacs the year before, which was the first time they'd lost in international competition. But the Olympics were something else. I still get emotional about it. On paper it looked improbable, the Americans so confident that their anchorman, Gary Hall Junior, bragged they would 'smash us like guitars'. But we had a strategy. The Americans always swam the race the same way, with their fastest man, in this case Gary, at the back. We also had an advantage because three of our four swimmers all had strong finishes while the Americans tended to fall away in the last 25 metres.

If we could establish an early lead by putting our fastest swimmer – Michael Klim – at the front so they were chasing us rather than dictating the pace of the race then they might be distracted and fall off their game, just enough for us to beat them. But it almost didn't happen at all. As I got changed for the race I split my full body swimsuit and had to find and then squeeze into the wet one I'd used an hour earlier to win the 400 metres final. It took some doing and I managed to make it to the marshall whose job it was to tick my name off just as our lane was announced. We were close to being disqualified. Lesson learned? Always, always be nice to officials and volunteers – I thank that marshall, Margaret, to this day.

Michael was swimming against Anthony Ervin, who would win gold in the 50-metre event, and yet Klimmy beat him by almost a body length in a world record time of 48.18. To put his performance in perspective, Michael would finish fourth a few days later in the individual event, with a time of 48.74.

Chris Fydler was next, swimming against Neil Walker, who would beat him comfortably in the individual final – and yet Chris held him off and kept the lead. Chris's time of 48.84 was a full second quicker than he would swim in the individual final.

Ashley Callus lost the lead to Jason Lezak in the third leg but somehow swam up to the American and passed him to touch first, in a time – 48.71 – that would have been good enough to win a bronze medal in the individual final, a race which he hadn't qualified for.

As the last swimmer, I only asked for one thing – to make sure we had a lead when I dived in. We did have a lead, although it was barely a fingernail. I'd envisaged at least one full second so I could hold off Gary Hall Junior, but he caught me halfway down the first lap. I tried to stay calm and trust that my power in the second 50 would be enough.

As I turned I was shocked about how far ahead he actually was. I gulped, then put my head down and drove hard, concentrating on keeping my stroke long as his shortened in the last 25 metres. I got to him with 15 metres to swim, held on then stretched out with my left hand to touch him out on the wall. I had swum 47.9 seconds.

Looking back now, I don't think our strategy worked in the sense that it affected the Americans, who also recorded their fastest time and certainly swam well enough to win the gold medal. The difference was that *our* strategy inspired *us* to swim better than we had before. We got in front early and each swimmer refused to let their opponent pass because that would have let down the rest of the team.

It wasn't just the four of us but the whole Australian team. The victory meant so much to the squad – there was a sense that to win this event and break the American dominance could inspire everyone else to do the same over the next few days. We had just swum 3:13.67 and set a world record. We never got close to that time again while I was swimming. Interestingly, there was a time when making it onto a squad as a relay swimmer seemed second best but now each place is hotly contested.

The importance of that race as an iconic victory is enduring and people often tell me that it still ranks as their favourite win by an Australian team alongside the America's Cup win in 1983 when I was just a year old. It's probably because of the larrikin element of us playing air guitars to mock the Americans after winning.

Another important aspect was the psychological boost it gave the Australian swimming team. From then on the Americans, in particular, feared us. We'd created an aura around the team, and done it so successfully that the other teams wanted our gear, especially the T-shirts naming us as the Australian swim team. We weren't loud and boisterous like the Americans but the way we swam was intimidating. They knew we were capable of lifting as a team and it really unsettled them. I realised it the following year at the world titles in Fukuoka when I was up against Jason Lezak in the relay and lost the lead before coming home and winning in my fastest ever split time of 47.87. At the Pan Pacs the following year I did it again against Lezak.

But the opposite was true in Athens. We swam badly from a bad lane and finished sixth. It was sad, not because we hadn't won the race but because we had lost something special to the team. I think it showed a few nights later when we finished second in the 4 × 200 metre relay. The Americans turned the tables on our Sydney strategy, swimming Michael Phelps first to try and get a lead, holding it through the middle of the race and then challenging me to swim over the top of Klete Keller, who had finished fourth in the 200 metre final a few days earlier.

I was a body length behind at the changeover and had almost caught Klete by the first turn, which was not my usual tactic (and was later criticised unfairly by Don Talbot). I was trying to intimidate Klete into making a mistake but somehow he was able to respond. I surged twice more in the last 50 metres, with 30 metres to go and again with 15 metres to go, but I simply couldn't get past him and he beat me by a hair's breadth. The US coaches were astounded that I'd been able to commit twice from a position of defeat. I still regard it as one of my most incredible races.

While we'd created a special – and powerful – aura around our team, my colleagues still had to deal with the circus that came with my involvement with anything in the pool. For the most part, they enjoyed the media attention created around me. They knew I hated the fuss but were fascinated by the whole thing, like the scene when we arrived to screaming fans in Japan for the 2001 World Championships – and later, when we dominated on the first night of competition and the vanquished Americans had to board a bus which had a giant picture of me emblazoned across it. Talk about rubbing it in.

Everyone referred to it as The Thorpe Show and for the most part it was said without malice. But the constant attention could also be wearing, not just for me but for the others.

165

I got along with most people but it was inevitable, I suppose, that a few people resented what I was doing and the attention and money that flowed from it. At one team meeting I remember someone asking why there was one person on the squad who made more money than the sport itself. Everyone turned to me for a reaction. In reality the comment was as much about the poor promotion of our sport as it was about me, but it still stung.

I can't and won't apologise for being financially successful but the resentment wasn't just about money. My own success and the media's infatuation with my life meant the success of others was overshadowed at times, and I really regret that. I can't explain the interest in me and I can't help it. I'm not someone who seeks attention; in fact I'm quite the opposite, and I have to deal with it. I suppose I'm used to doing that most of the time now and people get the impression that I'm comfortable with it. But I'm not – and I never really have been.

And the attention since I've been back in Australia hasn't helped my anxiety levels. I just hope I can rid myself of the monster when I line up in Mebourne next weekend.

16 JANUARY 2012

I'm in Sydney, packing to leave later tonight. The temperature is hovering near 30 degrees, a far cry from the minus 7 expected when I step off the plane in Milan tomorrow to collect my car and drive back across the border into Switzerland. The European winter, which took so long to arrive, is now in full swing and for once I'll be glad of the tent over the Tenero pool.

It's sad to admit but I'll also be glad to be out of Australia, at least for the time being. I loved being home, in this city which is so at ease with itself at this time of year, but the pressures of being me within it are too much. I've now made three re-entries into competitive swimming – my first race in Singapore, my first long-course meet in Riccione and my first Australian swim at the Victorian championships at the weekend – and the focus of attention is suffocating. I can't even train without the cameras clicking. I have to expect it, I suppose, but it makes me appreciate the peace of Switzerland.

I got some advice and tried breathing exercises before the 100 in Melbourne to contain my anxiety levels but it didn't work. I might as well have had a coffee and chat with someone for all it was worth, and it's just entrenched my view that I should tough it out on my own. The race itself was a mess, even worse than Riccione, and sent me right back to square one: the 51.05 I swam was the same time I swam back in Tenero in September, four months ago.

I had expected to swim around 49 seconds at this stage in my preparation and there is no reason, based on my training times, that I shouldn't be hitting the mark. Gennadi says I look like I'm thinking too much in the first 25 metres and I need to open myself up to the competition and the urgency of the situation. He's undoubtedly right but I haven't been able to flick the switch. As I touched the wall next to Michael Klim, who's also on the comeback trail, I smiled and quipped: 'At least yours was good.' We both laughed at the strange place we'd found ourselves in.

The 200 the next night had a different feel to it. I swam comfortably within myself to qualify for the final, which was a relief given the circumstances. But I should have stopped there and not swum in the final that evening. I was very tempted, although pulling out would have been controversial, so I swam anyway, even though I felt the job had already been done and I'd had my swim for the day. Neither my time in the final – 1:50.79 – nor my fifth placing meant anything beyond confirmation that I'm within target to swim much quicker when it counts in March.

Someone pointed out that Michael Phelps had swum slower times at a meet in Austin, Texas, this same weekend in both events. I wouldn't place too much stock in that but it's interesting nonetheless and gave me reason to think back on my own performances at smaller meets over the years. I tended not to compete too often but when I did, my times weren't all that special, which confirms that I need a big event to perform well.

Everyone around me – Gennadi, Leigh and Dave among them – continues to be positive and insists that it's all about timing, that 'it will happen'. I believe it will too, and that motivates me to keep diving back into the training pool. But I'm sick of hearing it. I just want the talk to stop while I get on with it.

Ahead of me isn't just work in the pool and the gym. In the search to redefine my stroke, aerobic fitness out of the pool has been put to one side to some extent. It wasn't planned that way but Gennadi and Leigh reckon I have to get fitter and even leaner now because my shape may be contributing to my poor form in competition. The gym work, designed by Swimming Australia's sports science manager Bernard Savage, has been about adapting muscle structure to work with the new stroke and building core strength, and the pool training has concentrated largely on technique, so I need to do the work out of the pool, which will be very new to me. So is the concept of being lean. In the past I've been happy to swim at a heavier weight because it suited my swimming style. In fact my 105 kilograms at Athens made me the heaviest elite swimmer in history. That, apparently, has to change.

For all my issues about being in Australia with the pressure of competition bearing down on me, representing your nation elicits a pride that transcends individual achievement, not just when you're standing on a dais singing the national anthem but also when you're walking down the street shaking hands with well-wishers. But that same privilege opened my eyes to some of our flaws as well and I feel strongly that a person in my position should care and be confident enough to draw attention to the bad as well as the good.

In July 2009 I was a guest speaker at a conference in London called the Beyond Sport Summit, an organisation which promotes, develops and supports the use of sport to create positive social change across the world. The inaugural summit, chaired by former British prime minister Tony Blair, has now become an annual event, bringing together those who use sport as a vehicle to create social impact with influencers from the world of business, government and other organisations.

The speech I gave focused on issues close to my heart and my sentiments haven't changed in the three years since. Re-reading it reminds me that although I care very much about what happens in the pool, there is so much more to achieve than medals and records.

My travels with my sport since I was a very young and shy 14-year-old opened the world to me, but I didn't realise at the time that this adventure would turn into a career beyond my wildest dreams.

I was the youngest male to ever represent Australia in swimming. By 15 I was the youngest-ever male world champion. At 16 I broke four world records in four days and at 17 I was an Olympic champion. I had fulfilled my life-long ambitions as a child – and I quickly realised I was a child in an adult world. It was the child in me that throughout my career asked, 'Why? Why is it so? Why is it done that way and why is the world the way it is?'

In my travels, competition took me to places where sometimes I was met with abject poverty, while I simply swam. Why was my life so blessed when others were born with less opportunity than I? I guess I witnessed at a very young age how sport is an international language; a language that transcended borders, boundaries, cultural ideology, politics and even socio-economic disadvantage.

I have only mentioned my career up to when I was 17. That's because when I was 18 I established my charity, Fountain for Youth. I didn't realise at the time that this might be my biggest accomplishment; an achievement not in the sense of doing something right, rather a stepping stone allowing my values that I had gained from sport to be transferred to something that is bigger than sport and, in my opinion, far more important.

That said, sport was what has made me who I am today and has afforded me the privilege to work beyond it. But my charity work didn't begin at 18. In fact, I was just 15 when I began working with those less fortunate than myself. Those years shaped my understanding of what charity was and it gave me an insight into the power of celebrity and sport, especially in sport-mad Australia.

I realised that my value to organisations who were trying to bring positive change was the weight my name lent to their causes. I must say, though, this should be an outrage, because as an athlete I'm not as qualified to comment on health or education as the health professionals and educators who daily tackle the big issues. In fact it's a bit disappointing that my teenager's opinion could garner more attention than those who'd been working on their chosen causes before I was even born. This realisation of the opportunity that my voice and name could lend to an excellent cause became the simple foundation of my very own charity.

I continued to win medals, breaking world records and travelling around the world, recognising the needs of people, particularly children, in many places I visited. By this time my charity had enough money to commit to larger projects. I sat at a board meeting and stated that I wanted to help the world's most disadvantaged children.

I started to think of what impact my effort could have in places like Africa or South-East Asia. I then visited some of the world's neediest communities; places that seemed to be a world away but were actually at my back door.

The communities I visited had illiteracy levels of 93 per cent. In other words, only seven percent of the population could read and write. Up to 80 per cent of the children in these communities have serious hearing impairments because of 'glue ear', middle ear infections neglected from infancy. These kids will never hear a teacher in front of them in a classroom – that is, if there is a teacher and indeed a classroom to begin with.

Malnourished mothers are giving birth to seriously under-weight babies and this early disadvantage only gets worse throughout a life born into poverty. Here, diabetes affects one in every two adults. Kidney disease has reacted in epidemic proportions in communities where living conditions, primary healthcare and infrastructure are truly appalling.

In this part of the world even the community leaders are afflicted by 'clusters' of chronic illness. Syndrome X, the doctors call it – diabetes, renal disease, stroke, hypertension, cancer and heart disease. Some people die with four or five of these chronic illnesses.

Rheumatic heart disease among the children in these places is higher than in most of the developing world. But I wasn't visiting communities in the developing world. I was in the middle of Australia – remote, yes, but this was my country, a nation that can boast some of the highest standards of living of any nation in the world. How shocked I was that Syndrome X was afflicting so many of the 460,000 Indigenous people of my country? As a result of these chronic illnesses and conditions, Aboriginal life expectancy has fallen 20 years behind the rest of Australia. For some of my fellow countrymen life expectancy had plunged to just 46 years.

Australia's grim record on healthcare for Indigenous people is by far the worst of any developed nation. Developed? How can a country be 'developed' when it leaves so many of its children behind? Australia has not provided its citizens with equal access to primary healthcare, education, housing, employment, let alone recognition and a life of dignity.

Now I don't expect you to just take my word for it. I'm not a doctor, I'm simply an athlete. But ask Australian health professionals like Doctor Jim Hyde, Director of Public Health at the Victorian Department of Human Services, who says that while our nation has plenty of medical problems, only Indigenous Australians are facing a genuine health crisis.

The Governor of New South Wales, Professor Marie Bashir, an eminent child psychiatrist, has repeatedly pointed out the national disgrace of allowing the 40 per cent of Indigenous children under the age of 15 to put up with health problems found in no other developed nation.

Patrick Dodson, winner of the 2008 Sydney Peace Prize and one of our greatest statesmen, identifies health as a human right for Indigenous Australians: 'Only the most urgent government action could change the inequality that has created this health tragedy in our own backyard,' he has said.

How could citizens with the greatest need be so underfunded? If we were to recognise the severity of this gross neglect, funding to these communities should be extradited. A commitment to the First Australians is well within the means of my country, and this is what I find inexcusable. I'm talking about an issue with a solution. For Australia to heal the wounds that have been weeping for 200 years, we must not ignore the issue, we must start the healing.

Like many people in Australia I was completely unaware of the huge gap in health and education outcomes for Indigenous people, let alone the differences of life expectancy. I, as many had, made an assumption – Australia is a rich country. Don't we throw a lot of money at that problem? It disgusts me to speak those words now but that was what I thought. This wasn't just my lack of knowledge in this area – it's echoed throughout the nation.

An Aboriginal health expert, Professor Shane Houston from the University of Sydney, says:

Aboriginal people are viewed by too many in the Australian community as an unwelcome burden on the nation. Governments say they have spent a lot of money on Aborigines but where do you see the results in this squalor? So the mainstream concludes that Aboriginal health is a waste of money. It's all the fault of the poor blacks. My people are somehow expected to just extricate themselves from this maze of life-threatening conditions. And if we can't manage to do that, then many white people will shrug and say our end is inevitable.

Visiting Aboriginal people, in their homes, their communities, on their land, has allowed me to listen and given me some idea of the problems that they face. I listen to the concerns of mothers and fathers for the betterment of their children, and see their unwavering strength in the face of social injustice. Within these communities I witness poverty, despair and pain. But I also see hope from those men and woman who want more for their children.

With the words of these people in my head, I became part of a campaign in Australia called Close the Gap, a program that recognises the difference between Indigenous and non-Indigenous life expectancy in Australia and the huge gaps in all of the factors like education, jobs and housing that leave Aboriginal people so deeply disadvantaged.

Close the Gap is a commitment to the understanding that this difference is unacceptable. It was supported by the Australian federal government and the opposition. This is the kind of action that is required in Australia. But the issue of Indigenous health and education goes beyond government; it's a fundamental human right. I hope all sides of government continue to commit to this policy as a starting point and that it will not be another hollow promise that falls short.

The truth is that none of the problems I have mentioned can truly be rectified until our government and my fellow Australians recognise the injustice faced by Aboriginal Australians and how they are denied so many human rights. This has been highlighted once again by what is known as The Intervention – the federal government's takeover of 73 remote Aboriginal communities.

The Intervention was conducted by the previous government and has since been reported to have been planned in the space of just one day. The irony is that Aboriginal people had been campaigning for decades about the living conditions and the neglect of children within their communities. The programs to protect and nurture children had been grossly neglected and underfunded by the government over the last decade. What appears to be a political stunt and a grab for government control over Aboriginal people continues to this day.

Once more an Australian government claimed it was doing its best for Aboriginal Australians by taking over their communities, appointing white managers and more government bureaucrats, and promising all kinds of things, if Aboriginal people would just sign over their communities to the federal government under forty year leases. And politicians wonder why Aboriginal people don't trust them.

The truth is for over 200 years Australian governments have forgotten and patronised Aboriginal people. The Intervention is unlikely to provide any lasting benefit to Aboriginal people because it tries to push and punish them, to take over their lives, rather than work with them. One of Australia's oldest and wisest Aboriginal leaders, Galarrwuy Yunupingu, says the only way forward is for Aboriginal communities in these remote areas to be led and organised by their own organisations. Assimilation will not work.

So the way I try to contribute through my organisation, Fountain for Youth, is to work with Aboriginal teachers, health workers, parents and children, with the health services and the schools, to encourage people to believe that we can move forward together. We support pre-schooling and health education, and provide literacy backpacks that let kids carry home reading for the whole family. And we use sport where we can to make a difference.

As a swimmer, who would have thought I'd have ended up supporting Flipper Ball, junior water polo for little Aboriginal kids in the mining communities of Western Australia? As a swimmer, who would have thought I'd be studying for a degree in psychology at university and at the same time working with young Aboriginal university graduates on a mentoring program to help get more kids to complete high school and go on with their studies? As a swimmer, maybe I was expected to just be satisfied with the gleam of those gold medals. But all sportsmen and women know the truth – there is something beyond sport.

There is the challenge of playing a part in the human family, to contribute and make a difference. We can use sport and use our sporting status to improve the lives of children and whole communities in so many places. We can make it a fairer, safer playing field for everyone. In 20 remote Australian communities, thousands of Aboriginal children will have some extra opportunities in life if I commit to work hard on this. I do intend to work hard at this for the rest of my life.

seventeen

26 JANUARY 2012

Australia Day in Tenero. There'll be no fireworks over Lake Maggiore tonight or barbecues on its icy shoreline. It's a relief in many ways, the quiet and isolation are comforting and my times in training are already plummeting. I've never swum faster sprints in training – and I mean never. Perhaps it's finally happening.

I have a new training exercise – I swim 16 sets of 25 metres. The idea is to sprint for one lap, which is timed as my head crosses the halfway mark. Then I rest for a few seconds before pushing off the wall for the next set, which is timed, and so on. The other squad members are supposed to do them at the pace of a 200-metre race, which is roughly 12.5 seconds for each 25 metres. I start at that pace but then my speed increases, yet maintains the ease of the stroke. In other words, I'm going faster for the same effort.

Yesterday I got the splits down to 10.5 seconds. It felt great and it looked great. The coaching staff, who haven't seen me for a month, are shocked at my progress. Even Gennadi is excited. This is the way he's wanted to see me swim – not in a time which suggests I'm on the right track but in a way that shows I've arrived at the destination. That's why it was so important to get things right in the training up until this point. My stroke is now even more unique and rhythmical, as if I'm turning my arms almost without effort.

There's another exercise which involves swimming three sets of 1000 metres with a rest of 30 seconds or so between each set. The idea is for me to find a speed which feels efficient and comfortable – around 70 seconds for each 100 metres – so that I can concentrate on my stroke rather than the clock. At the end of the third set I was told that I'd dropped the time by six seconds per 100 metres which meant I had swum the last 1000 metres a full minute quicker than the first without realising.

I knew when I came back to the sport that I'd have to make some changes to my stroke but it's Gennadi who's filled in the blanks and helped me evolve it into one that's not only working but one I like the look of. Gennadi and I gelled because I look like a swimmer he could coach, with many of the same feelings about the sport that he espouses. Then there's the connection with Alex Popov. I didn't know until recently that Alex used to do long swims as part of his training, even though he was a sprinter. Not many people can do it because of the concentration required. It emphasises that the distance component of the training I've been doing is more than just aerobic fitness – it's about repetition to perfect the stroke.

The important thing for me is that I now have the training times to back up my sense that everything is coming together. It's not unreasonable for me to make a good guess about my performance at the trials in March based on my times a couple of months earlier. If I calculate a reduction of somewhere between two and three per cent, I'm confident that I can swim around 1:46 for the 200, which would almost certainly qualify me for an individual swim at the Olympics. If I use the same calculations for the 100 then I'm pretty confident of swimming a 48-second low. It's not an exact science and depends very much on how my body responds in the taper but the bottom line is that I don't have any choice if I want to make the team.

I'm swimming at another meet this weekend, in Luxembourg. To be honest, I'm going under sufferance but Gennadi and Leigh insist it'll be good for me and I trust their expertise. I'm not convinced but I'll do it anyway, although it'll probably be my last race until the trials. Then again, they may think otherwise and I'm in no position to argue. I'm not expecting much, but then again I might swim well.

I'm just hoping it's low key so I can get in, have a swim and get out again as fast as possible. If the administrators insist on my career record being read out again at least it will be in Luxembourgish, which is a mix of French and German dialects, so I won't understand it.

Thinking about the speech I gave in London about my Close the Gap inititiave reminded me of how personal my work with charities has been, and when and why it began. Many families are touched in some way by hardship and we were no exception when, in 1997, the younger brother of my sister's then boyfriend was rushed to hospital with a massive tumour.

Michael Williams was 11 and just three years younger than me when he was diagnosed with an aggressive, life-threatening cancer. His seemingly overnight transformation – from a happy, healthy kid with whom I spent hours playing computer games and watching movies to a boy at death's door – was an important lesson for someone who had just made the Australian swimming team and appeared to have an amazing future.

Michael survived but he would be sick and in hospital for a long time. I visited as often as I could and soon found myself saying hello to other sick kids on the ward. It had struck a chord with me; I realised just how fortunate I was, and that I should give something back when I could.

I started doing bits and pieces for a number of different charities, always concerned with children. I made occasional visits to hospitals to see the kids and have photos taken, and every Christmas I bought a heap of toys and took them to various children's wards. I found it really fulfilling because the impact on the kids and even their parents was immediate; especially the parents, many of whom can't sleep at night for worry. Being there was a simple message of support which, in some ways, was as important as a cheque – it meant someone was going out of their way to make a difference.

In 1998, as interest in the sport ratcheted up toward the Sydney Olympics, money was being pumped into Australian swimming with events like the Telstra Grand Prix series and Qantas Skins. Even then I hated swimming for money. Earning money from endorsements was one thing, which is the business aspect of professional sport, but I didn't swim to win a car or a few thousand dollars. That would devalue what I love.

I broke my first world record in 1999 when I was 16. It was at the Pan Pacs, which was held at the brand-new Aquatic Centre at Homebush. Telstra had offered $25,000 for the first world record at the venue and I stepped up and beat Kieren Perkins' long-standing 400-metre record.

The cheque was presented after the medal ceremony and I was asked on the spot what I would do with the money. My answer was instinctive, if reluctant, because I would have wanted to spend it without fanfare. The money would go to charity. I think everyone was a bit surprised because elite sports careers cost a lot of money to support, but it's simply the way I felt. I split the money between Lifeline Australia, which provides services for suicide prevention, crisis care and mental health issues, as well as providing programs for young people, and the Children's Cancer Institute, which I knew about because of Michael's situation.

By then I'd already decided that I wanted to start my own charity but for legal reasons had to wait until I turned 18. On 24 November in 2000, six weeks after I legally became an adult, everything was in place to launch my Fountain for Youth, which was set up to help disadvantaged children.

One of the lessons I'd learned watching other charities at work was how distracting the in-fighting between state and national organisations was and the impact it had on where and how the money was actually funnelled. I didn't want my charity to get caught up in the politics of it all. There are also very tight restrictions on what the charity could and couldn't do with money raised, so we started funding small groups who wouldn't ordinarily get money from other sources – always for children and always in areas such as health and education.

We even went overseas. On my first visit to China in 2003 we put money into the Zhi Guang Special Education School in Beijing, which supports orphaned children with disabilities. The school was established by an incredible woman, Madam Wang, who literally built the facility with stones that she'd collected from the streets on the outskirts of Beijing. And as she gathered the stones, she gathered the orphaned children who'd been dumped in the streets, including a bright four-year-old, Ping-Ping, whose name translates roughly as apple crate – which is what she was found inside.

At about the same time I'd invited former *Sixty Minutes* reporter Jeff McMullen to join the board as director (he's now the foundation's honorary CEO) and it was during a discussion about investing in some of the world's most disadvantaged areas that he suggested we should first be looking in our own backyard, at the plight of Indigenous people.

I was sceptical at first, an ignorant, suburban white boy raised in the belief that everyone was treated equally – that is, until I accepted his challenge of travelling into the ignored, ancient heart of our country to witness the shocking truth first hand. We spent several days visiting remote communities near Katherine in the Northern Territory – and I mean *remote*; I flew in a plane from Darwin to Katherine and then drove off-road for 90 minutes through the scrub. What I saw struck me both for its raw beauty and its tragedy.

Some of these settlements were established after World War Two and hadn't been upgraded since. The first one had a few dozen rundown buildings housing around 400 people in varying family groups and a shop where people bought cheap biscuits rather than the rancid fruit and vegetables, made inedible because of the lack of refrigeration.

I sat under gum trees and listened to the weary cynicism of tribal elders who'd only told the children that I was coming to see them when I reached Darwin because they didn't want them to be disappointed as they had in the past by other white people of influence who'd promised but didn't show up. I spoke to women who had pooled their 'mummy money' to establish a kitchen and cook school meals so their children ate at least one decent meal per day to counter the malnourishment, diabetes and glue ear so rife among them. I talked to a woman called Milly who had lost both of her sons, one to disease and the other to suicide. She was translating the Bible into the local language.

One of the locals, Wayne Runyan, taught me how to launch a spear with a woomera, aimed at a wallaby painted on a box, joking that I'd 'scare a real one off'. Big John taught me traditional painting techniques like cross-hatching and using very fine brush strokes, and he and some of the kids took me out on a 'bush tucker walk' to collect bush carrots and lemon ants, which they use when cooking fish.

I left a changed man. The statistics relating to the dire health and poverty faced by Aboriginal people weren't numbers anymore – they were people and I knew them by name. The trip had been a culture shock, as if I'd visited a different country; a place trapped between two worlds – ancient and modern – that most people prefer to ignore or, even worse, wish away.

There are a lot of things which open up for you as an Olympic champion. The world becomes an exciting place of opportunity and access, a continuous red carpet experience. It's all very exciting and flattering but ultimately it's superficial. I see my charity as something of substance, and it allows me to work and share experiences with people I'd never dreamed of meeting, and to have a real impact on their lives. That's something of worth. That's the real red carpet.

After that life-changing experience, Fountain for Youth began supporting health education and early learning for Aboriginal children in four remote Jawoyn communities east of Katherine – Wugularr, Manyallaluk, Barunga and Minyerri – through organisations like the Sunrise Health Service Aboriginal Corporation in Katherine.

Two years later, backed by research which showed that improved education was the key to improved health and buoyed by a $1 million federal government grant, we launched the Literacy Empowerment Project to provide education resources and staff support for literacy and numeracy. In 2008 the $1 million grant was renewed and then boosted in 2011 to $1.3 million. Over that time, the Foundation also raised over $3 million from public donations and fundraising enterprises.

The Literacy Empowerment Program provides early learning books, CDs, toys and other equipment for developing fine motor skills in children and encourages parental involvement, which is sometimes as simple as adults joining their kids for four hours a day under the spreading gums. These are the stepping stones for school readiness.

The accompanying Literacy Backpack Project provides selected books, magazines, newspapers and audio-visual reading materials for schools and their students as well as materials to be taken home for the families. Early surveys showed that in many communities, illiteracy rates were as high as 93 per cent and most homes were bookless, with no access to libraries or book stores. The Backpack Project now reaches about 2600 children and their families in 21 remote communities and school attendance rates and results have improved in those areas. A survey of schools in the Katherine area showed that participation in the National Assessment Plan for Literacy and Numeracy (NAPLAN) had risen significantly and was now close to 90 per cent between Years 3 and 7. There had also been a noticeable improvement in the percentage of students achieving national benchmarks, particularly in lower primary where the pass rate had jumped from 27 to 40 per cent. It's a long but hopeful battle.

We've also helped foster and develop a series of other projects, including the community storytelling program, which focuses on Indigenous life, culture and community; we support Djilpin Arts Aboriginal Corporation and its Walking with Spirits Festival which celebrates Aboriginal culture, as well as the establishment of the Ghunmarn Culture Centre, which houses one of the oldest collections of Arnhem Land art, the Blanasi Collection.

In November 2010 when we celebrated our 10th anniversary, his Royal Highness Prince William of Wales released a video in support of our work, which he described as inspiring. He said:

Giving those in our societies who have been left behind the tools to rebuild their lives for themselves, to rebuild confidence and self-belief, is truly profound. That is why I applaud the work that Fountain for Youth is doing to support education, health, cultural awareness and opportunity for Indigenous people in Australia. No work can be more important.

I agree. There's never been a better time to remedy what has happened and get it right for future generations. And in doing so there's a great opportunity for us all to gain because it's a two-way process. Australians are missing out on learning about an incredible culture that has survived on this continent for thousands of years.

To be honest, it surprises me that Indigenous people are still willing to work with white Australia, given the appalling way they and their ancestors have been treated over the last two centuries. But when I ask Indigenous Australians what they want for their kids, they say 'we want them to be able to walk in both worlds – blackfella and whitefella'. I think that's the least we can do.

At the moment there's a debate about the need to recognise Aboriginal Australians in our constitution, something that hopefully will be addressed in a referendum at next year's federal election. It's not before time.

eighteen

31 JANUARY 2012

Things aren't always as they appear. That's certainly the way to describe my races at Luxembourg last weekend. I wasn't looking forward to the meet but the four swims in the 100 and 200 (I made both of the finals for a change) have turned out to be very useful at this stage in my preparation – and in more ways than one.

The important aspect of the races, particularly the 200 metres, wasn't where I finished or the time I swam but the 50 metre splits. I wanted to take the races out faster in the first 100 than I've been doing to see how it felt and what I could do in relative comfort, and then not to worry too much about the back half. What's really hard in competition is getting the pace right, so I decided the best way to make use of the race was to experiment.

I faded in the back half, but not because I was cruising. I think training fatigue set in to some extent but it was more to do with the fact I let myself slow a little too much in the third 50. If I'd gone a little harder then, I probably would have had a better last lap.

The media coverage was more interested in the overall times, which showed little improvement from Victoria a few weeks ago and was read as more disappointment and doubts about my performance. Imagine what they'll think when I swim in Zurich in a few weeks' time and completely ignore the 200 in favour of the 400, which I haven't swum in competition since Athens. Perhaps it will be read as desperation on my part instead of the real reason – I just feel like swimming a 400. In the meantime, my training is being mixed up a little with a camp overlooking the ocean at Tenerife in the Canary Islands, followed by a boot camp in the late winter cold of the Bavarian town of Lindau in the far south of Germany.

The 100 metre heat on the second morning was my best swim of the meet because the 50.82 seconds I clocked was well within my comfort zone. In the final I tried a lot harder but got very little out of it. I tried to swim it with force and determination and may have gained a marginal improvement – I did it in 50.76 seconds – but I lost a lot of technique.

But there was another bonus. Of all of the competitions I've swum since November, Luxembourg felt the most comfortable, and by quite a margin. I may even have solved the anxiety problems, although my solution is a little drastic and ill-formed – I made myself anxious before the warm-up to the point of not wanting to race so that by the time I walked out onto the pool deck and stood on the blocks I'd chilled out a little and could handle the nerves a bit better. I don't even know what you'd call it – pre-race or pre-onset anxiety maybe.

One of the issues, I think, is the unknown. When I swam before, I'd reached the top of the plateau and knew that, with a reasonable training schedule, I could perform almost at will at major competitions. There was no need for interim meets and experimentation. If I prepared well and remained healthy then it would simply happen.

I also had the naivety of youth on my side. Back then I couldn't see the top of the hill I was climbing and didn't know or care about pressure because every step up was a win. This time I'm coloured by the fact that I know where I've been and I want to get there again. Thinking about it this way, the pressure is unavoidable, really. If I had another year to prepare, I'd have forced myself to put my achievements aside and been satisfied by improving at every meet. But I don't have that luxury.

Even with the demands of competition I'm always an interested tourist and Luxembourg was no exception. A tiny nation state, it's mountainous and cold like Italy and Switzerland and feeling the sting of economic and political pressures like the rest of Europe. I've been watching it all unfold over the last ten months – the politics are brutal and never far away.

My own family is split when it comes to politics. My mother's parents were small business people and always voted conservative, while my father's family were working class and hard-wired Labor voters. It wasn't something we generally discussed around the dinner table when I was a kid but I was always aware that my parents came from opposite sides of the political fence and it was okay to think and vote differently in a democracy.

Actually, my parents' views are a pretty accurate reflection of the way I see the world politically – I lean strongly to the left when it comes to social policy and firmly to the right when it comes to finances and the economy. It's probably why I've been approached by both sides of politics over the years. For the record, I've never wanted a career in politics, although I am very interested in policy and have used my high profile to speak out on issues like Aboriginal affairs.

The attention from both quarters has come in the form of subtle suggestions rather than blatant offers of a parliamentary seat, but the intent is there. Catherine Keating, daughter of former prime minister Paul Keating and a friend of mine, has tried to tempt me on a few occasions over the years. She's convinced that I fall on the same side of politics as she does, probably because of my charity work, and that my views are close to her dad's.

Talking about proximity, I have actually been close to Mr Keating on two occasions. The first was when I was in primary school and he, as the local MP and prime minister, came to the school to hand out some prizes. I received one for academic achievement and shook his hand. That afternoon when I told my nan (Christina and I always went to her house after school), she snarled and said I should have spat at him. Her vehemence took me by surprise given that she's normally the sweetest woman you could ever meet.

Years later I sat next to him on a plane between Darwin and Sydney. It was probably just after the Athens Olympics and I was on my way home after doing some work with my foundation up in the Territory. From memory there was no formal introduction – there was no need – but at some point in our conversation I recounted our earlier meeting and my nan's reaction. Mr Keating wasn't offended – in fact he laughed, and said that it might surprise me how many people feel the same way.

We chatted for a couple of hours, mostly about Australia's relationship with Asia. He was aware of the time I'd been spending in Japan and remarked that I should open myself up more to China because that was Australia's future. 'If it doesn't work out,' he quipped at one point, 'at least the tucker's good.'

Alan Jones, the broadcaster, is another person who tends to divide people. I was about 14 the first time I was interviewed by him and, in contrast to her attitude to Mr Keating, my nan warned me that I must call him Mr Jones, and not Alan, as a mark of respect. He and I have met many times since and I do have a great respect for him. Even though some people say terrible things about him, I've never seen any of it. I can only judge him on what I've seen and in that regard I think he's a gentleman.

We can have a wide-ranging political discussion and agree to disagree on issues such as climate change. He admits to being a sceptic. He's also been very encouraging personally and once said to me: 'Ian, if you were to write down five things you'd like to do in your life and one of them was to lead this country then that could happen.' He wasn't suggesting that he could make it happen or that I should aspire to be Prime Minister, rather that it was something I was capable of doing.

For the whole period of the first part of my career, John Howard was Prime Minister and with all the functions and ceremonies I was attending then I became quite comfortable in his presence. Looking back now, there were times when I gravitated to him and his wife Janette at some events – friendly faces in a large room filled with many people I didn't know.

I'd just turned 18 when I invited Mr Howard to launch my Fountain for Youth foundation. Sitting next to him, I naively launched into a dissertation about my views on Australia's taxation system. As I told him I didn't think it was right for anyone under the age of 18 to have to pay tax, he nodded patiently with a fatherly smile on his face. My rationale was that I'd been paying tax since the age of 14 and yet I had no way of influencing how my taxes were being spent by his government. I argued that unless he was prepared to lower the voting age, which was unlikely, then we shouldn't have to pay until we were old enough to vote. Instead, the government should be encouraging young people to earn and spend their money. I thought it was a marvellously constructed argument, and his reply, as far as I recall, was a gentle suggestion that the issue was a little more complicated than I might imagine. But his support of my foundation was generous nonetheless.

The other enduring image I have of Mr Howard is watching him crowdsurfing at the Sydney Olympics. It happened in the village after the closing ceremony. A couple of people – I'll blame the rowing team, who always seemed to be at the centre of anything unruly – picked him up and, despite his obvious discomfort, kept him above their heads for quite a while. It was a bit of fun but it was also an acknowledgement by the athletes of his backing of such an incredible event.

But although I have a lot of interest in government policy, it doesn't mean I want to be a politician. I'm intrigued watching the chess game of the parliamentary process but being involved at that level just doesn't sit comfortably with me because the result of those games affects the lives of real people. I can't get my head around that.

I was about 20 when I first encountered the kind of game-playing that goes on. I was trying to secure government funding for the Fountain and I realised I needed to ensure that I was evenhanded with both sides of politics if I wanted to protect my project. If funding was cut then the lives of the hundreds of people we work with could be affected. One frontbench MP was dead against us because we had dared to be outspoken about the terrible conditions Aborigines were living under. The message was clear: either we accepted government money and spoke positively or we didn't bother applying. It's a part of the game I dislike immensely.

I have strong views on a number of other policy areas. On the subject of economics, my main concern is that Australia has to learn the lessons of the past and understand that it's been living beyond its means for too long and relying too much on our natural resources. We have to find a way beyond simply digging holes and exporting raw materials offshore for others to refine, build and send back as expensive imports. That means a better-educated workforce and more emphasis on technology industries and high-value manufacturing because

Australia will never be able to compete with other countries on cheap exports.

I grew up believing that everyone had access to free health care and education but, sadly, it's not true. I was so shocked when I first visited Indigenous communities in Central Australia, and I still am. They just don't have access to the same services that most Australians take for granted and we need to address that seriously.

I think our education system is also lacking. We've all been waiting for this government's promised education revolution and it hasn't really happened. Not only do we need to start investing more heavily in education but we also need to look at evolving the system itself. My own experiences as a student were mixed. I support public education but I also think it needs to be able to better respond to the individual.

Children tend to be told that the mark on an exam paper will define what they can do with their lives and I just don't agree. There are so many success stories of people who have struggled at school for various reasons and yet gone on to achieve great things. I dislike the way we segregate children from an early age into streams of achievement and promise. Not only does it say to the achievers that they're different but it tells the masses who aren't that they're under-achievers. Why can't we keep everyone's minds open to achievement for as long as possible?

The Finns have the right idea. There's no streaming, not even in private schools, and the first years of school empha-sise social interaction and individuality. The philosophy is that children 'learn how to learn' rather than being 'taught'. Exams only start in high school. What I like about their system is that it's not just about academics but bringing up children to be well-rounded. Their results show that it works.

Drugs are another area where we have to be brave. The evidence shows that the problem should be dealt with as a public health issue rather than a criminal issue. I agree with harm reduction and safe houses for drug addicts. I'm not for or against the legalisation of drugs but think each needs to be assessed and that we should keep an open mind.

Drug use among young people is still on the rise and we need to look at why they're using drugs, how we can make it as safe as possible and how we can stop them. Perhaps we should look more closely at the Portuguese system where drug use offences are regarded as relatively minor infringements rather than criminal issues, and there has been a massive increase in government spending on harm minimisation. The evidence so far suggests a significant reduction in problem use and deaths, a reduction in the criminal policing and justice workload and yet an increase in the amount of drugs being seized. That, of course, requires a mature and broad-minded approach by politicians of all persuasions.

nineteen

4 FEBRUARY 2012

I'm glad to be back in Tenero. I've really been able to concentrate on the daily training, which is crucial as we get closer to the trials in Adelaide. Not long now. As we move into the final phase my routine is changing; it's more about sharpening my skills and refining my physique.

The aerobic training outside the pool has kicked up a gear, something that's been long in the planning. It's aimed at reducing my weight by about six kilograms before March. The theory was to get the swimming right first and then add everything else afterwards. I like walking so I have to do an hour each day or 40 minutes cardio – either skipping, the bike or the treadmill plus an extra 20 minutes before each swim session to get my blood pumping. I've also increased the tennis to three times a week, not on Gennadi's orders but because I prefer swinging a racquet to slogging it out in the gym.

I'm never going to look like the other sprinters, tall and skinny. It's simply not realistic. I have an odd physique for a swimmer – the only one who looks like he could play football. It's a matter of working with the assets I do have, such as my range of movement and flexibility, and using my weight which means I should be able to propel myself off the starting blocks a lot quicker. I also have unusually big shoulders and legs, which should give me a power advantage and make up for the fact that I don't sit as high in the water as some of the lighter guys.

I also have a sparring partner. Andrey Grechin is a Russian 100-metres specialist who swam at the Beijing Olympics, was a semifinalist in the 100 at the world titles in Shanghai last year and has posted a time of 48.59 seconds. I initially spoke to Gennadi while we were in Australia about getting someone in to challenge me in training. I rejected the idea of bringing in Massi Rosolino but even though I knew little about Andrey, Gennadi assured me he was the right type of swimmer. I took his word and I'm glad I did.

Gennadi knows that I'm like a dog during training. It's my pool and nobody is going to beat me in it, so having a sprinter the calibre of Andrey will really spark the sessions. We train together most of the time and the benefits have been immediate, particularly when we do drills like the 25-metre sets. My times are consistently quicker with Andrey in the pool.

Gennadi, as usual, didn't comment on my performance in Luxembourg, although he did say probably the most reassuring thing I've heard. He told me he'd seen how I would swim at the trials: 'Now we need to work on it,' he added, clearly deep in thought. It was a significant moment for me, given that he has a knack of seeing how people will perform in competition based on the way he sees them swim in training. He continues to be very solid about how I will perform in Adelaide and I take a lot of confidence from that. The problem, of course, is that he didn't tell me what time he thought I would swim.

I've conceded that James Magnussen is probably going to swim under 48 seconds at the trials, which means I'm going to have to swim under 48.5 to have a chance of getting the second spot for an individual swim. So that means swimming against swimmers like Matt Targett, James Roberts, Matthew Abood and Eamon Sullivan – as well as setting a personal best time, given that the fastest I've swum in an individual event was 48.56 seconds, which won me a bronze medal in Athens.

If I get past the first hurdle, which is making it into the team, I have three months to really make some gains. It's one of the rare advantages I have in my return to the sport. While others will be working to get minuscule improvements in their times in that period – and I mean tenths or even hundredths of seconds – I'll be carving chunks out of mine, almost like an age group swimmer.

But first, the trials.

Most people don't have enough time in their busy lives for passive thought. I've been lucky in that regard – the endless laps in a swimming pool are a perfect opportunity to let my brain wander into areas that most people don't have the time to consider. It appeals to the nerd in me; the kid playing alone on the lounge room floor, and who, at school, would rather be in the library at lunchtime than playing handball in the playground with the others. One of the few pluses about not finishing high school was that it made me learn about the world in a way that was different to other people. The system may not have suited me but I still had a thirst for knowledge which I satisfied with experiences or by inhaling books, which then raised more questions.

It's the way I do everything and why I continue to seek answers in the pool. I was always the guy who asked questions. That's what's driven my interest and passion for public policy and why I've read about education in Finland and drugs in Portugal. Travelling the world a lot, on planes in particular, makes me think about how transport routes might work in the future as aircraft ranges increase and our travel habits change. All that travel time and the space to think have also been behind many of my business interests over the years, satisfying the creative side of me outside the pool, and linking my commercial life with my philanthropic interests.

It's fair to say that some of my past choices in business ventures haven't been the best for my image, but I have no regrets. Besides, if I worried too much about critics then I'd never have done anything. I'm proud of being brave enough to decide that if something felt right for me then I'd prefer to take the risk and challenge perceptions. Hopefully, if I continue to show that I don't really care what others think, then people might begin to see that being a little different is okay.

The line of men's jewellery I helped design in 2002 is probably the best example. When Autore, a family company, approached me to help design a pearl choker I was dubious, because it was clear that my involvement would just feed the comedians in the media. I knew I'd cop the pearl necklace jokes – and I did – as they strived for schoolboy innuendo about my sexuality, but it was a chance to be involved in an industrial design project, so I said yes and decided to weather the storm.

The product line was based around a cultured pearl the company was producing which was shaped a little like an abstract torpedo, hence my involvement. We had the option of producing something that was ultra-hippy, with the pearl hanging off a choker of cord, fashioned to look like rope, but the real challenge was to turn it into something beautiful but masculine enough to appeal to both men and women.

We decided to set the pearl at throat level on a neoprene black strap between two cylinders that could be in brushed silver, gold or platinum, which gave the impression of the pearl being a stud. I was really proud of the finished product because I think it achieved the aesthetic balance we were after and was something that a young generation – people my age – could begin to appreciate. It ended up selling well, particularly through Qantas inflight sales to Japan, and we only stopped manufacturing it because it was copied by other companies using cheaper pearls. It became too expensive to compete.

A few years later I spent some time designing a range of men's jewellery for Omega, the watch company, when I was still representing them. They'd seen what I'd done with the pearl necklace as well as some other designs I'd done privately and were keen on my ideas. It was just after I'd stopped swimming in 2006, when I was based in Los Angeles, so I had time and the creative energy to try something new. I came up with a range of pendants and rings using only Omega watch parts. Sadly, the plan fell over because of the global financial crisis, but I've still got a box full of prototypes at home.

My underwear collection, which was manufactured between 2002 and 2006, was another project that appealed to me, this time because of my interest in fashion, although I didn't realise how much work went into creating a decent pair of undies. I still wear them, although I'm running short of stock!

I went through the process of buying almost every pair of underpants on the market, trying them all and deciding what aspects I liked and what I wanted to change in the cut. Then I needed to decide on the fabric. I wanted to appeal to the high end of the market and went through swatch after swatch of combinations until I found the right mix of cotton, lycra and silk, which would otherwise only be used for a high-end T-shirt.

The colours were straightforward – plain black and white are the biggest sellers in the undies marketplace – but the marketing was a different challenge. As I discovered, there had to be a unique selling point. Mine was that it was under-wear designed for sport and leisure, and I spent 80 per cent of my time coming up with a theme for the collection which was essentially for shop windows.

My other significant project has been the low GI active

sports drink, the Thorpedo, which some have labelled a failure, but in reality it's been a reasonable and ongoing success. It didn't work in Australia but that's because we simply weren't able to counter some very aggressive strategies by some of our bigger competitors who made life difficult for us, like buying all our stock from small shopkeepers and replacing it with their own. The shopkeepers came out ahead because they were able to sell drinks that had cost them nothing and so did the manufacturer, because it took our stock off the shelf. In any case, the drink was designed for Japan and was sold in Australia mainly to establish credibility and market history, which is needed to satisfy the Japanese market. The drink has been doing well there, thanks to the fact that there's something like 44 million vending machines throughout the country.

Even now, we're the third most popular sports drink in Japan, with four products including one marketed as 'Sparkring' (the Japanese language has no sound for the letter L). It contains a fruit called yuzu, which looks like a cross between a lemon and a lime but tastes like something between a grapefruit and a mandarin.

There are certainly aspects of the business world that I dislike, like the red carpet experience – and I detest the clipboard carriers who time my appearances at a store opening by the hour. I also find it embarrassing to watch my races on giant video screens when I'm making a presentation, but I enjoy the adrenaline of public speaking and live television and I'm passionate about the brands I represent, particularly the companies I've had long-standing relationships with, like Adidas and Volkswagen Group.

I guess that's life. You have to roll with the changes, which is what I face over the next few weeks as my training schedule intensifies and peaks as the trials approach. I'll be moving from Switzerland to the Canary Islands, then on to Germany, back to Switzerland – and finally to Australia.

twenty

9 FEBRUARY 2012

I almost broke my ankle yesterday. Imagine coming this far only to be thwarted by an accident on a tennis court! It happened as I turned quickly to chase a backhand and my left foot got caught in the movement. It's the same ankle I broke less than 12 months out from the Sydney Olympics.

I thought I'd done the same thing until I realised there'd been no snapping sound. I bent down, rubbed it, retied my shoelaces and breathed a sigh of relief. Mind you, if tennis is the highest-risk activity you do in preparation it means I'm pretty well wrapped in cotton wool.

I'm just as likely to break my ankle walking to the pool each day. It's just me. It could happen any time. I'm not accident-prone as such but I have thin bones for my size: the slightest twist, turn or fall means I could snap something. In 2006, while I was still swimming, I walked into the ensuite off my bedroom, slipped on a wet floor and landed on my right wrist, breaking it. I once broke my scapula – the shoulder blade and one of the hardest bones in the body – just by stretching.

Apart from my mishap, tennis has been the enjoyable part of my week in the Canary Islands. Not only is it warmer here than the rest of Europe – around 22 degrees during the day compared to sub-zeroes further north – but we get to train outside, which really does make a psychological difference.

Now we've entered the aerobic phase of the preparation, I've been swimming more kilometres but the real difference is being made in the work out of the pool. I've being doing a ridiculous amount of cardio exercise. I don't mind it so much, but I find it really, really boring. I don't understand how people happily can run or walk on a treadmill or pedal on a stationary bike – or do spin classes, for that matter.

Some people make the same criticism of swimming: that it's just like following a black line up and down a pool for hours a day, but if all they see is a black line then they're missing the point of it. You have to succumb to what you're doing and where you are, rather than simply trying to make it to the other end. If you can let go of the concept of counting laps you get to enjoy how you're moving and the way you're feeling.

There's another faintly ridiculous part of the training here. It's called the flume, a small pool which pumps out water at increased speeds so you can swim on the spot, just like a tread-mill, in fact. I understand the concept and perhaps my view is excessive, but it simply doesn't feel like swimming. It's unnatural, because your hands are automatically pulled back by the current as they enter the water. It's a great novelty but that's about it.

Having said that, the results were interesting if nothing else. I began by swimming for five minutes at a speed of 1.4 metres per second (mps), which was comfortable. Then I swam for one minute at 1.6 mps, followed by 1.8 mps and finally 45 seconds at 2 mps, which is the equivalent of a flat 50 seconds for the 100 metres (without taking starts and turns into account). After that I really ramped up the speed – I'd like to say I managed to swim for 30 seconds at 2.2 mps but it was more like 20 seconds before I was slammed against the far wall. Then I cranked it up to the maximum 2.5 mps. I lasted for four strokes. That bit, I must admit, was a lot of fun even though I'm bruised after being slammed against the wall.

I'll continue using the flume for the rest of the week, although I'll stop getting back into the pool afterwards because you lose the sensation of moving through the water – it feels as though the bottom of the pool is moving instead, again like a treadmill. It's pretty weird, a bit like getting off a trampoline and jumping. Instead of the bounce it feels like concrete.

I'm dreading the move to Lindau next week – a week and a half of boot camp in Germany's frozen winter is far from appealing when you're gazing out over the blue water of the Canary Islands while you're churning out laps. After that it's the meet in Zurich and then I start to taper for Adelaide.

The way I swim is largely about the way I feel. Rather than analysing it or explaining why I swim a certain way, I prefer to just let it happen. Sure, a lot of the things we do and the way we train is determined by science but that doesn't answer everything.

I find science limiting to the extent that it only raises more questions. There's a reason why scientists write papers rather than books, because by the time a book is published they have moved on, often challenging what has been discovered. What this says to me is that we will never know everything, and that's where religion falls into place. It's like looking at life through the eyes of a child who doesn't question how glass is made but just wonders at its beauty, or picks up a rock in a river bed because it is wet, smooth and shiny and not because it might answer questions about geology.

Religion has always been an important part of my family's life. We define ourselves as Congregational and when we were growing up, Christina and I went every Sunday to the local church in Padstow with our parents. They still go regularly and it remains an important part of my life, although my beliefs have changed – or perhaps 'broadened' is better way to describe it.

When I'm asked to define what I believe in spiritually, I struggle. I'm not the same kind of Christian as my father, for example, whose beliefs have strengthened in recent years. Although I identify myself as Christian, I have a very different view on things like the Bible and the way I feel about God. The way I see it is that I believe in a greater being and there are things that happen that can never be explained. This is the foundation of my spirituality, and the more I learn the more I realise that we will never know all the answers.

I believe in a God because I couldn't imagine some of the amazing things that have happened to me in the pool – or some of the things that *didn't* happen to me, such as being harmed in the September 11 attacks in New York – unless there is a greater being. I have Christian values but I don't want to categorise them. Some of the things I think and feel fall under a Buddhist sensibility; also, I don't think being a good person is the territory of any one religion. My book-keeper is Jewish. He was raised very differently to me, with a different set of religious beliefs, and I admire him because, above everything else, he's a person of morals and a first-rate human being. I've found the same with Muslim people I've met in Abu Dhabi as well as Buddhists and Shintoists in Japan, which confirms to me that there are similar sets of values behind all religions.

I've read the Bible and plan to read the Koran because I'm inquisitive about other beliefs. I've found that aspects of other religions, like some Chinese concepts, fit with my strategies in life. I'm not afraid of investigating or trying new things. I once went to the Sheikh Zayed Grand Mosque in Abu Dhabi, a massive structure of 82 domes which is big enough to house 40,000 worshippers. Its design, described as a fusion of Arab, Mughal and Moorish architecture, makes it one of the most beautiful buildings I've ever seen. Before we entered the mosque, my host washed himself and I wondered how I, as a visitor and a Christian, should act in this situation. Should I simply watch politely or follow his lead? It seemed no different to cleansing myself when visiting a Buddhist temple in Japan. When I asked him, he looked shocked and I thought for a moment that I'd offended him. It turned out he was just surprised and appreciative that I would be open to taking part in the ritual. As he showed me how to wash my feet and hands, then my face – even my nose – in preparation to enter the sanctity of the temple, I knew I was gaining an important life experience which taught me about the world.

It was a long way from Milperra, that's for sure.

When I was growing up, my father was a very traditional man; forceful in his way and insistent that his word was law in the family home. We had our share of differences and difficulties, just as it's normal for families to have problems from time to time, but I always considered Mum and Dad to be model parents. While Dad was brusque and tended to shout when I was in trouble, I knew I could always talk to Mum. And if it got too tough at home I knew I could always run away to my maternal grandmother's house. I never did.

Religion is an area where my father and I continue to have our differences, particularly since he refound God ten years ago. As kids we always went to church on Sundays but I seem to remember Dad being quite reluctant to go at times. That changed when he stayed home (he hates flying) when Mum and I went to the Manchester Commonwealth Games in 2002. While we were away, Dad renewed his relationship with the church and found a commitment which has been maintained ever since.

Our worst argument happened at my grandmother's house a few years ago when he was questioning my own commitment to religion. He was angry because I'd stopped going to church regularly. I regard the church as the middle man and don't believe that I have to go every week to have a relationship with God.

Things got pretty heated as we went back and forth. Dad argued that going to church meant I was around like-minded people who would support me, and my response was that it wasn't something I need, that I preferred a direct connection with God.

'Do you pray?' he asked me at one point.

'Yes, I pray when things are going well,' I said, 'and I pray when things are going badly. It's a release for me.' I'd thanked God when I won my first Olympic gold medal, the 400 metres at the Sydney Games. It had been my goal to be an Olympian and my dream to win a gold medal, so who else would I have thanked when I achieved them, despite a broken ankle, drug accusations and controversy that was building over my swimsuit? Sure, I may have got great genes from my parents but why did I get the right genes from each?

Dad and I were getting nowhere. He believed that the church itself was integral to being a committed Christian and I disagreed. To me, it's just a building. The world is my church. Thankfully my grandmother is slightly deaf and wouldn't have heard most of it. The argument got pretty loud at one stage, and then Dad relented, realising that he didn't want to bully me into changing my view. He backed down, he said, because he didn't want to repeat the mistakes of the relation-ship he had with his own father. He still prompts me from time to time on the issue but he never questions my spiritual commitment and neither do I question his.

Although our relationship isn't always smooth, my father has spent the last 15 years trying to draw me back into the family, sometimes successfully and sometimes not, although, to be fair, he hasn't been fully aware of some of the issues which made me isolate myself. His concern stems from the moment I became a world champion at the age of 15, the night he told Michelle Flaskas that he'd just lost his son to the world. I hadn't heard about that until recently, and it demonstrates his foresight. It must have been difficult for him and Mum; excited and supportive of my achievement but apprehensive about how it would change the dynamic of the family forever.

I know Dad had a difficult relationship with his own father, but I never saw the demanding aspects of my grandfather's character, although I do remember one of the games Christina and I played with him which hinted at a steely nature. My grandfather had a special chair – only he could use it – and Christina and I would sneak in and sit on it, challenging his authority. If he caught us he'd take off his belt and, with a smile on his face, pretend he was going to smack us – with us squealing with apprehension.

But there's no time for kids' games at the moment. I've got my work cut out for me over the next few weeks before Adelaide and the trials. Next stop is German boot camp.

twenty-one

19 FEBRUARY 2012

I was right about Lindau. It hasn't been a high point in my preparation so far and I'm struggling to maintain enthusiasm. Two weeks ago I was training outdoors in Tenerife with the sun on my back and the smell of salt in my nostrils; here, it's near zero degrees outside and I'm swimming under fluorescent lights with chlorine pounding my nasal passages 24 hours a day.

The facility has a nice enough pool but the complex design is debilitating. The pool and gym are on the ground floor, with hotel-style rooms, where we are staying, on the floors above. It means you can never get away from the chemical smell of the pool and, worse, you have to pass by it to get to the food hall, which is on the lower ground floor beneath. Talk about putting you off your dinner.

I don't mind hard work, in fact I usually revel in it, but there's no stimulus for me here beyond training, training, and training. That's fine if there's something pleasant to look, like in Tenerife, or if I'm doing things of value outside the pool like I do in Tenero, but the problem here is that it's literally living and breathing training for 10 days. I brought a couple of books with me but I finished them in the first few days, including Paul Ham's huge tome – 700 pages – on the bombing of Hiroshima and Nagasaki, so I've got nothing left to read in the hours between training, and German TV is a bit tough to follow.

Even the one thing which gets me through these sorts of training schedules – eating as much as I like – has gone badly wrong. Actually, it's bloody awful. When we arrived there was no protein in our nightly main meals – or if there was, it was well hidden. Everything is served cold, mainly different types of ham, or bologna (Devon as I'd call it) which is chopped up and smothered in something resembling mayonnaise. It slops around on your plate like workhouse gruel. Granted there is a pasta dish on the menu but it doesn't compare with what we normally eat living on the Swiss–Italian border. Besides, on inspection we found it was prepared like milky creamed rice.

When we asked why there wasn't more protein – for example, portions of chicken or fish or steak – particularly since it's a facility catering for live-in professional athletes, we were told it was a budget decision and if we wanted better food we'd have to pay for it. We happily paid up but the very next night we found that the bonus protein was just half a chicken breast each, which is ridiculous given the size of the appetites in our training group. We had to pay more the next day just to get the other half-breast. I'll be glad when we finish in the next few days.

The training routine doesn't make things any easier but that's why we're here. It's the final slog before I begin to ease up and taper, rest up for the competition, which is only a few weeks away now. I always knew time was my enemy but it seems like I'm on an escalator whizzing toward 17 March, when the final of the 200 metres will be swum in Adelaide. We're on a routine of eight swimming sessions every three days – a rotation of three, three and two – which is the heaviest load I've had in this preparation. On top of that, after each swimming session I'm doing up to an hour of cardio exercise on a treadmill or a stationary bike, which means that on the heavy days I'm training for up to eight hours.

It's hard to measure what impact this kind of training will have. I do know that I'm tired, though, which is probably why I lost my temper with another swimmer the other day. I regret it now, or at least the way I went about it, but it seemed to me that he wasn't putting in enough effort and was affecting everyone else in the process. The only good thing about my sharp words is that he's now pulled his finger out.

When we're finished here, thankfully I'll get a few days back in Tenero and the comfort of my own bed before heading to Zurich for the final swim meet. Then it's another short high altitude camp and finally, out to Australia for the trials. It should be thrilling but I still haven't felt it yet. Trepidation, even a touch of fear, but the wings of excitement haven't yet fluttered in my belly. I just hope they wake up soon and quell the smothering sense of anxiety which I'm sure is contributing to my fluctuating moods.

One thing I don't have to think about as Adelaide approaches is what to wear in the race. That decision has largely been made by rules brought in to limit the impact of swimsuit technology.

I fall into the unusual position of having broken world records with and without a full body swimsuit. I swam in traditional swimmers at the Pan Pacific championships in 1999 when I was 16 and broke my first world record in the 400-metres freestyle in the time of 3:41.83. My last world record was three years later, also in the 400 metres, when I swam 3:40.08 at the 2002 Manchester Commonwealth Games as a 19-year-old. To me the difference of 1.75 seconds was due to my greater age and strength, the training I'd done, what I'd learned and improved on and the way I prepared – not because I was wearing a full body suit.

Having said that, I do concede there's an advantage in wearing a suit, in the same way that technology has improved swimming since the days of woollen suits, which progressed to silk then nylon and then Lycra and ranged from neck-to-knee to tiny briefs and then back again to full-length suits.

The question is how much effect did they have? Nobody has been able to accurately assess what improvement the fabric made to times but my own guess is that it's probably about 0.1 of a second for every 100 metres – in other words, less than half a second in the 400 metres.

The suit I used to wear was the most refined product ever made by Adidas. I could use each suit only once, after which they were thrown away. At $20,000 a pop, they were hand-stitched in a small Italian factory, and were so specialised that even my measurements had to be done by one particular person – a woman named Kim who flew out from the UK to take three or four marginally different combinations, which would be tested a couple of weeks out from competition in order to make a decision. The whole process took three months and the finished product was so tight that it took 15 minutes and help from two other people to get into one. They were also tested for colour, which found that black is the fastest shade because of the way dye goes into the material and how that, in turn, can compress the fabric on the body. There is another slightly faster colour – white – which we couldn't wear for modesty reasons. They're the rules.

Strangely, for all that effort, the biggest advantage wasn't a physical one for me but a psychological disadvantage for the other swimmers, who seemed to be intimidated by me wearing it. It seemed to add to the sense of invincibility about me swimming at my peak.

Like everyone else, I began using a suit out of curiosity. Suits had been around since the early 1990s but I had no real interest then; I found them constrictive. Then, in the lead-up to the 1999 Pan Pacs, a couple of the swimmers – Michael Klim was one – began using a neck-to-ankle suit made by Speedo, who claimed it reduced drag. Fédération Internationale de Natation (FINA), the world governing body for aquatic sports, had approved the technology, so we all started experimenting as other companies stepped in and made their pitches.

I'd been in discussions with Adidas about their product, which was based on alpine skiing suits and designed to compress the muscles so they were tight in the water. I was impressed with the theory but decided to wait until after the Pan Pacs before making a decision. When I began to trial their 'off the rack' suit in the months afterwards I still wasn't convinced. It was only after the company agreed to make one to fit my unusual shape that it seemed to be worth the effort and I decided I'd wear one for the Sydney Games.

The benefit for me was that it changed the way the water felt. I could tell the water was cold when I dived in but I couldn't feel the sensation of it being wet. It took time to adjust to but in the end I loved the feeling, which isn't unlike the heightened sensitivity we get from shaving down for competition.

There were people, including current and former swimmers and coaches, who were against the use of the suits. Forbes Carlile, Australia's great pioneering swimming coach, reckoned they should be banned and Kieren Perkins was also against the suits, although he ended up wearing one during the Sydney Olympics.

For me, the suit caused two problems at those Games, and neither of them were in the water. In the 12 months before there'd been a huge battle over the legitimacy of the technology. FINA had stood its ground and insisted they were legal and the Australian Olympic Committee (AOC), fearful of legal challenges from swimmers after the event, demanded a ruling from the international Court of Arbitration for Sport (CAS). In the end, CAS decided it didn't have the authority to cast judgement on FINA's rule book and the suits were cleared, but the problems for me were just beginning.

The AOC had declared the suits to be specialised equipment, which cleared the way for me to swim in the Adidas product even though Speedo was the official sponsor and provider of swimwear for Sydney. But that's where the AOC support ended; they insisted that there were contractual agreements in place which would prevent Adidas from going ahead with its planned promotions during the Games and demanded that a television advertisement showing me swimming with a seal was dropped and that any in-store branding, which included T-shirts and cardboard cut-outs of me in the suit, be removed.

I was blissfully unaware of this behind-the-scenes battle, as was Dave Flaskas until the day before the opening ceremony, when he was told by the AOC that my accreditation would be withdrawn if Adidas didn't follow through. The threat was clear – I'd be frog-marched out of the Games village, my Olympic dreams in tatters. Even a decade or so later it seems ludicrous, but Adidas wasn't going to risk what would have been a farcical scene. They withdrew the advertisement and branding and I swam, although I would know nothing about what had happened until after the event.

The first night of competition was probably the most exhilarating of my career but it could so easily have been the most embarrassing. There was very little time after my win in the 400 metre final, the medal presentation and the compulsory media conference before I needed to be ready for the final of the 4 × 100 metre relay, which we'd targeted as an event in which we could really challenge the American dominance.

I'd brought two suits with me from my room in the village, where I had several more backups just in case, given they could only be worn once. In hindsight, I should have brought a reserve because as I squeezed into the second suit I heard a tearing sound. In the haste to get me ready for the relay, a zipper had burst open and the suit, so carefully measured, was now useless. The only option was to try and re-use the suit I'd just worn in the 400-metres final only an hour before. It was fished out of my bag and I somehow managed to force myself back inside it. The zippers held fast and I rushed to the marshalling area just as our team – Michael Klim, Chris Fydler, Ashley Callus and me – were being introduced.

'So glad you could make it, Ian,' quipped Fydler.

I began to have mixed feelings about the supersuit era after the 2008 Beijing Olympics, when world records tumbled like ninepins. I think the mistake was that the governing body, FINA, fiddled and delayed acting as it should have to introduce rules that would have allowed technology to improve the suits gradually, instead of the free-for-all which ensued.

What resulted were suits made of a polyurethane composite, like a really thin wetsuit material, which created floatation but was also very rigid. It meant swimmers didn't have to move through the water but pull themselves across it, almost like a boat. The fabric was supposed to be porous but in the end the opposite was true and the suits prevented water from moving through them. Some competitors even started wearing more than one to boost the improvement.

At the 2009 World Championships, German swimmer Paul Biedermann was wearing suit when he beat my 400-metre record by one one-hundredth of a second. He beat his own best time by three seconds that day which, unlike my own experiences with the suit, showed that it was the difference between the two times. A few days later, he created a new record in the 200 metres. Despite this, I don't begrudge Biedermann the record and I believe it should stand as the fastest 400 metres ever swum. I don't hold much stock in world records – they're all personal best times and will all be broken eventually. Part of being a champion is knowing and accepting that there will always be another athlete to replace you.

Between 2008 and 2010, when polyurethane suits were allowed, there were 147 world records set, including 43 at the 2009 world titles in Rome. All this happened after I left the sport. FINA finally acted in March 2010 and allowed textile-only, knee-to-waist suits for men and knee-to-shoulder suits for women.

Yet I still think that too much attention was paid to the swimsuit, rather than the athletes and their performances. People have continued to create records and always will. I don't have an issue with technology because I believe that training harder than anyone else and understanding how to ensure my body will perform under pressure are bigger advantages. It's almost impossible to define an unfair advantage. Is it unfair because someone is better educated or knows more about recovery methods or nutrition or has access to a better thera-pist, even travels first class? The list goes on and on. Where do you draw the line?

twenty-two

28 FEBRUARY 2012

One of my first swimming teachers, Jenni Ashpole, used to make us practise races at Padstow pool with our goggles halfway down our faces. We complained about it at the time but looking back, it was a smart way of teaching kids how to deal with problems in race situations. With equipment that wore out quickly through sheer use, losing goggles was a frequent occurrence and something that has happened to me on and off over the years – like last Friday in Zurich.

To be honest, I wasn't looking forward to it. I was fatigued after the training slog at Lindau and would have been much happier training at Tenero before getting on the plane for

Australia, but Gennadi insisted I needed one more hit-out in a competitive environment. The Zurich International Meet was the only option and the competition was average, other than my training partner, Andrey. It reminded me of the club meets we used to swim years ago, which were considered an extension of training and only involved senior swimmers as an incentive for the younger ones.

Still, if I was going to compete then I wanted to swim fast and convince myself that things are finally coming together. Something under 50 seconds was really a must. Then my goggles came off.

It's my nightmare. Not only are you swimming blind but the anxiety goes through the roof because the pool seems to close in on you. If it happened in a longer race, like the 400, then I would seriously consider touching the wall and stopping to readjust them, even if it cost me a few seconds, but in a 100-metre event you just don't have that luxury. I swam as well as I could but it was useless and my time – 52.28 seconds – showed my state of mind and frustration.

It was clear that something had gone amiss but the media coverage suggested I was not only struggling but going backwards. I didn't see the stories, thankfully. Instead I got ready for the 400 metres the next day, which I had decided to swim instead of the 200 and really only as a training session to practise turns and stroke technique. Even then, I won the race in a tick under four minutes. Within an hour or so of finishing I was on board a train headed back to Tenero, a pleasant three-hour ride through the heart of the Alps, and playing cards with the other guys. Halfway home I'd forgotten about the meet, even the gold medal stashed somewhere in my training bag, my first 'win'. I just hope it's not the last of this campaign.

Since then training has really stepped up. Yesterday I was swimming faster times than I had at the Zurich meet. I was doing repeat 100-metre sets – six of them at under 51 seconds each time according to Gennadi's stopwatch – and yet it felt like one of the most comfortable training sets I've ever done. Andrey, who won the 100 metres in Zurich in 50.06, came up to me after training and wanted to know what was happening. He wasn't aware that I'd lost my goggles during the race and when I explained he laughed and told me he had wondered, 'Where is Ian?'

It feels like things really are coming together. Bernie Mulroy, a West Australian-based coach who will train me once we reach Australia for the trials, and Bernard Savage, who has been handling my strength and conditioning program, know the times and they're both really happy because it's a strong indication that we've broken through and there are some much better performances around the corner.

Better late than never.

The 400 metres is both my triumph and my frustration, the race for which I am most remembered but also the reason why I never reached my potential as a sprinter, because my training was based on middle-distance stamina. It's still my favourite event if only because there's more time to set myself into a comfortable stroke and play around with race tactics, depending on how I feel. It means that even in the heat of competition I can enjoy the artistry of swimming.

I discovered my race tactics almost by accident. It was the

1998 World Championships in which, as a 15-year-old, no one expected me to finish in the medals let alone to win. Doug Frost sent me out with instructions to keep on the shoulder of the race favourite, the Italian Emiliano Brembilla, but after 250 metres I realised that I'd conserved so much energy that the pace was too slow and I was uncomfortable. So I changed my stroke, increased speed and won the race.

I realised then that the race wasn't about crawling slowly for 350 metres and dashing madly over the last 50; it was an event in which strategy could be built and tested; where the last half of the race should actually be the quickest – what we call the negative split.

The speed of the first 50 metres depends on how I'm feeling. There have been races when I've swum it in 25 seconds without effort, and others in over 26 seconds. For me the key word is effort. Over the next 100 metres I want to be as effortless as possible while I settle into a stroke. If the stroke rate isn't working or I'm not comfortable in the water then I change up or down until I find the pace that seems right.

The idea is to swim as much of the first half of the race as easily as possible – smooth, economic strokes at a good pace – and waste a minimum of energy. The second half then becomes almost like a 200-metre race, with similar tactics as I lengthen my stroke which, in turn, means I kick harder to increase my pace through the 300-metre mark.

The last 100 becomes a sprint. I can feel the pain before I reach the last turn, which is when I have to dig into my reserves of energy and grit my way through the intense pain that comes with the build-up of lactic acid. I concentrate on not letting my stroke fail even though I feel like curling up into a ball.

I broke the 400-metre world record five times in my career, the first time at the 1999 Pan Pacific Championships, when I beat Kieren Perkins' long-standing mark of 3:43.80, set at the 1994 world championships in Rome. I wasn't focused on the world record, even though I knew, based on my training times, that I was capable of it. I just wanted to set my own fastest time and hope I could win the race.

I was up against Grant Hackett and the South African Ryk Neethling and we all got to the 200-metre mark in a line. This is where my race strategy kicked in, turning what was traditionally the weakest sector of the race – the third sector – into a strength. By the time I reached the final turn I'd established a seven-metre lead. Then I just clenched my teeth and swam through the pain with the noise of the roaring crowd audible under water.

It was the first time I'd swum the race the way I wanted to swim it. Kieren, who hadn't qualified for the final, came onto the pool deck to say congratulations, which was a friendly gesture.

I should also remember the Olympic trials in May 2000. It was the first time I'd worn my bodysuit in competition and I took half a second off the record, but my ambitions were no more than just making the Australian Olympic team. You get that chance only once every four years. The time – 3:41.33 – meant little compared to the joy I felt after winning the race and realising I'd made the team for the first time.

The Olympic final that year was another matter altogether. As I dived in, all I remember – apart from the noise in the stadium – is that the water felt cold and that I swam the first 50 metres probably a little too quickly, spurred by the excitement. If I look back at the race, which I'm sometimes forced to when making presentations, I notice all sorts of little mistakes, like breathing as I came into the turns and lazy kicks off the wall. They're both habits picked up at training – when you swim a ridiculous number of kilometres day in day out, you tend to look for moments of rest. The problem is when those bad habits creep into the race itself.

I had the race pretty much to myself, although I was surprised at how close the Italian Massi Rosolino had got to me. It was annoying, actually, because he was at my feet through much of the race – it meant he was just in my peripheral vision, and also affecting my clear water. With 20 metres to go I had a look around to make sure there was no one near me. I couldn't help smiling to myself because I realised I was about to win an Olympic gold medal. Then I admonished myself that I hadn't got to the wall yet and to keep concentrating. I touched in 3:40.59.

I would have loved someone else to have developed a different race strategy and issue a challenge, to be enjoyed like a game of chess. Grant Hackett was the only one who could really get close to me but I felt that he didn't put himself out there. I was always surprised that Grant didn't swim faster than he did. During poolside interviews after races he would sometimes comment about my performance and how I'd beaten him in the past, so it seemed to me he may have been psychologically beaten before we even got in the pool.

I swam the 400 metres at the 2001 World Championships in Fukuoka very differently to Sydney, almost two seconds slower in the first 200 metres and then powering home, swimming the last 50 metres in just 24.26 seconds and setting a new record at 3:40.17.

The fastest 400 metres I ever swam was at the 2002 Common-wealth Games in Manchester and yet my overwhelming sense of that swim was one of regret because I cruised over the last 100 metres. I could have pushed myself harder but was simply going through the motions. The reason was that I'd just had a fight with Doug Frost. I was swimming in seven events at that meet and another seven at the Pan Pacs less than a month later so I was conscious of managing my performances to get the best results over the two competitions.

But Doug wasn't listening. He'd told my parents he was concerned that I hadn't done enough training for the event and wasn't going to swim well. All he seemed to be interested in was how Grant was going to swim the race. Eventually I said to him, 'I'm not Grant, I'm Ian,' to which he said, 'Yes, but you've got to understand how he'll swim it.' I replied: 'If you want to talk about how Grant will swim the race then go and talk to him. I don't want to hear about it.'

In the end I walked away because everyone was watching and it was about to get really heated. He had no idea how I was feeling or what I needed to hear. The relationship had finally gone. It put me in a foul mood, although I hid the way I was feeling by almost dancing onto the pool deck.

It was only after I dived in that I sensed how good I felt physically. I was a second under the record at the 300-metre mark – and then switched off. I touched in 3:40.09 and yet, when I look back, I realise how much more I could have pushed myself. It would definitely have been under 3.40 seconds and possibly under 3.39.

As it turned out, I would never swim as well again and the fated 400-metre swim in Athens two years later effectively

Above My popularity in
Japan remains a mystery
to me but I'm grateful
for the enthusiasm. It's a
wonderful country and
I love to visit.

Right Being mobbed by
autograph hunters at the
2002 Commonwealth
Games.

I suppose you could call this a career fall. Not even my big feet could save me from gravity as I toppled into the pool at the 2004 Olympic trials.

I will be forever grateful to my friend Craig Stevens for giving me a chance to defend my 400-metre title.

I couldn't hide my relief and delight at winning the 400 metres in Athens. Grant Hackett pushed me but I managed to hold him off.

© Newspix/Gregg Porteous

A bronze in the 100 metres was a bonus, making me the only man to medal in the 100, 200 and 400 metres at a single Olympics.

© Newspix/Gregg Porteous

After the dramas of the 400 metres, my win in the 200 metres was pure joy.

© Newspix/Mark Evans

At a post-Olympics street parade, with Michael Klim. It was always good to celebrate as a team with the public.

Deidre Anderson, psychologist and Deputy Vice-chancellor at Macquarie University, guided me through my decisions to leave swimming and to make a comeback.

Announcing my 'retirement' from competition – a day of regret, but I felt I had little choice at the time.

Refuting the *L'Équipe* drug allegations was probably the most traumatic media conference of my life.

This was a welcome I enjoyed as much as any Olympic parade. In the Northern Territory in 2009 for my charity, Fountain for Youth.

Education and reading are the keys to improving health standards. And it's the next generation that's heeding the message.

My face tells the story of my return to the pool. I didn't realise how much it meant to me, nor how much work lay ahead.

Gennadi Touretski and I chat during my return to competitive swimming in November 2011, which raised more questions than answers.

Older and wiser at the Victorian swimming titles in February 2012, with Michael Klim.

After the 200-metre semifinals in Adelaide: the moment of realisation that my Olympic campaign was over.

Facing the cameras after a performance had been easy when I was winning, but I was still proud of my effort at the trials.

The next generation: My work with Aboriginal communities is a great joy outside the pool.

sealed my future with the distance. I intended to swim it again for the Beijing Olympics, along with the 100 and the 200 but, of course, by then I'd quit. This time around, Gennadi and I haven't had the luxury of time to train for it, and though I miss the tactics and psychology of the distance, I don't know if I'll ever swim it again seriously.

twenty-three

6 MARCH 2012

I'm finally back in Australia, but not in Sydney. I've landed on the other side of our vast continent. Flying in to Perth from Europe was a better travel option; it means I can just travel on to Adelaide in a few days' time. I was also hoping to avoid the media doing it this way, but someone apparently tweeted that I'd arrived and I was caught as I left the airport car park. Social media seems to have added another level to the scrutiny.

There are other good reasons for being in Perth. I love the swimming pool here. It brings back happy memories of my first world title in 1998. The weather is hot and dry here, too, unlike the wet summer they've been having on the east coast. What's also satisfying is the general public's reaction to me swimming again. I felt it in Sydney at Christmas and I'm getting the same sense of support here. People are simply happy that I'm back racing; having a go. How very Australian! They seem to understand my motives better than the media. After all, I want to do well but winning isn't everything. I can't give people an answer about how I will swim. Once I might have been able to assure them, because I could rely on my training times to be repeated and bettered come race day, but this time around it's the great unknown. I'm feeling positive. What more can I say?

I started my taper at a three-day high altitude camp back in the Italian Alps. It was more about my psychological health than anything. Gennadi wanted me to clear my head. Instead of doing three cardio sessions a day, he limited it to one and insisted that I spend the other two sessions relaxing, in the sauna or the spa, even walking.

We started to back off the swim training as well. I wasn't allowed to swim any faster than what we've been calling 'Easy Look Good' speed. I left Switzerland really happy and knew when I arrived in Perth that I had four days to swim within myself and avoid the possibility of going too fast too soon.

Because of the time spent travelling, there's a great risk of thinking you're okay and then wrecking months of training by pushing too hard. It's happened to countless Australian swimmers over the years because of the distances we have to travel to compete. Patience is needed. It's why we spend so much time in training camps before competing. The only place it counts now is race day.

Of all the sciences associated with swimming, the taper is the most uncertain. It's not a science really, given that athletes respond so differently to the process. I followed an almost identical path in my early career and yet the result differed, good and bad, from season to season. This time, given the enormous changes to my program, I'll have to rely on external observations to ensure things are working. There's a bit of guesswork involved and I'll need Gennadi's experience because I have absolutely no idea how my body is going to react.

Tapering might as well be called resting up. It's the period where training eases so the body can re-energise and be at its best for the event. But equally, it's about preparing your mind for the job ahead. You want the two working in sync and that isn't always easy, particularly when your body is on edge and your mind is wondering about what might be ahead.

Training is a constant conundrum. The workload feels easier because I'm rested. Does that mean I should push myself harder or will that simply reverse the process? After all, it's how I perform in ten days' time that counts – not any of the training sessions I've done in the Alps, which nobody has seen. It's like taking a cake out of the oven: either it hasn't risen or it's collapsed, or it's miraculously survived and looks perfect. That's where Gennadi's experience comes into play.

I've had good and bad tapers over the years and it isn't necessarily a good indication of performance. The Sydney Olympics was a bad taper, partly because I hadn't been able to get my head around going to an Olympic Games, unaware of what it would be like and how to deal with the huge publicity hype, which was very difficult to ignore. I also had nagging doubts because I'd broken my ankle 12 months out and had to change my training program to accommodate not only the injury period but also strength work to get my leg muscles even.

But it all changed the day I walked into the Olympic village six days before the Games began. The size of the event and the number of athletes was staggering. It would have been easy to get carried away with the moment, to walk around in disbelief that it was actually happening and I was a part of it, but I knew instinctively that I had to crush those feelings in order to perform at my best. I had to force myself to quash the excitement and not spend my emotional energy too quickly.

I was still calm and telling myself – and others – that it was no different to any other event when I lined up for the heat of the 400 metres on the first morning, which I swam in a pair of briefs rather than my suit. I broke the Olympic record. That afternoon I slept easily but woke up feeling a little flat. I remember wondering, was it possible to come this far, to do everything right and then, for some inexplicable reason, regress physically just as the race start beckoned? I could only hope that the feeling was a blip.

When I walked out onto the pool deck that evening with the other finalists, the noise was incredible – screaming, chanting, thumping, people calling out my name, all at the volume of a football grand final crowd rather than a normally polite grandstand of swimming supporters. It suddenly hit me how big this occasion actually was for me – an Olympic final in front of my home crowd.

Suddenly my heart was in my mouth, too nervous to even smile at the crowd. I had to try and hold the feeling and settle, not allow it to overwhelm me on the starting blocks. It was a feeling to embrace rather than fight. I was thankful when the gun went and I could finally race. This was my environment, my city, my pool and I could now pour all my energy into the competition.

My tactic was simple – get out in front and stay there – which is exactly what I did. Once I was in the water safely and swimming well, I simply wasn't going to get beaten. I knew the Italian Massi Rosolino was behind me but I had him covered. I swam the last 20 metres with a smile on my face and the sound of the crowd in my ears. I touched the wall, turned to confirm what I knew on the scoreboard and thanked God quietly.

I couldn't have stopped the emotion, even if I'd wanted to. I allowed everything which had been bottled up to pour out. As I got out of the pool, the realisation of what had just happened hit me. Everything seemed to have stopped. I was the conductor so I faced the grandstand and raised my arms. They responded and the noise reached a new crescendo.

Will I feel the same way in Adelaide? Can I hold myself together physically and psychologically to ensure I make the team?

Swimming is a game of millimetres and fractions of seconds. I broke the world 400-metre record five times between 1999 and 2002 and yet improved by less than two seconds over that period. My best time of 3:40.08, which I set at the Commonwealth Games in Manchester, was only beaten seven years later by German Paul Biedermann – by 0.01 seconds. Another example: the most exciting race of my life and the victory which gave me the most joy was the 4 × 100 metre freestyle relay at the Sydney Olympics when we broke the American dominance in the event and famously celebrated by playing air guitars on the pool deck.

We set a world record – that of 3:13.67 – and won by 0.19 seconds, despite having to swim eight centimetres further than the Americans. How do I know? Because one of the officials on duty that night sent me a printout of the lane measurements which showed that Lane 5, our lane, was one centimetre longer than Lane 4, where the US team swam. It might not seem like much but the difference can make a huge impact in the pool.

The regulations, handed down by FINA, the Switzerland-based world governing body for swimming, demand that all lanes are slightly longer than 50 metres but even then there will be marginal differences in the way the touch pads are attached to the pool wall. Nothing is perfect, everything is filmed. The price to challenge FINA on a result is 500 Swiss francs, which is why all team managers carry the cash in their pockets.

FINA tends to be a stickler for these rules and, like the progression of race times, is a slow beast to move. It'd be fair to say that I'm not the poster boy of our international federation. We've had a stormy relationship over the years, with me repeatedly 'bringing the sport into disrepute' by speaking up about my concerns over drug use and what I saw as the organisation's inaction.

But I should give credit where credit is due. I'm confident the sport is now virtually free of performance-enhancing drugs. It'd be naive to suggest that there aren't any cheats but I'd be shocked if any of the finalists at the London Olympics tested positive. And Olympic, World Anti-Doping Agency and FINA officials deserve some accolades for finally moving to clean up the sport. If someone is caught at London then it should be seen as a good thing; not a reason to cast aspersions on all swimmers but evidence that officials are alert and on their game.

But in other areas, swimming administrators are still moving too slowly. In 2004 I described the swimming administration as being in the Jurassic period, particularly in its marketing of the sport and its drugs policy. I've already given them credit for the latter but the former issue is far from resolved.

Part of the problem is that FINA is still operated as a gentleman's club which treats its stars like performing monkeys who should be grateful for the peanuts they get and refrain from having opinions. I don't believe that's any way to run a business – or a sport. It's mired in old ways and desperately needs fresh blood. There should be frequent elections for executive roles, limited terms for board members and broad representation from around the world to re-energise it.

We have to look beyond the traditional European markets and go where the growth is, not only to survive but to flourish. And that means going to Asia. We're already seeing it with an upsurge in performances by competitors from countries like Japan, Korea and China and I'm sure that, eventually, we'll see talent emerging through South-East Asia as well.

Also, world cup competitions will simply disappear unless FINA moves to win a big financial backer, like an airline who can get swimmers to and from meets. Depending on the sponsors which emerge, there could be one or two events in the Middle East, another couple through Asia in cities like

Singapore, Beijing and Tokyo, one alternating between Australia and the US, and perhaps even Brazil.

Things have to change and the best FINA seems to be able to do is copy athletics and make swimmers wear sponsors' bibs. World Cup events lose money at the moment because most of the top swimmers don't compete, finding it difficult to justify the costs and time spent away from training, and so the events don't attract crowds. People want to see the best swimming; the sport at its peak. Where's the incentive for world record-holders or Olympic medallists if the best you can hope for is $1000 appearance money – usually cash delivered in an envelope to the hotel when you arrive, which is a pretty unsettling way to be paid.

One of the few elite swimmers who competes regularly at World Cup meets is the 34-year-old Swedish sprinter Therese Alshammar, a short-course specialist who's made the two-month series her speciality, demonstrated by the fact that she's won four to date. Therese's had a great career, including two long-course world championship victories in 2009 and three Olympic medals at Sydney. But there are few others.

Swimmers have at least one major long-course event each year, from the Commonwealth Games and the Pan Pacs to the biennial world championships and the Olympics, and every other region will continue to take part in events that are relevant to them. It's not unreasonable to have short-course events mixed between them, but it means the timing of the series is critical and I think they should be tightly coordinated to allow top swimmers to fit them into their training schedules and racing calendars.

As with FINA, I have strong opinions on how the Olympic Games are administrated. People criticise how commercial they have become, and say that it's against the spirit of the competition, but without having a responsive commercial base it just wouldn't be possible, for example, to broadcast the event to the world, and we'd lose the impact it has on younger generations. It's a matter of balance and I think they've mostly got it right.

It's difficult to capture the incredible atmosphere of the Olympic Games as an athlete. I remember being criticised at Sydney for suggesting that it felt like any other swim meet but in fact I was trying to convince myself and hold onto my nerves rather than downplay the importance of the event. As a 17-year-old with the weight of expectation on me I couldn't afford to lose myself in the event itself – at least until my races were finished.

My biggest concern for the future is the choice of sports that come and go. Golf, for example, is one of the more ridiculous suggestions and I disagree with the IOC's decision to include it at the 2016 Games in Rio de Janeiro. I realise that it was included as an event in the 1900 and 1904 Games but the sport itself already has four major tournaments which athletes aspire to attend and an Olympic medal isn't going to mean much to them.

I realise that it's not an easy issue. After all, tennis has found its place at the Games even though, like golf, its four grand tournaments are the pinnacles of the sport. Even so, the players now regard the Olympics as a significant event. I remember seeing the Williams sisters, Venus and Serena, walking around the Olympic village in Sydney wearing their gold medals. It was clear they were very proud.

If there are going to be changes then we need to look

at some of the amateur sports with high participation rates. The martial arts are an obvious area, given that judo and taekwondo (which should be retained) are already Olympic sports. I think there's room for more traditional sports such as karate (which has twice been rejected) although I'd draw the line at something like mixed martial arts or cage fighting. Netball would be another sport worth considering, given that one-third of the world plays the game and since it's already included in the Commonwealth Games.

I've had an interesting relationship with the Australian Olympic Committee over the years, although, by and large, I think the athletes have been well served by the board. I was furious when they declared after the Sydney Games that the event had been so successful that funding was in place for the next three or four Olympics, and yet the first thing they did was cut the medal incentive scheme, which rewarded athletes who won medals, although it now seems to have been reinstated.

We've had arguments about sponsorship, about what swimsuit I could wear and even selection policy, but I think vigorous discussions are part of the relationship between athletes, coaches and the governing body. They've also introduced terrific changes like the decentralisation of Olympic sports training and facilities, which means there is broader access for athletes, even those who come from regional areas. It could have descended into an ugly grab for cash by state bodies but I've been pleasantly surprised that the funding has been handled even-handedly as well.

Funding for athletes will always be an issue because there's so little money to hand out to so many. I think there could be better ways to distribute funds to individuals, ways which help them and give greater accountability. Rather than just handing out money, for example, it could be structured by giving an athlete a budget from which they can bill back costs such as flights to competitions, accommodation or living expenses like electricity, or even dietary protein. What also has to be addressed is the 'me too' approach. It doesn't work in sport. I agree that we should fund as many swimmers as possible, but only to a base level, beyond which there should be incentives based on performance. It's the reason I feel comfortable with the funding I've received from Swimming Australia. They decided that my past results warranted financial support to help with my return.

I'd really like to see sport funding come out of government health budgets. I'm not suggesting that spending in traditional areas is trimmed but that more is pumped into sport because, in the long term, it provides financial and social dividends that far outweigh the initial investment.

Our success in sport is due in part to our champions. Kids get involved in sport because they're inspired by watching great performances, so I think funded athletes should be required to connect with their local communities through participation, perhaps several times a year, in organised events. That way there's a social benefit, too. I'd love governments to take this option seriously – they could save themselves a lot of money in the future by getting kids active in order to prevent the currently ballooning health problems associated with obesity and bad lifestyle. Of course, just like the issues facing many Aboriginal Australians, programs that aim to help in this way are going to require some foresight beyond the next election.

twenty-four

10 MARCH 2012

My swimming stroke has felt good from the moment I reached Perth. I expected to feel a little rusty for a session or two, simply because I'd been cooped up in an aircraft for more than half a day and travelled through several time zones. Instead, my pace has been good and my efficiency has been terrific. But yesterday's morning session was exceptional.

There wasn't anything special about the morning as such. I didn't stretch (because I don't do that sort of thing) and I did a few old-fashioned warm-ups which didn't feel any different to my normal routine. But when I dived in, I knew the session would be special. The water felt right and my stroke slotted into place immediately. I was smiling under water, before I'd reached the end of the pool.

Everything I touched seemed to turn to gold; every stroke as close to perfection as I could imagine. I haven't had a bad day since I arrived but yesterday it reached a level that I've either never swum at before in training or I simply can't remember doing. I stopped midway through so Bernie Savage could check my heart rate. It was low.

'Looks pretty good this morning,' I said as he finished.

'Bloody amazing, mate,' he answered, typically brusque.

As good as it was, the session left me in a quandary. I was due to swim one of the important training combinations in the afternoon – two 100-metre sets at 200-metre pace, followed by two 50-metre sets at 100-metre pace and then a 600-metre warm down before getting lactate readings between each set. Then I'd do it all again. It was the same set I'd done at Tenero when Gennadi used his stopwatch back in September, and a great pointer to what I might swim at the trials.

The problem I faced was the freedom Gennadi had given me to decide exactly when I would swim the combinations. Should I do them there and then while everything felt right – or should I wait, be careful and rest, using the psychological momentum of the morning in the afternoon session?

Instinct said do it now, my head said to wait. I would have loved to have swum it super fast and felt like my training had peaked at the right time but I decided there was no point taking a risk at this stage, when all I had to do was rest for a few hours and return to the pool with those positive thoughts still in my head. I went back to the apartment and ate and slept and read until it was time to get back in the water.

And that's when the joy of my earlier swim turned to dust.

The difference was disturbing. Compared to the morning, the water felt uncomfortable and my first few laps were edgy and hesitant. I immediately abandoned the idea of doing the planned combinations because I knew it would only make me more frustrated. I replaced it with another routine – 16 sets of 25-metre sprints – and forced myself to clear my head and finish the session without disappointment.

I walked away feeling as if I'd made the wrong call; that I should have done the set in the morning when I felt like it. The question mark is playing in my head. It also shows again what an imperfect science I am dealing with here. Why was there such a significant change in the way I felt in the morning compared to the afternoon? Nothing happened to affect my performance and yet the difference is stark.

And my decision not to swim the training set? Rationally, I know it was the right choice but it also went against my instinct, which was to keep going when I felt so great in the water. I keep coming back to that – my feeling for instinct and the need to trust myself.

Still, I have to keep everything in perspective. There's still a week left before the trials begin and apart from this blip, my preparation and taper have been great. The decision to make Perth my base has paid off, too – the media has only expected a little each day and then given me space and I feel as if all the work is coming together at the right time. Even the schedule of events works well. The 200 metres is my first event which, if all goes to plan and I make the team, should give me a psychological boost for the 100 metres a few days later.

This close to the trials, I find myself revisiting some of the best moments of my career, but also some of the saddest, like the impact on my family of the unfounded accusations on the eve of the 2000 Olympics that I was a drug cheat. At the time it seemed to be a ham-fisted attempt to unsettle me but it only served to inspire me to train harder and swim faster to prove the doubters wrong. But just when I thought the issue was over – dead and forgotten – I was wrong.

Fast forward seven years. Disillusioned with the sport that had dominated my life, I'd retired and was looking forward to exploring my new life and finding out what I'd missed that other 'normal' young people regarded as a part of growing up. Even so, I couldn't ignore swimming completely and in the last days of March in 2007, while I was travelling to Victoria and South Australia for some sponsorship commitments, I decided to make time to go and watch some events at the World Championships, which were being held in Melbourne. That World Cup was a significant meet for me in many ways – if not for my decision to retire just four months before I would have been competing and, as if to cement the changing of the guard, Michael Phelps, the US swimmer, came out and beat my 200-metre record, which I watched from my hotel room in Adelaide. I spent the Friday night of that week at a relaxed dinner in Melbourne and went to bed feeling pretty good about the world, looking forward to watching the next night's competition from the stands.

That all changed at 7.30 the next morning when Michelle Flaskas phoned. She and Dave had been inundated with calls from the media after the French sports newspaper *L'Équipe* had posted a story on its website that said I had given a positive reading for two banned substances, testosterone and luteinising hormone, in an out-of-competition sample I'd given the previous May.

It's difficult to find words to describe my response. Shock barely covers it; I was physically shaking, my stomach twisting. I didn't know what to say or how to react. I couldn't understand what had happened – how or why. As I'd tell journalists at a media conference the next day, it was the flipside to winning an Olympic gold. Even worse, it put a question mark over all my achievements, everything I had ever done or said. The moment was truly awful.

In contrast to the drug allegations in 2000, which had unfolded in front of me and were uttered by men I could see, refute and ridicule, this was different, and far more serious. I had no idea who'd spoken to *L'Équipe*, what their original remarks had been, where they got their information or, indeed, what it meant. I could only presume that someone had improperly accessed my records and leaked the results of a sample I'd given before retiring. I knew I'd never used performance-enhancing drugs of any sort and yet a sample – one of dozens I gave willingly every year, which would have amounted to hundreds over my career – seemed to have returned an irregular result. And while *L'Équipe* had published their information, I hadn't even been notified by the swimming administrators.

As it turned out, I *had* returned an irregular result but the Australian Sports Anti-Doping Authority (ASADA) had decided not to take it any further. FINA, however, had decided it wanted the samples retested. But that didn't explain why my name had been leaked.

I sat in my hotel room for a long time trying to digest the news, took a few calls from my family and close friends and then switched my phone off. I'd had enough. I wanted the outside world to go away. This was what I'd been trying to escape when I retired and yet the pressure was still chasing me, thoughtless and unyielding. Now it seemed that someone wanted to sully my career and use the media to disgrace me. I was guilty without charge, let alone proof.

When I finally turned my phone on around lunchtime there was a traffic jam of messages from friends and other swimmers. Everyone was very concerned, and I realised that instead of isolating myself, the best thing to do was go ahead with my plans to attend the swimming that night. I asked to be able to sit with my former teammates in the stands, not knowing what the response would be, and watched Michael Phelps win another gold medal, this time in the 200-metres medley, one of seven victories for the meet. The sport was already moving on without me. Why couldn't I be left in peace?

The media conference was one of the most difficult I've ever done. I couldn't hide my emotions, unable to pretend that I was okay, because I wasn't. The journalists seemed to understand the predicament and my fears. They noticed my red eyes, my cracked voice and my nervousness and treated me with a level of respect that I really appreciated. I still had no real idea about what was going on and, in an attempt to offer some explanation, I suggested it could have been the result of an anaesthetic I'd been given a few weeks before the sample was taken, when I had an operation to repair a broken hand.

Then I tried something which was, in hindsight, probably a bit too clever. I was asked who I thought had leaked the story. In my mind, I already knew the person responsible – someone associated with FINA. I couldn't name them but

I tried to allude to the connection by referring to the pink outfits the officials were wearing at the championships in Melbourne. I quipped that I thought the Pink Panther had done it. I was really hoping that one of the journalists would take the hint and look into it. Unfortunately, they saw it as gallows humour.

As I tried to clear my name in the next few months, it was a really tough time for me. The sample had shown raised levels of two hormones which occur naturally in the body – testosterone and luteinising hormone – and there didn't appear to be an explanation. The concern wasn't the levels themselves, but the fact that both were raised at the same time.

I sought medical advice in Los Angeles. The tests there, which were rather uncomfortable and carried out with my trousers around my ankles because the two hormones relate to sexual performance, were all normal and offered no further explanation other than the fact that the initial result made no sense. As it was explained to me, it's a bit like a blood pressure test, which can show one reading in the morning and a different reading in the afternoon. I understand why we test for irregularities but that's all they are, and they should never be made public.

It took four months before ASADA cleared me. The chairman, Richard Ings, said it was common for athletes to show slightly elevated levels without any suggestion of an offence. He also stated: 'The evidence available does not indicate the use of performance-enhancing substances by Mr Thorpe and he has no case to answer. Experts were unanimous in their opinion'. It would take another two months for FINA to drop the case. In the end I attempted to get *L'Équipe* to explain themselves but after spending a small fortune on legal fees, I realised that the company wasn't going to answer to an Australian court and had no assets here, so I dropped the matter.

It leaves one final question – why my name and results were leaked. To me it was clear – I felt it was payback, plain and simple. I'd been an outspoken critic of FINA's drug-testing procedures for some years and the irregularities in my sample provided the perfect opportunity for someone with a bone to pick to get back at me for daring to speak my mind.

In particular I'd been very vocal at the 2001 World Championships in Fukuoka, where I described FINA as made up of a bunch of dinosaurs who couldn't manage their sport and questioned their commitment to addressing the drug problem. My beef was that, not only was it unacceptable that we had to compete against swimmers who were drug cheats (and I've swum against a few), but the image of the sport itself was being tarnished. I was also sick and tired of the innuendo about me and my performances.

My comments didn't go down well and created a media furore. I never intended for my comments to spark the public debate that they did, but I'd made them in response to a specific question about FINA and their drug-testing regime and I didn't want to lie.

Two years later, at the World Championships in Barcelona, I was asked the same question and I repeated my comments, although this time I avoided the term dinosaurs. I said: 'I don't think it will ever be a clean championships, which is an unfortunate thing to say. I've been critical in the past and I'll continue being critical in the future until it's a clean sport.' Nothing much had changed since 2001 and I wasn't going to pretend otherwise.

And so in 2007, four years later, someone saw an opportunity to get back at me. I think leaking my name was a spiteful, despicable thing to do and I know the shadow it has left over my career will never fully be erased.

I have never taken performance-enhancing drugs, and have always been at the forefront of anti-drug campaigns, even volunteering to have my samples frozen for testing in future years. I feel as though I've been an asset to the sport and its battle against drug cheats. But it's not only the illegal performance-enhancing drugs that I feel strongly about. Just because the rule book says athletes can take Creatine, which aids the provision of energy to muscle, doesn't make it morally right. I don't even take multivitamins, although like other swimmers in the Australian team I have used sleeping tablets like Stilnox on occasions, to sleep between training sessions. I found them helpful and always used them sensibly.

Although drug-testing policies and procedures have improved, I still have grave concerns about several aspects of the process. With a system that dictates athletes are guilty until they can prove their innocence, there's little or no protection. It should be the other way around. Athletes need to be able to trust the integrity of the system and have their privacy assured unless there is a case to answer. I would even argue that their identity is protected until they've had the opportunity to defend themselves.

I think it's also time that the concept of drug abuse in sport – not just swimming – is put firmly into context by sports administrators. It's still common for the public to see any kind of improvement as potentially tainted by drugs, or that the exposure of a few is seen as the probable actions of all. The fact is that drug abuse, for the most part, has been curtailed. It still goes on, but certainly not at the same scale that it once did.

I think the one area that still needs a major overhaul is the way the drug war is funded and managed. There's just no consistency in the levels of funding around the world, with too many authorities playing a role. Instead, there should be a pool of funds provided to a single authority – probably the World Anti-Doping Agency – which would then administer all testing.

twenty-five

14 MARCH 2012

There are a few pools which have been particularly important to me in my career. Perth is one, and Adelaide is another. Not only did I swim well here in age championships as a kid but it was where I made my first national team at the age of 14.

That was 15 years ago, more than half my life. I was a medley swimmer then but when Doug Frost and I arrived we realised there was an opportunity to make the senior team in one of the prestige events – the 400 metres – so I pulled out of the 200-metre medley to concentrate on the longer event. It was a punt and it worked. It seems that fate has made this pool the place to gain my spot in the team again.

I was thinking about how well Adelaide had treated me as I flew in last night. The weather was amazing. There's something very special about this country, particularly noticeable when you've spent time overseas. It felt frontier-like as I walked outside; warm and fresh, the smell of eucalypts and the sun about to disappear below the horizon, reflecting orange light everywhere and highlighting this most Australian landscape. I felt it in Perth, too.

The colours are bigger and brighter here than in the northern hemisphere; so are the flavours of the Australian red wines that I love, so different to the lighter, more subtle tastes of Europe. There's a different quality to the light here, too – you can tell if a film has been shot in Australia before anyone even speaks.

I flew in with Bernard Savage and my Western Australia-based coach, Bernie Mulroy, and we discussed what would happen and how we'd react to the media, who'd be certain to be in the airport car park. Bernard, looking like a burly security guard, paved the way through the lines of photographers. I stopped for a few minutes; happy to say how nervous but pleased I was to finally be at the trials. The nerves were there but, for once, I wasn't worried.

I slept well last night and drove to the pool this morning for a light training session, as much to get a sense of the venue again as anything else. I could feel my excitement growing but I was waiting for the *wham* sensation – the moment when I feel I'm back in competition. There were a lot of swimmers and coaches already there when I arrived; old faces and new, the hallways and change rooms full of noise and chatter. I tried to get a sense of whether it felt threatening – a bad sign – and I didn't, which was promising.

Then I got changed and got into the warm-up pool. That's when it hit me; that same chlorine pong that had ruined my appetite in Lindau three weeks ago but this time it meant something entirely different. The same sights and smells had been there in Asia, Melbourne and in Europe but those meets didn't mean anything to me. I'd felt under-prepared and anxious then – even awkward – but this time it felt right. In the stink of the chlorine was the whiff of competition.

I inhaled it; thrilled because it confirmed that I belonged and I was ready. This was my time to perform. I felt like getting up on the starting blocks and racing there and then. It was just like it used to feel, all eyes looking at me. Earlier in my life it was because I was the one – the force. This time it was because I was the unknown quantity, a curiosity in many ways, but still someone with an aura of possibility. I could use that as motivation. It was energising.

Tracey Menzies, my old coach, was there on the pool deck. I was pitted against one of her swimmers in the 200 metres and she looked me up and down and commented that I was looking good. It was an acknowledgement that I belonged there among the Olympic hopefuls even after such a short preparation. Other coaches came up as well. They could tell that I'm a different swimmer to the one who turned up to Victoria in January. It added to the sense of expectation in the air, that I'm here and ready to race. It really fed my confidence. Frankly, I couldn't have felt any better.

It was a critical moment. There's no way I could swim if that feeling of competition was missing. It would have made me question why I'd begun this journey and endured all the training; ask myself whether I'd been lying to myself all along;

even discover that my values were askew. But I've felt it, and now I have to pull back my enthusiasm, concentrate and be patient. Tomorrow is the day.

There has been one sour note, although I'm trying to make sure it doesn't affect my preparation. I had to do another media conference this afternoon, which was dominated by controversy created by a newspaper about the payments made by Swimming Australia to help my training. It wasn't pleasant. I was accused of being a self-indulgent prima donna being handed preferential treatment who was either foxing about his chances or hopelessly out of his depth. I find it not only ridiculous but set up and pushed by people with dubious agendas.

At any other time I might have been tempted to expose the people pushing this controversy and their motives, but I feel a responsibility to Swimming Australia. I don't want the trials to be hijacked by it but driving it are people who see an opportunity to take a shot at Swimming Australia management.

I gave my explanation. It's pretty simple really. Swimming Australia supported my preparation as they had done for any other swimmer they believed was worth supporting. I'm grateful they agreed to help contribute toward my training costs and sports science services, which were higher than others because I had decided to train overseas.

'There have been a number of athletes who have been Olympic champions or world record-holders who have been supported by Swimming Australia,' I said. 'The money that has come from that is not dissimilar to what has been funded to other people in the sport. We're not all cookie-cutter athletes and if we were we'd have a pretty ordinary swim team. It's not my decision who does or doesn't get funded. That's a decision that happens within Swimming Australia.'

Had I been foxing? 'There may have been a period when I first started back in swimming and I was hoping I might be able to do it but my struggle against time and anxiety means I haven't had that luxury. So, frankly, no. I'm nervous about the upcoming days.'

Sitting there in front of the media conference, this was the hardest question. Am I worth it? We'll know tomorrow I suppose, but I think most people would agree that the event itself is better and more interesting with me in the field, struggling alongside everyone else for a place on the Olympic team.

Isn't that the point?

Kieren Perkins seems to think I'm worth it. He's been a vocal supporter since I made the announcement I was returning to the pool, dismissing the naysayers after my underwhelming performances in Asia last November and continuing to defend me in the row over the Swimming Australia payments. I'm grateful for his support although it feels a bit strange, considering we haven't been close over the years. In fact when we were teammates our relationship was cold at times, even bordering on hostile, especially when he retired and began voicing his opinion from the sidelines.

Kieren was one of my childhood heroes – I even wrote him a letter once when I was nine years old – but he seemed to find it difficult to accept the new blood coming through the ranks when Grant Hackett and I appeared on the scene in the late 1990s and began putting pressure on his times. Grant has spoken publicly about the sense of intimidation he felt from Kieren so I'm not alone in my experience. That said, even though, in the past, Kieren took issue with me in his comments about my use of swimsuit technology, times have changed and he's been clearly and publicly supportive during my comeback, including this generous statement in this morning's papers:

Ian's got nothing to lose. Even if he does fail in this bid, it won't in any way diminish his extraordinary achievements. But the big winner is the sport, which has really enjoyed having his profile and persona back. What is so exciting is that he is putting the sport in front of a whole new generation. And he is showing young swimmers what it is to be more than a swimmer. Brand Thorpe is about more than being a world record-holder. A lot of world record-holders you've never heard of, but what Ian did was reach beyond swimming.

Relationships are difficult in such a competitive environment. I'd count people like Grant Hackett and Michael Klim as good mates, as well Craig Stevens, with whom I trained for years and owe a great deal for his generosity in standing aside from the 400 at Athens after my blunder at the trials.

The Dutch swimmer Pieter van den Hoogenband, who was one of my biggest rivals, is one of the few swimmers I've remained in contact with over the years. I think we connected because we were both alike in our laid-back approach to competition – that is, until the race started. Strangely enough, I think our friendship was cemented in the moment he beat me to win the 200 metres at the Sydney Olympics. Even though I felt crushed I remember offering my congratulations while we were still in the water, but by the time I'd climbed out of the pool and was doing the post-race interviews I'd already started feeling a sense of comfort that a friend of mine was now experiencing the same feeling I'd had the night before when I won gold in the 400.

It's difficult to express how it feels to become an Olympic gold medallist. When Grant won the 1500 metres on the last night of competition at Sydney all we did was just look at each other — it was an unspoken bond, I suppose, no words required.

Michael Phelps was the flipside of Pieter for me; we were never rivals as such, because our careers overlapped rather than clashed. We only raced once seriously before I walked away from competition, in the 200 metres at the Athens Olympics. When I met Michael he was being touted as the next big thing in swimming — the American Ian Thorpe, as it was put to me at the time — and someone who had the capacity to dominate his events in the same way I had been. In that sense we might well be considered rivals given that our impact on the sport itself is often judged side by side.

Michael and I became friends despite our very different personalities and styles. He's an intense competitor who races to beat his opponents and I'm a quiet participant obsessed with self-improvement. He and I also swim very differently and yet he's one of the few people I would describe as a natural swimmer, as opposed to an athlete who becomes a swimmer. I'm sure he'd understand what I mean when I talk about my sense of water.

It certainly wasn't intentional that I missed seeing Michael beat my 200-metre record at the 2007 World Championships in Melbourne. My life had moved on in the months after announcing my retirement and I needed to be in Adelaide for some sponsorship commitments. I remember watching the race in replay the next day, sitting alone in my hotel room. I viewed it from an analytical point of view rather than with an emotional attachment to the record; the same way I always looked at my own races in replay – at the performance, not the result. I always wanted to know how I was able to go so fast and what could I do better to go faster again.

I was fascinated by Michael's performance, not because of the time he set but his strategy of starting quickly and fading slightly as he came home. It looked to me as if he could go faster, which he did at the Beijing Olympics less than a year later. At no time, though, did I even consider that Michael had taken my world record – it wasn't *my* world record, it was *the* world record. He certainly hadn't taken anything away from me; his performance didn't change the best time I had set. He had simply set his own best time and it was the fastest ever timed.

That's the attitude I've always taken with world records. My view is that all I was doing was setting my own fastest time. If that happened to be the fastest time ever set, I received enormous adulation for the achievement, but that didn't change the fact that it was my best time – to date. To judge my career on the idea of being the fastest to have ever swum would have meant my self-worth was wrapped up in being better than anyone else rather than the best that I could be.

But world records are the last thing on my mind at the moment. Where once I was expected to set a personal best whenever I dived into a pool, tomorrow is about just making the team.

twenty-six

20 MARCH 2012

It's over. I didn't make it, not even in the event I thought I stood the best chance in.

I'm gutted. I know I looked it, interviewed on pool deck in the moments after the final of the 200 as I tried to accept what had happened, my agony complete with snot hanging out of my nose, which no one thought to let me wipe away. As I stood there I struggled to contain my churning stomach, smiling at the gracious applause from the crowd and wanting only to flee to the warm-down pool.

There's no other way of looking at the events of the past few days really. The truth in elite sport is brutal; black and white, win or lose. The sob stories never last as long as the entries in record books; they only note those who made the Australian Olympic team – not those who failed to. Not only did I not qualify for the 200 metres, I missed out on the 100, too. As I commented poolside, the fairytale had turned into a nightmare.

So what happened? I'll start at the beginning to see if I can make sense of it all.

I'd taken a sleeping tablet the night before the 200-metre heats. I usually do in competition, because my head tends to race with thoughts which keep me awake. I slept eight hours and woke up just before the alarm went off. I made myself a cup of coffee as I always do and it was only after I sat down and took a couple of sips that I remembered I was going to race – the day had finally arrived.

I'd stopped drinking coffee before competition back in 2004 and used caffeine powder instead, mainly because I wanted to know exactly how much caffeine was going into my system and didn't risk getting too close to the legal limit. I usually stopped two weeks out from race day to make sure I didn't have withdrawal symptoms but this time I'd forgotten, perhaps because I hadn't been in this situation for a while.

Pushing the coffee away, I realised I had to get my gear together and get to the pool on time. I'm afraid my brain isn't the kind that allows me to prepare early. I can't understand people who begin packing days before they're leaving. It makes no sense to me. I like doing things at the last minute so I know exactly what's in my bag – spare goggles and caps, for example. Do I need to take my training bag or not? Can I borrow someone else's kickboard at the pool for the warm-up? I was getting stressed out because I was out of practice.

I drove to the pool, iPod on but deaf to the music because my head was full of thoughts about the race ahead. I had a parking space inside the gates of the aquatic centre but media crews were waiting so I politely made my way through, smiling and saying I was there to race. It was true. I felt good; a bundle of nerves – but good.

My pre-race routine was fine and when I walked out onto the pool deck the place exploded. It was a morning heat but it looked and felt more like a final. Channel Ten, which had the television rights, were broadcasting my race live.

My one serious concern was the anxiety. It had affected me in Zurich and at Luxembourg and I could only hope to manage it as best I could, not to mention tying my goggles even tighter. The crowd was cheering so loudly that the marshal had to stop and ask people to be quiet. As I stood, ready to get up on the blocks, I could feel the anxiety bubbling but it also dawned on me that it was okay to be nervous. Instead of being a threat, it was something natural. I relaxed a little and it made all the difference. The old feelings of control were back and so was I.

I swam the race perfectly, just the way I'd planned, with the first 150 metres at a fast but comfortable pace and the last 50 metres with the luxury of being able to turn off the *Titanic* – which is how it feels when you deliberately slow down – to coast home.

I had swum 1:49.16, the fifth-fastest heat time as it turned out. It meant I had a good lane in one of the semifinals later that night. I got out of the pool feeling great, already with plans to drop my time by two seconds. I'd done it before. I felt that the two seconds would be easy to find in the semis, not just because I'd backed off in the last 50 in the heat but because my pace would naturally increase in the next swim. It was just a matter of resting, trusting my training and letting it happen.

I could already foresee dropping that time even further into the 1:46s in the final, which would mean not just qualifying for London but winning the national title. I also knew that others were watching and could probably tell from my split times that I'd slowed down at the end. I was starting to scare the shit out of them.

I swam down for a kilometre, had a massage and went back to the hotel but couldn't sleep. That's not unusual but it was a mild frustration, given that I'd practised sleeping in the middle of the day in the week leading up to the event. Instead I read some of Osho's *Innocence, Knowledge and Wonder*, a book that explores our search for meaning. Maybe it's the wrong book to be reading this week.

I tried to dismiss any thoughts about the semi so that my mind was clear and I could rest and relax. Lunch was normal but I forgot to take a snack to the pool for later. Instead I had to find a protein drink when I was there to fill the hole in my belly, although I always like to feel a little hungry before a race – if I'm hungry I'm chasing something to fill that need and that works for me in a race.

I went out about half a second quicker over the first 50 metres, and even as I started down the second lap I felt as though I was in front and planned to stay there. But then, in the second half of that lap, something didn't feel quite right. Turning into the third lap the feeling only got worse; things weren't quite as comfortable as they had been in the morning.

Then, in the second half of the third lap I tried to accelerate – only to find that it simply wasn't happening. I was very worried now.

Turning at the last 50 I knew I needed to do something special and just had a sinking feeling. I realised then that my whole Olympics campaign was falling apart and there was nothing I could do about it. I knew my fate long before I touched the wall. When I did, it was hard to turn around and look up at the clock, but eventually I did. It wasn't the time that was hard to take in – which was more than half a second slower than the morning – but the number of swimmers ahead of me. I couldn't qualify. I was dusted.

The whole place was gobsmacked. Where there'd been noise and excitement and cheering before the race, now there was silence. Then I had to do the poolside interview, which was broadcast around the arena. It was probably the hardest interview I've ever done. I can't remember exactly what I said but I know my response was honest. As destroyed as I was, I still really wanted to thank people for all their support, something I'd wanted to do whether I qualified or not. I felt grateful for the amazingly positive response.

After that I started swimming down but I couldn't face more than a few laps. I looked up at Bernie Mulroy, who was by the pool, and told him I wanted to get out. I felt as if everyone was looking at me. He agreed it was the right thing to do, and I went to have a massage. As I lay there thinking about what had happened, I just wanted to cry but I couldn't allow myself the luxury. Instead I decided that when I walked out of the room I'd begin focusing on the 100 metres, which was two days away.

Before the competition I thought my chances of qualifying for the 100 were 50-50 but after my performance in the 200 they'd plummeted to about 10 per cent. I was now a very dark horse for the sprint and I knew it, but I didn't want to think that everything was over, no matter how dire it looked. I still had another chance, as slim as it was. I had another media conference and wanted to get everything straight in my head about what I was doing next. I have to say that for all my complaints about the media, on this occasion they were very supportive. The tone of their questions echoed the fact that they appreciated the effort I'd made.

Leaving the aquatic centre, there was a crowd outside. Rather than getting into my car and driving away, I stopped and signed autographs and had photos taken for about 15 minutes, determined not to let my disappointment show. As I finally got in my car to leave, Mum stuck her head through the window. She'd been in the stands and would have been as shocked as anyone.

'I love you, mate,' she said.

The way she spoke to me was as much as a friend as my mother. Wanting to get out of there as quickly as possible before I lost it altogether, I brushed it off, replying with something like 'Yeah, I know.' It was only later that I realised how dismissive it must have sounded. I didn't mean it that way, of course, but I should have told her how much I loved her back.

Driving back to the hotel was hard. The only other time I'd felt anything like this was back in 2004 when I was disqualified for the false start in the 400-metre trial for Athens. And this was worse. Gutted is really the only word I can think of that comes close. I'd been prepared to find it tough but I'd always expected to reach the final and be competitive, at least for a relay spot. And after such a great heat I'd expected to compete for an individual place. Now I hadn't even made the final.

I had a quiet meal then planned what to have for dinner the following night, in effect trying to speed up what was a grieving process. I wanted to look forward as much as I could. I knew it was a terrible time to reflect on what had happened. That would come later.

I've always swum multiple races in competition and trained myself so that when a race is over, whether I'm successful or not, I'm already thinking about the next one, which helps me avoid becoming too emotional about what has happened. I've always been very good in that respect, and was probably learned from my young days when I'd swim almost every event during a competition. I just had to hope that I could achieve that psychological distance from my disappointment this time.

When I prepare to race I don't really to talk to anyone, even Mum. As soon as I go into taper mode I can be moody and difficult to be around so it's best to shut off and simply concentrate on what I'm doing. I might chat around the pool or talk to coaching staff but the mobile phone becomes a no-go zone. I read text messages but rarely answer them. It might appear selfish from the outside but I just have to be in my own space. I may have picked up some of this from others but I've discovered over the years that the separation is essential. Competition is a process of preparation, racing and then recovery, which is then repeated over heats, semifinals and finals. It's gruelling to say the least.

All I could do the next day was pretend; go to the pool and have a swim to make it feel as if I was still involved, even though

I wasn't. Despite everything that had happened I wanted to see the final that night, partly because I believe in supporting the other swimmers but also out of curiosity. I wanted to know how fast they'd go. I was searching for motivation.

It was hard sitting in the stands, feeling as if I should be out there and knowing I was capable of winning the race. But they'd all swum faster than me and I wasn't going to begrudge them their chance to go to the Olympic Games.

Still, it was frustrating to watch their tactics. Rather than build the race they all seemed to amble for three laps, watching each other, and then have a mad sprint home on the last lap. I was hardly in a position to critique them, but I couldn't help myself. That kind of strategy is limiting and doesn't do anyone any justice. The 200 is a very tough race and swimmers need to learn how to hurt themselves early in the race and build up a tolerance to lactic acid if they want to challenge to be the world's best.

As hard as I tried to move on from the disappointment, there's no doubt in my mind that it affected my performance two days later in the 100 metres. It's not an excuse, but a realisation that it put a great crack in my confidence. I'd come to the competition very confident, had a boost after the heat swim – and then been shattered. In all my experience I've rarely had a disappointment, let alone something as big as that, but it wasn't until after the 100 that I realised that this episode has come to a close.

There's not much I can say about my swim in the heat of the 100. It was colourless. I started well and turned well but just didn't swim very fast. My time – 50.35 seconds – was almost half a second quicker than I'd gone before but again it felt sluggish. I turned at the wall, looked at the numbers and realised that this time I was going to miss the semifinal. My campaign had ended.

I swam down for a few hundred metres but got out of the pool because I could sense that people were watching and felt sorry for me, and the last thing I wanted was pity, no matter how genuine. Instead I had a massage to give me time to think about what had happened so I could face a media conference. As I lay there on the table, my thoughts kept coming back to the question of whether it had been a failure. From a pure racing perspective, the answer was obvious – yes. But as the minutes ticked away, I could also see that it had been a great success: I had rediscovered my enthusiasm for the sport that had once burned me out.

When I appeared, the journalists were generous. I could tell that they were disappointed like everyone else. In the lead-up to the trials I'd been asked many times if I'd been foxing. Now they all knew – no, I hadn't, and neither had I ever hidden the enormity of the task I'd set myself.

17 APRIL 2012

I went to inspect a house in Tenero today. Actually, the place was quite a way up on the hill behind the town. It was 10 degrees at the lake when I left and zero degrees and snowing when I reached the house. Still, the views were spectacular.

The lease on the apartment where I've spent the last year is due to end around the time the Olympics start and I'm interested in buying if I can find the right place. Perhaps that says something about my state of mind at the moment. I want to stay and continue swimming but I have to be sure about it. I've now had a month to think about what happened in Adelaide and how I feel about the future, and the answer still isn't easy.

No matter what happened I'd always planned to go on after the Olympics, but for most of my preparation I hadn't even considered the idea that I might not make the team. The trials were just a hurdle in my mind; something to be wary of but negotiated with a degree of comfort. But that all changed over the Australian summer as my training times failed to translate into racing times as expected. The trials became a wall and one that, in the end, I couldn't scale.

I'm feeling 50–50 about it right now, but I won't know until I train for a few more months and see if there is any progression. My plans have been further frustrated by a bout of bronchitis which has kept me out of the pool for the last week. I'm better now; I've almost stopped coughing up rubbish, which means I can get back into training. I'm looking forward to that – it means I can answer some of the questions about where I go from here.

What about how far I've come? Did I fail? Was it a waste of time?

I was certainly disappointed with the results but what I'm pleased about is that I had the balls to do this. It would have been a lot easier to sit in Sydney, playing with the dogs, tending the garden and cooking for my friends while trying to shut out this part of who I am. Whether it was successful or not, I gave it a go. I've answered a big question inside of me that would otherwise have haunted me for the rest of my life and in the process reignited a passion for something I loved, and had ended up hating. For that I'm really grateful. Despite this, I keep asking myself what went wrong. The answer is still as clear as mud.

I did everything right in the taper. My training times suggested that I should have been able to swim faster. One of the explanations I've been given is that my body was simply unable to back up from heat to semifinal. I didn't feel fatigued as such but because I hadn't been swimming and competing for such a long time, my body wasn't used to the effort. It happened to Michel Klim in the 100 metres as well. The truth is that 18 months just wasn't enough time to reach elite form, even with my background in the sport. I knew it deep down but hoped that I'd somehow make it through and have an extra three months to peak for the Games.

Before I made my return, friends would ask me what it would take for me to swim again. I always replied that it would take three years of hard work, more as an excuse for not doing it than anything else. But looking back now, I was spot on. If I give myself another six months and aim for next year's World Championships in Barcelona, then I'll be pretty close to being competitive, but in reality it would take another year to get back to my peak, so the Glasgow Commonwealth Games in 2014 seem to match the timing a bit better.

But I'm hesitating at the moment. It's not a question of wasted effort but a life question. Do I have the willingness to do it, particularly when I have so many other opportunities to use the tenacity I've shown in training to accomplish other things? Hopefully I'll find an answer soon. But what's interesting is that I have a new perspective about my past achievements. I didn't realise before just how much I'd accomplished before I retired in 2006. Everyone else was amazed but I couldn't really see it, perhaps because I was in the middle of it, in the eye of a storm, and was concentrating so hard on making it happen. Sometimes it's only when you stand away from something that you can truly see what's happening and why.

As I continue to train it's become clearer that it's important to acknowledge to myself just how good my early career was, and put my recent performances into some kind of perspective. I have to consider that I have a new best time, which is necessary so that I can see myself improving rather than trying to catch up all the time. My best time for the 200 metres, for example, is now 1:49.16 and not the 1:44.06 I swam in 2001 in Fukuoka. Likewise, for the 100 metres my best time is now the 50.35 seconds that I swam in the Adelaide heat swim and not the 48.56 seconds I swam in the final of the Athens Olympics. I've hit the reset button like the scores on a computer game.

As I wonder what lies ahead for me in and outside the pool, I realise it's also a good time to reflect on what has happened to me and why. My successes have been played out publicly but there's a very dark shadow which has frequently dulled the way I see things, even the glitter of Olympic gold. I've never spoken openly about the complications of my life; in fact, not even my family is aware that I've spent a lot of my life battling what I can only describe as a crippling depression.

I feel as though I'm in a good place at the moment, which is probably why I can allow myself to think more about it. In a way I wish I could talk about it, not only to clarify it for myself but to show others that it's possible to manage a serious illness and still achieve great things in life. I know the illness can't be blamed or used as an excuse for poor results – I was able to swim some of my best times through some of the worst periods. And it also wasn't a reaction to the high life of red carpets and speeches, and neither can I blame the media intrusion – although it certainly hasn't helped and might explain my reticence to discuss my private life.

It's a terribly dark place in which to hide.

Even when I was a child I knew I was different. I don't mean in a physical sense, nor that I had a feeling of superiority over other people. Quite the opposite. I didn't have words then to describe what it was but there were times I'd feel sad for no apparent reason. It's probably why my early school reports annoyed me so much, glossing as they do over individuality to assure parents that their children are good and coping well when the truth is often very different.

By the time I was in my mid-teens, those sad periods were getting more frequent and longer but I just tried to ignore them and get on with what I was supposed to be doing, which was plenty. I still had no words for what I was feeling but that wasn't the only reason I didn't tell my parents. Life had become complicated by what was going on for me in the pool and I could already see that they were struggling to come to grips with the world I was entering. Even at 15 it just seemed that I needed to shield them from the fuss. Besides, I wanted to be the perfect child and what I was feeling was a character flaw as far as I knew. I was also hoping that they knew intuitively that something was wrong and that there was no need for me to try and explain it. But now I realise it's time to be open. I need to talk to them about it.

It's going to be tough. I've always told Mum and Dad that I want the way I live my life and my family relationships to be as normal as possible. I don't want to be treated like the superstar, I want to be treated like their son. I know how Mum will react; she'll cry and ask me why I didn't tell her and then she'll tell me how proud she is that I've finally talked about it. Dad is different. I'm not sure how he'll react. I know it'll take time for him to come to terms with it and how it fits in with his religious beliefs. I hope it does, because family means a lot to me. He once said that he felt he'd lost me as a son. I hope, in my honesty, he'll feel as though he's gained me back.

It's taken me a long time to accept that being depressed wasn't my fault and rising above it is actually a strength of character. Just as I believe sexuality to be a genetic disposition, so too is depression. It was something that I would have had to deal with whether I was a swimmer or not.

I was 19 when I finally decided to try and get some answers. The Sydney Olympics had come and gone, I'd moved out of home and had begun my initial preparations for Athens, which was still three years away, but the illness had become crushing and I knew I needed to seek out other ways of managing it. The freedom of moving out of home had given me space but it also meant I was more alone with my thoughts than ever before. And my success in the pool only compounded the misgivings: I should be feeling great; happy and invincible. Instead, there were nights when I would contemplate ending it all.

A clandestine visit to my doctor had provided some help, including medication, but little in the way of explanation. If anything it isolated me even more because I felt as if I now had a secret and no one to share it with. It was something I'd already found as a 15-year-old world champion, a child among adults, someone without peers with whom I could share my fears and questions, let alone a classroom and school playground.

I suppose it was inevitable that I'd turn to other, artificial ways of managing my feelings, and I found alcohol. Ironically I was never really a drinker, hating my first sip of champagne at a family wedding where I recall agreeing with Mum, a lifetime teetotaller, why anyone would want to drink something that tasted awful. There wasn't much room for it through my teens, either; my training schedule too full to party with my contemporaries. I succumbed rarely and when I did it there were other motivations, like the night I found myself in a nightclub after a function and accepting a glass of vodka to impress a girl. There were a number of other swimmers there, all older than me of course, including Samantha Riley, whose then boyfriend, the speed skater Johan Koss, frowned at me and warned it would ruin my brain.

The more I tried it, though, the more I found it suppressed my feelings. And a few years later, when my black periods grew more frequent, I found that the more I drank the better I felt – or rather, the less bad I felt, although that only lasted until I woke up the next morning to go to training. My poison was always red wine, at times drunk in quantities that now seem unbelievable.

I'm not an alcoholic, because this isn't about addiction; I'm not dependent. I used alcohol as a means to rid my head of terrible thoughts, a way of managing my moods – but I did it behind closed doors, where many depressed people choose to fight their demons before they realise they can't do it without help. Now I am getting that help and managing my depression properly.

But in the past it was a different story. There were occasions when I would have friends over for dinner, drink moderately through the meal, enough to suppress my thoughts, then wait until my guests had left before opening another bottle and getting plastered. It was the only way I could get to sleep. It didn't happen every night but there were numerous occasions, particularly between 2002 and 2004 as I trained to defend my Olympic titles in Athens, that I abused myself this way – always alone and in a mist of disgrace. I know I never did anything really bad when I was under the influence but there are definitely nights that I regret.

Yet I never missed a training session. Somehow, the reality of the morning always forced me out of bed and into the pool where I worked as hard as anyone, as if to erase the memory of the night before. And even though I was training for the Olympic Games with a hangover, my performances were some of the best of my career, including the world record for the 400 metres which I set at the 2002 Commonwealth Games in Manchester.

I was also able to hide my drinking from the battery of sports psychologists and coaches who work with the elite athletes. I appeared psychologically strong, a determined, dedicated athlete with all the answers about goals and directions to satisfy their criteria, yet beneath it all I was a wreck.

What strikes me is that it demonstrates it's rare for even the most successful people not to have problems. It seems that whatever you want to do, having a desire and a determination to succeed is powerful, even in the face of depression. I can imagine how some people, when they look at my life and all its opportunities, could say that I have no right to be depressed. For a long time I thought so, too, and questioned myself constantly, but if it's something inside you that's different there's not a lot you can do about it on your own. But somehow I swam, competed and won in spite of an illness I didn't understand and was too fearful to admit. It's the reason why I chose to study psychology at university – it wasn't just a desire to finish school and get a degree but to satisfy a craving to find answers about myself.

I can only remember being caught out drinking once. It was a Saturday morning, probably at Caringbah pool, and another swimmer told me I smelled of alcohol. I brushed it off, saying I'd had friends over the night before, and completed the session with a blazing headache. Exercise can play a very powerful role in managing stress – when you feel like crap, just go for a walk and you'll feel better – but I sometimes wonder if the relentlessness and intensity of my training schedule over more than a decade did the opposite and exacerbated the condition, the physical exhaustion wearing me down psychologically.

It's another reason why I believe athletes shouldn't be seen and managed as a single group of identical people. The media – even some swimming professionals – couldn't understand why I needed to spend periods outside the pool between major meets. As far as they were concerned, even a week off training meant a loss of condition and potential, but I saw those breaks simply as a way of being able to *stay* in the sport, one that I could easily have fled before competing at my first Olympics, felt tempted to quit many times before competing at my second, and ultimately left prematurely on my way to a third.

My illness was so severe that, at times, I considered suicide. I believe it's actually quite normal for people to think about killing themselves because it's part of the great conundrum of life and death, but the difference between those superficial, inquisitive kinds of thoughts and some of my bleakest periods of introspection was that I took the next step and planned how and where to do it.

My blackest periods would often last a month, and it was during those times that I thought about 'it' happening. I even considered specific places or a specific ways to kill myself, but then always baulked, realising how ridiculous it was. Could I have killed myself? Looking back, I don't think so, but there were days in my life that, even now, make me shudder.

My worst moment came when I was playing by the rules, so to speak – getting out of the house, communicating with friends and family and not drinking – but I wasn't getting any joy out of even the simplest things which made me happy, like being with my dogs or cooking. All of a sudden the suicide notes in my head started to feel rational. I needed help.

The psychiatrist asked a series of questions which gave me a score on a depression and anxiety scale that was quite scary. He concluded that my medication had stopped working and it meant I had to change – not a pleasant experience – and also that I had to go on anxiety medication, something I'd never had to take before.

Even today, at a time when I'm pretty happy with my life, I have to manage what is quite a severe illness. It's a day-by-day proposition. When I wake up, every day is potentially a dark one and I realise that it's something I'll have to live with all my life.

I want the message to be positive: that things can get better. The key is to accept that it's an illness that can be managed properly. Like so many others before me, I wanted to fight it by myself. It felt embarrassing – particularly for an elite sportsman – and it became a weakness that couldn't be shown. In hindsight, I realise that it would have been much better to share it with my family and close friends.

I sense that the incidence of depression is quite high among elite athletes, probably much higher than in the general population, and not just because of the enormous physical and psychological stresses we put ourselves under. Perhaps we're attracted to sport in the first place because the exercise helps the way we feel. The first person I told about my depression was another swimmer because I recognised that they suffered it too. I felt we shared common ground. It was only last year. I had been living with my secret all my life.

It's another reason why athletes shouldn't be seen as a robotic group of super humans. We're all different, each with our own problems. Depression has never been discussed openly and with the honesty that's required to tackle it properly. But I don't want my depression to define me. I've lived with it all my life and have now reached a point where I'm comfortable acknowledging it. Beyond it, I have a life which is empassioned by other issues, particularly my charity. I'm fortunate to have access to many services that others find difficult. I would support the role that organisations like Beyond Blue and the Black Dog Institute play in society.

Once I was worried I didn't have the mental strength to return to swimming, but I realised it was more important to get back in the pool than deny myself something that is a critical part of who I am. Others may look at my performances so far as a failure but, like many of the responses to me and my races over the years, it's far too simplistic a description for something that is so complex, a complicated spectrum of grey.

I may not have made the Olympic team for London and been gutted by it, but my return to swimming has been a success in a much broader sense. Certainly, I have had some bad times in the past 18 months, times when I called Gennadi to say that I couldn't make training because I was ill, when the truth was that I was feeling down. Thankfully, they have been short and relatively few, and for some reason when I am in competition mode I'm able to manage my feelings a lot better. But in the end, swimming has been my salvation.

twenty-eight

14 MAY 2012

Gennadi and I sat down after training today because we needed to have a conversation about what it is that I'm supposed to be doing. He wants me to race again in a few weeks and I'm just not interested.

I'm actually in a great space at the moment, content and enjoying the life of an athlete in training. It's intense and tiring but my life is now also unhurried; not held to ransom by the deadline of competition. I told Gennadi that I can't see the value in racing so soon after the disappointment of Adelaide. I want to be in form and confident the next time I race, ready to show what I'm capable of doing.

He understood immediately, nodding in his thoughtful

Russian way. He's going on holiday actually. It's been six years since he's had a decent break and he probably needs some time away from the pool deck; somewhere warm and beautiful where he can be alone with his thoughts during the day and among friends in the evening, which is when he likes to mingle. I'll be here in Tenero when he gets back, churning out the kilometres, which will give me the aerobic base that I missed in the last campaign. My routine feels challenging but normal, the weariness at the end of the day almost comforting.

Apart from the physical conditioning, the key to the next phase is enthusiasm. When I arrived here in Tenero fourteen months ago I was keen to try something new and was excited by the results it might bring. But that excitement dried up in the lead-up to the races for the World Cup meets in Asia last November when I lost my way a bit because of the anxiety about racing. I've got the feeling back now and I want to bottle it and keep it close by.

And I don't want to be ruled by time. I just want to train and enjoy the process rather than feel bogged down by the pressure and expectation of performance. For my two targets, the World Championships in Barcelona next year and the Commonwealth Games in Glasgow in 2014, I have all the time in the world and it feels great. It gives me a chance to smell the roses, not in terms of taking time off but taking pleasure in the training. I feel as though a weight has been lifted.

Perhaps there was a silver lining in failing to make the Olympic team. It's made me take a step back and look at what happened. I should have qualified – I really believe that – but even though I didn't, the experience only reinforced the knowledge that I made the right decision to come back to the pool. I can walk away from what happened and accept that I'm disappointed that I won't be swimming in London, but I also know that I want to continue.

Swimming is in my blood. I don't know how I managed to live away from it for four years. I enjoy aspects of training that most people would think as drudgery; for me it's an exploration of what I can achieve. I know now that, no matter what happens, I want to continue to swim – and also that I want to swim at a level I haven't reached before. I still believe that's possible.

There's also been another change in my thinking. When I retired in 2006 I couldn't see myself being involved in swimming ever again. I didn't even want to be around a pool. Now I feel the opposite; that I will always be involved with the water in some way, whether it's competing or in a role in the background – perhaps even coaching.

I have an odd relationship with Los Angeles. It could be such a beautiful city. If only someone could just hose it down every night. Instead, it's an ugly concrete sprawl with only slivers of beautiful landscapes and homes, the kind of place that could just disappear overnight. On the other hand, I like the people who choose to live in LA; it's because they go there to succeed. Their sense of purpose, their energy and drive, is clear and palpable, and it's one of the numerous reasons why I chose to base myself there after the Athens Olympics.

Despite all my misgivings in the weeks leading up to those Games, as the competition went on the event got better and better for me – there was the enormous relief of being able to successfully defend my 400-metre title, the win in the 200, making amends for my loss to van den Hoogenband in Sydney, as well my snatching of a surprise bronze medal in the 100. Those performances made me the first swimmer ever to medal in the three distances at one Olympics.

Teetering as I was on the brink of giving up swimming, it was the bronze medal rather than the two golds which made me want to keep going. The pressures of what swimming had become for me then were all consuming and, combined with the constant hounding from the media, not to mention the darkness that had been my companion for so much of my swimming life, I was close to quitting on so many occasions. In Athens, if I'd only swum and won the 400, I would have most certainly retired then and there. The 200 was a joy, but it was the 100 which made me think about a fresh challenge. How far could I push it?

Suddenly I could see a reason for swimming on, but I knew it could only be for just one more Olympics. Everything in between Athens and the Beijing Games – even the Pan Pacs and the World Championships – seemed largely irrelevant. And I needed a good long break from the pool if I was going to survive the pressures of the elite training life for another four years.

I was still fragile psychologically. It's not as if I could just stop feeling black and confused. And the lure of alcohol was still powerful. The last thing I wanted to do was jump back in the pool straight away. Desperate to enforce order over a life that seemed so out of control, I decided that a break from swimming was my answer.

Of course, what I didn't realise was that I needed help from those around me, not the isolation I craved.

The period following the Athens Olympics turned out to be the longest time I'd spent out of a pool since I was a kid, and it was almost four months before I dived back in. Even then I didn't train seriously until February 2005 and it would take another six months before I got back to a decent fitness level, which told me this time around what a battle it'd be to come back. During this time I managed to tell Tracey Menzies and Dave and Michelle Flaskas that there was something wrong – but I also insisted they didn't worry about it; that I wanted to work it out for myself.

In the months after Sydney I smoked cigarettes as a way of exploring life away from swimming, knowing full well that it was stupid and made no sense. I remember buying my first packet after trying a cigarette in a nightclub. Again, I was trying to impress a girl and only ended up looking like an idiot because I didn't know how to hold it, let alone inhale. And yet I still found myself sneaking into a petrol station late at night pretending to be buying a packet for my sister. It was an act of rebellion, I suppose – even though I couldn't stand the taste. The attendant clearly knew who I was and didn't believe a word, especially when I asked for the only brand I could think of – Cartier.

It seems almost funny now but it was yet another example of my lonely battle to understand what life was about and how to fit in. Four years later I was revisiting those same questions but this time in a much more desperate state, afraid to really open up to anyone about my moods and the self-medication with alcohol.

In the first few weeks of my time away from the pool, learning how to relax was a new skill in itself. The regime of an elite swimmer requires periods of intense activity followed by periods of no activity – rest and recovery – with very little flexibility in the routine. Relaxation is something you do in the periods in between those gruelling programs, and it's hard to find ways of wiling away the time when you're used to spending seven hours in the pool each day.

So I filled my days travelling between my business and sponsorship commitments, which had reached a new and higher pitch post Athens. Opportunities were opening up in China as well as in Japan and Europe, with projects like the underwear range, the health drink and the necklace, not to mention the television work with the Foxtel network, including opportunities to make documentaries on the environment.

It was then that I discovered LA. I already knew people there so I immediately felt comfortable socially, helped along by the fact that the lifestyle and climate are similar to Australia. It's also an easy transport hub between Europe and Asia, so I found myself drawn back to the city often and was immediately interested when a friend suggested I should buy a house there.

Our search yielded nothing until, on a whim, she drove past a house that she'd once stayed in soon after moving to LA herself. It was a quirky cottage perched on a hill among the treetops above the city with a funicular the only way to get inside. There was a For Sale sign outside it and she rang, telling me excitedly, 'I've found your house. You must buy it.'

By this time I was back in Australia, deep in a full training schedule with Tracey but already thinking seriously about splitting my time between Sydney and the US. Despite my disrupted training I was in reasonable form when I swam in the New South Wales 2005 titles that December and won both the 200 and 100 events. Then I flew back to LA to inspect the house – and fell in love with it straight away. It was irresistible to the child in me, the treehouse I'd never had as a kid because my father lopped the branches off anything higher than the house for fear they'd fall on the roof.

It was built back in the 1960s as a hunting cabin and was later changed into a house with a huge deck on its roof with views on one side of downtown LA. If I looked to my left I could see through the lower canyon, which reminded me of the Italian countryside, and if I turned to my right I could see gum trees which, of course, reminded me of home. There was also some history to the place. John Lennon had lived there for a few months after splitting up with Yoko Ono in 1973 and, so the story goes, almost got shot one night when a neighbour took aim at him taking a leak off the deck, probably stoned off his head. I even had his son, Sean, stay over one night after I bought the place.

The deed done, I flew back to Sydney where I was due to swim at the Australian titles, which doubled as the trials for the Commonwealth Games. There I won the 100 and 200, having decided to drop the 400 from my schedule since Athens, at least for now. Things were going okay. I believed I could win all three events in Beijing but the question was how and where to train.

It was then that things began to go horribly wrong. In March 2006 I contracted glandular fever, which forced me to pull out of the Commonwealth Games. Then, in April, I broke my hand when I slipped over in the bathroom and had to have a screw inserted. My plans had been thrown into disarray. By now I'd begun working closely with the American swim coach Milton Nelms, then the fiancé and now husband of Shane Gould. I'd been introduced to Milt by Tracey in 2003, and we'd worked together occasionally in the lead-up to Athens. With all the recent dramas and interruptions I wanted to feel different, find a fresh challenge and be focused by it. Milt agreed to spend three months on an intense program that would help me regain my health and physicality and get back on track.

It was the perfect excuse to base myself in LA for a while, away from the constant hype. There was nothing wrong with the media interest and no inappropriate questions but the pressure itself never seemed to let up with photographers often at the top of my driveway or at the pool. Tracey graciously accepted my plan which was to head back to Australia that December and her coaching in time for the final preparations for the World Championships in Melbourne in March 2007.

Working with Milt was so invigorating. He changed my posture and where I sat in the water and we worked on utilising my spine and enhancing the natural flow of movement with my kick. He also changed my stroke to lessen my bent elbow, among many other things. We sometimes trained in the ocean so that I could concentrate continuously on my style. He also got me to do a lot more dry land work. I did running sessions through the Runyon Canyon in the Hollywood Hills behind the city, a lot of work with rope ladders, rotational exercises, skipping and high knee lifts. The idea was to learn how my body moved and to take that knowledge to the pool. It was all designed around posture – a high-intensity and advanced mix of yoga and pilates. It was very similar to the experience I'm enjoying with Gennadi. I was excited, intrigued about exploring swimming again.

The interesting thing about the time I spent in the United States was that my profile there was quite small compared to many other countries throughout Europe and Asia. Even American Olympians, perhaps with the exception of the high-profile track and field athletes, struggle for recognition against the stars in the professional team sports like baseball, basketball and football.

I felt as if I was hiding out in the open, rarely recognised in the street, and even then people struggled to remember my name. It was a joy to watch the expression on the face of the woman on the checkout of my local supermarket as she tried to place my face with a name. She even glanced at the name on my credit card and still looked puzzled as I walked out. The relative obscurity meant that I didn't need to worry about the media for a while, hoping they'd received the message that I wanted to be left alone to train and swim well for the Beijing Olympics. And indeed I was for a while, happily recovering from a sequence of unfortunate events, as well as battling my own ongoing demons. Despite this, there was still a mentality that I'd given up on Australia, which I had to ignore.

My peace was short-lived. In early August it started again. First a local newspaper reporter knocked on my door and asked for an interview about why I was training in LA. When I declined she was shocked but it wasn't long before the Australian media smelled blood in the water and made its way to America.

I wanted desperately to be well again, physically and psychologically, which meant having space and room to breathe. But here they were, following me to and from the pool, even photographing me eating lunch. There's a restaurant chain called In-N-Out Burger and I was in the habit of eating there every Wednesday as a high-protein, low-carbohydrate treat. I'd have two double double protein burgers, which is two meat patties and two slices of cheese inside a lettuce 'bun'.

Then they began questioning my friendship with Australian actor Heath Ledger and his then fiancée Michelle Williams. I liked Heath, not because of his high profile as a movie actor but because he was an interesting and unique person. It was the period before and after *Brokeback Mountain* was released to rave reviews and launched him as a major Hollywood actor. His daughter Matilda Rose was born in late 2005 so I knew Heath and Michelle as young parents, normal people away from the spotlight.

Yet it was insinuated that I was sleeping with Michelle after a photo was taken of us in the carpark of what looked like the back of a seedy motel. It was actually the back entrance to the offices of an interior designer we were both using. I saw the photographer and knew what was about to happen. My instinct was to give him the finger but I knew that would only exacerbate the situation.

The media also began following Milt and me to training, which forced us to use rented second-hand cars and regularly change swimming pools, even travelling to Seattle for a few days, which then led to suggestions that I wasn't going to training. When you have to change the way you drive to a training session or you can't go home and need to hide at a friend's house, then it becomes serious.

In desperation, I agreed to do an interview with the Foxtel network in September to counter the stories about my body shape, fitness levels and enthusiasm. I talked about quitting and said it was something I thought about every day. But it was a half-truth – I didn't want to quit, I just wanted to swim. I meant it as a warning shot to the media; that if they continued with their onslaught I wouldn't go on.

Even if they were right and I was struggling, what was the purpose in hounding me and publicising my struggle? I was an athlete and a private citizen, not a politician on the public payroll. I'd won gold medals for Australia at two Olympics but that didn't mean I should have to justify my actions to the media – or the nation. Surely I'd earned the right to some privacy, particularly when I was clearly pleading for help?

The last straw came toward the end of October, the day after I'd arrived back in Sydney. The paparazzi had surrounded Caringbah pool and then followed me home. The next morning, during a dry land session with Shane Gould, it hit me – I couldn't go on. I stopped, looked at her and said: 'That's it. I can't do this anymore.'

It would be another month before I announced anything. I wanted to make sure that it wasn't simply a petulant reaction on my part. Even in the midst of my despair I realised that it could be an overreaction; that there was a potential for paranoia. There was also a lot at stake. I knew I'd be letting people down. I was halfway to the Beijing Olympics and despite the setbacks I still believed I could perform well. There were financial aspects to consider as well; I'd signed four-year deals with sponsors like Adidas, Omega, Qantas and Foxtel, agreements that peaked in 2008. I'd be throwing away a bucket-load of money. But this wasn't a decision about money.

It was then that I went to see Deidre Anderson, on Shane's recommendation. She knew the moment I walked through the door that I was about to retire, but I wasn't even ready to say the words. It took me a few weeks to come to it; but interestingly, others already knew what was about to happen. My parents in particular could see that it had all become too much; they understood. Their response was amazing.

The way I saw it then was that the attention had become like a cancer. It had corrupted my sport and my only option was to stop. Only then would it disappear.

twenty-nine

6 JUNE 2012

This week I baked a coconut and banana cake and built myself a barbecue table. It seems a strange combination but it sums up the way I'm feeling at the moment; settled in a funny sort of way but a bit uneasy about the future and what it holds. Besides, the two projects remind me of my maternal grandparents and their influence on my life and it's comforting to think that a part of them is here with me in Switzerland.

Poppy Hathaway taught me woodwork in his garage workshop where I spent hours after school watching him use the lathe. I haven't made anything for 20 years, and thought I'd forgotten everything, but even so I managed to draw up a design for the table, order the timber cut to length and then bolt it together on the balcony. It seems to fit but it won't be staying because I'll be moving in a few months. I'm not going far, further up the mountains and out of the village where the view across the valley and lake is even better. I'll also have more room to breathe. I'm going to continue renting, at least for the time being.

Nan taught me to cook, hence the cake. She's tiny and laid-back, always with a spark and a witty remark but tough as nails, especially when it came to Christina and me learning our times tables in her kitchen after school. But she's starting to show signs of being her 89 years. So is Pop; he's 85 and doesn't do woodwork anymore. Both have handed in their driver's licences, happy to walk everywhere. They're still at home in their two-storey house. The staircase is the best thing for their health.

I'm heading home to Australia next week and I want to have a conversation with them, one that's long overdue. It's to tell them about the positive influence they've had on me, the sense of protection I've always felt. I want to know if they want me to be there, in Australia, for them as they get older. I know the answer already; that they're fine, happy exploring the internet, and couldn't stand it if I didn't get on with my life.

The family worry about me living outside of Australia. They fear I'm running away, afraid to be in my own city; also that I'm isolated from them. It's definitely been true in the past, partly because of the media pressure and my own demons; now it's even more so because my life has so many different parts. I've recently sold my house in Caringbah and will look for a more suitable apartment near the centre of Sydney because I've decided that I want to spend about half my time in Australia each year, and half here. I've fallen in love with this area of Switzerland and am looking at a couple of options to set up a home here as well. And I still have my treehouse in Los Angeles.

I officially walked away from swimming at 2.53 pm on Sunday, 19 November 2006. I remember the exact time because I glanced at my watch when I made the decision, sitting with Dave Flaskas at my kitchen table. We'd spent the last hour discussing the pros and cons of the situation and there was nothing more to talk about. In the three weeks since I'd announced my intention to family and friends, and despite the impact my decision would have on the sponsorship deals we'd struck, Dave hadn't once tried to talk me out of it.

As our discussion came to a close, we looked at each other and then Dave asked quietly: 'You haven't changed your mind, have you?'

I shook my head. And that was that.

Three days later we held what I hoped would be my last media conference. I spoke passionately and honestly. I was struggling with motivation, I said, a struggle exacerbated by illness and injury. And I wanted to explore my opportunities and find some balance in a life that, so far, had been lopsided. It was all true but, as I'd done so many times before in my career, I didn't reveal the whole truth.

I didn't mention my continuing struggle with depression, although I hinted at it when I spoke about a darkness in my life and described swimming as a safety net and a security blanket which I was about to cast off. But none of the assembled journalists, many of whom had known me for most of my career, read what was, to me, glaringly obvious between the lines. Neither did I blame the media for their role in my decision, even though it had, ultimately, been the deciding factor.

When I walked out of the conference that day I had no real idea about what I wanted to do, only a broad understanding that I now had time to answer the 'what if I'd never been a swimmer' question. If I was a more calculating person I would have hung in there for another two years, collected my financial bonuses from sponsorship deals tied to performance and then been in a much better position to explore the world. But I wasn't and I didn't. The money issue was still irrelevant.

Over the next few weeks I would concentrate on 'detraining', coaxing my body into normality, away from the peaks and ravages of elite training, and learning to ignore the cravings for starchy food. But the larger challenge was ahead. I'd just discarded the biggest part of my life and, for the first time as an adult, was no longer a slave to time. How was I going to fill the void?

For a while I roamed without intent. Los Angeles beckoned; a sanctuary now free of the media pack but with only part of the answer. I spent some time in Brazil – Australia without law and order – where it's more dangerous to stop at an intersection than drive through a red light. I love it there. Everyone eats late, sleeps often and there's always a party in the street somewhere, and everyone dances, good or bad, from grandparents to little kids. Life is exciting – and dangerous – yet somehow simpler.

But I was running away, and life with all its complexities was still in pursuit. The drug allegations published by *L'Équipe* emerged in March 2007, shattering any peace I might have gained since my retirement. The experience shook me badly, making me fearful that my swimming achievements were under threat. Couldn't they see how wrong it was; how much I'd championed the fight against performance-enhancing drugs?

I didn't know where to turn. Worse, no matter where I went I couldn't escape the questions. In the few months since I'd retired the demands of the media pack had lessened. Now journalists were following me again, to events around the world, even the opening of a watch shop in Beijing. I remained polite even though I was burning up inside. Finally the formal investigation was dropped in November, ending a very troubled first year in retirement.

I retreated inside the Los Angeles house or back home in Sydney, sometimes for weeks at a time; scouring the cupboards for food rather than forcing myself to go outside to face the world. This would be the darkest period of my life. Not only was I lamenting the loss of swimming and where my life was headed, but my legacy was being questioned – two mood triggers which had a devastating impact.

I would lie in bed for days at a time, in half dream mostly, delaying the most basic of things like going to the toilet or eating. I knew that I needed to get out but I couldn't raise myself. When I finally emerged I would find hundreds of voice messages on my phone. I knew people close to me were worried but I simply couldn't respond.

I still had my business interests to keep me busy – appearances for Audi at motor shows, opening stores for Omega in

China and doing television projects for Foxtel. I even worked for Westpac for a while, looking at programs aimed at school children. And of course there was my charity, the Fountain for Youth, whose work and profile was growing and whose legacy I could never have imagined. It seems a lot when I look back on it now, flitting back and forth across Asia and Europe as I was, but I was still searching for something else.

It was a key time for me in focusing on my own issues, which I was managing as best I could and the reason I enrolled at Macquarie University a few months later to do a degree in psychology and linguistics. The move helped me overcome my misgivings about not finishing high school and satisfied the craving I had for an intellectual pursuit. It also gave me direction in my search for answers to my continuing struggle against depression. I'd been able to shake the media but not the disease.

My timing wasn't great in some respects. Having already enrolled in the course I had to seek an extension on my first round of assignments because of my sponsorship commitments at the Beijing Olympics. I also fractured my shoulder blade in three places while stretching at the beginning of a gym session. The injury would be an ongoing frustration for a couple of years and, in hindsight, probably delayed any decision to come out of retirement.

Another question lay in wait for me at Beijing. How I would feel watching the Australian team in the pool without me? Yet instead of being torture, it was the moment that I realised I'd begun to come to terms with what had happened. Yes, I had a hankering to compete but my enrolment at university meant I finally had something new and meaningful to concentrate on. I seemed to have been angry for so long; angry that it hadn't felt like my choice to stop swimming, that I'd been pushed toward the cliff and had eventually toppled over. I was angry at myself for feeling like a victim and that I'd let other people down. I was angry at the sense of regret that I'd ever been a swimmer. I needed to find that other life so I could look back kindly on what I'd achieved, for my own self-preservation more than anything else.

The strange place I found myself in then was characterised by my verbal tangle with Michael Phelps, who was trying to become the first swimmer ever to win eight gold medals at the same Olympics. I'd been asked about his chances and I said I didn't think he would do it, not because I didn't think he was capable but because I thought the French would beat the US in the 4 × 100 metre freestyle relay, in which Michael was swimming. As it turned out, Michael's teammate Jason Lezak swam the fastest relay leg in history to catch Frenchman Alain Bernard and win gold for the US – and Michael. Somehow what I said was misinterpreted as a criticism of Michael's ability rather than a comment about the competitiveness of the racing, and he ended up pinning a newspaper article quoting my doubts to the inside of his locker as inspiration.

I was actually sitting in the stands with Michael's mum and sisters when the US won the 4 × 100 medley relay to give him his eighth gold and break legendary US swimmer Mark Spitz's record of the most gold medals at a single Olympics. I turned instinctively and congratulated them, glad to have been wrong and to have been there to witness such an incredible achievement. I was happy not just because of the physical triumph but because of the person he had become in maturity. I'd been one of Michael's childhood idols so it was even more important to acknowledge what he'd done.

I didn't dive back into a pool until the summer of 2008–09. It was Caringbah pool from memory, the morning after a big dinner, when a mate and I decided that we should be fit again. The water feels strange even after a few days off so it felt very weird when I dived in that day. As I made my way slowly down the first lap my injured shoulder made it even more difficult. I knew people were watching, but I didn't care much. I realised I wasn't very good at it anymore and that I wasn't prepared to train to get it back. The water felt different and I didn't want to distort my memories of training and swimming so I only went back to the pool two or three more times after that.

I still hadn't escaped the media attention, although by now the stories were sporadic and centred mainly on the trivial, like who I might be dating. Whenever that particular question arose so too did the debate over whether I was gay. I dealt with it each time, patiently repeating the denial and my weariness of the issue, but it was about to reach a new and cruel level.

In January 2009, a newspaper published photographs of me and a friend, Daniel Mendes, holidaying in Brazil. The accompanying article said, correctly, that Daniel had lived at my house in Sydney for the past three years while studying at the University of Wollongong, had accompanied me to a couple of red carpet functions and had also been on holidays twice with me and my family. The implication was clear: Daniel was my gay lover; I'd finally been outed. It was outrageous and stupid. I felt as if the last two years had been for nothing – the media was still chasing, still demanding, even creating answers that they wanted to their inappropriate, valueless questions.

It wasn't all doom. Friends told me they'd never seen me so creative. It was true in many respects. Apart from the seemingly bottomless well of work as a motivational speaker at functions and conferences around the world, my business interests had expanded to include an online mortgage venture, and I was promoting products for Adidas, Audi, the watch-maker TW Steel and Yakult Japan. I'd also thrown myself into the environmental movement, making two television shows, including *Fish Out of Water* which looked at the impact of global warming, and supporting initiatives such as Scouts Australia's application for government grants to install solar panels in scout halls across the country and feed the excess energy back into the national grid.

Occasionally I'd be asked about swimming and if I would ever consider returning to competition. The thought crossed my mind often but I always dismissed it because the idea of swimming was coloured with anger and regret. I honestly believed that the day I walked away from swimming was the end. In interviews I had deliberately used the term 'discontinued' because I'd wanted to leave the door open, if only slightly ajar. But I didn't really think it was possible because I'd come to hate what it represented. Why would I want to go back?

At the beginning of 2010 the media attention turned to my personal finances, with the claim that I was in difficulties because of the impact of the global financial crisis. Several newspapers produced intricate examinations of my business life, concluding that I could be looking for a return to the pool to boost my commercial worth. They justified their claims with reports of a then private conversation I'd had with swimmers at the Commonwealth Games trials in March in which I encouraged them to target the 4 × 100-metre relay at the London Olympics.

Both suggestions were untrue. My businesses had gone through a tough time like everyone else during the GFC but I would never have returned to swimming for money. It wasn't the motivating force when I began, it didn't tempt me to stay when I walked away and it certainly wouldn't be the reason behind a renewed commitment to 60 hours of training a week. The day-to-day life of an elite swimmer is one of asceticism and physical and mental discipline. There's no financial reward meaningful enough to lure a swimmer out of retirement unless there is a much bigger driver behind it – a love of the sport and a willingness to put everything to one side in order to give over to it and, in my case at least, some very personal issues to test and pass.

Life, however, was beginning to turn for the better, and it would be this alone that would be the catalyst for my decision to return to the pool seven months later in that plane above the Atlantic. In May I travelled to Tanzania after being appointed by the World Economic Forum as a 'young global leader'. On one of the stopovers we visited a school to talk to the children about tolerance. I loved the idea of being involved with young African kids but I admit I had my doubts about the subject. I dislike the word 'tolerate' because it suggests a reluctance to accept rather than a positive embrace.

After we'd addressed the children, they had just 30 minutes' preparation to make a presentation to us and the rest of the school. One boy, aged seven or eight and small for his age, stood on a chair and told the assembled audience, which included business leaders, politicians and even royalty: 'I may be short but I have a voice which is as valuable as yours. This is what tolerance is about; for me not to be judged by my height because I am standing here as a tall man.'

I couldn't believe it. Where did he find those words, so clear and simple so that everyone could understand? I was sitting next to the Crown Prince of Norway, Haakon Magnus, who was equally taken by the boy's words. I turned to him, smiled and said, 'The world's in good hands.'

My heart was lifted. There were good things happening around me.

thirty

26 JULY 2012

The London Olympics begin tomorrow. I'll be at the opening ceremony, not as the competitor I'd hoped to be when I began this journey but as a BBC commentator – and that's okay. I've come to terms with my disappointment in Adelaide. I did enough to glimpse what might be and I'm satisfied with that for the time being.

Having said that, I had a strange moment yesterday as I was moving into the London hotel, which will be my home for a fortnight. I began unpacking my clothes but stopped when I got to my gym bag, which also had my swim gear in it. I'd packed it in case I felt like doing a few sessions between on-air stints. It seemed so out of place here, with all my commentary jackets, pressed trousers and shirts, and I realised how much I wanted to be part of the swim team again; not here in a luxury hotel talking about my sport, but in the village on a single bed, my T-shirts and tracksuit dumped in a wardrobe that wobbles because somebody has assembled it in a hurry. Thankfully the moment passed quickly.

My future as a competitive swimmer remains undecided. I want to keep swimming at least until the World Championships next year in Barcelona, perhaps even the 2014 Commonwealth Games in Glasgow.

I'm settled in Tenero, enjoying the training regime, beside a tranquil Swiss lake, lost in thought about performance and the puzzles outside the pool. I've told Mum and Dad about my darkest thoughts and fears and they responded instinctively, as I'd hoped. I'm their son and they love me unconditionally. Now it's time to move on with my life, whatever that brings.

I still freak out a little when I consider what I've done over the last year and a half and what I am revealing publicly. Hiding away from the pool would have been the easier path but eventually I'd have looked back with regret. I needed to face the whole truth about myself and not just the pieces I felt I could manage.

I hope that people can now understand why the question of my sexuality has been so insignificant compared to my battle with depression, but I do wonder if they'll continue to ask whether I'm gay or not. There are far more important messages: that success in itself doesn't make you happy and it's almost impossible to win battles on your own.

I think happiness is a fleeting concept for most people. 'Content' would be the word I'd choose to describe how

I want to feel from day to day. Happy is hard for me, but there are times when I experience happiness in the moment. It's usually when I've let go of everything and am around friends or family, being silly and playing games.

There are times when I feel invincible: internally powerful, even arrogant. It's a feeling beyond happiness really; a combination of euphoria and pride. I feel as though I could do anything. Moments like these have come in the training pool where I'm alone with my own thoughts, when the water feels like magic. And even though I was hurting physically I knew that I was swimming in a way and producing times that hadn't been done before. I had that feeling in Perth on the way to the Adelaide trials; I was on an absolute high. I realised I'd recaptured the sense of performance I'd known before my retirement.

Some of my most euphoric moments have been while representing Australia – being selected in the national team for the first time, and being marched out to stand on the dais to celebrate a victory. I remember the feeling I had after the 400 metres at the Sydney Olympics very clearly because I was trying to suppress the bubble of joy inside of me, which was pushing up like champagne out of a bottle. I had another race – the 4 × 100 metre relay – soon afterwards and I couldn't afford to let it go. When we won the relay an hour or so later I couldn't hold it down any longer and the euphoria exploded poolside.

Australia will always be home, as they say, although I have a strange relationship with my home city. I miss Sydney and its freedom and space when I'm away, and I miss the water too, but I find it claustrophobic to be home for too long. My life, experiences and interests have expanded. Love–hate would be far too strong a description for my feelings but it's true to say that I'm confused and saddened by some aspects of our so-called egalitarian society.

Let's face it, I'm not the right person to front an advertisement selling Holdens, beer or meat pies. I simply don't match up with the symbolic and clichéd images used to promote the Australian way of life. The truth is that I just don't fit the mould of the traditional icons of our nation, which ironically derives its self worth frrom the success of its sporting heroes. I'm sure it's the reason why my sexuality began to be questioned when I won a world title as a slightly embarrassed, giggling teenager. The athlete people saw on their television screens was different and inexplicable. If I'd been a stereotypical Australian male then it would have been okay, but I wasn't – and I never would be, as it turned out.

That said, I've enjoyed enormous popularity and support from thousands of people who have cheered me in the stands and tens of thousands more who've watched me on television. But there have been times when I've been in the depths of despair wondering why I was swimming for a country that seemed, at least from my perspective, to want to tear me down.

I love the Australian appreciation of the underdog yet it's at odds with the treatment of the biggest underdogs in our society – the Indigenous community. Likewise, we applaud people who 'have a go' but then put a ceiling on success by cutting down tall poppies, as if too much success is something that's bad for us. It's something we have to get over in Australia. We have to celebrate and be proud of our achievements, whether it's in sport or science or music. We have to stop being so insecure and strive toward success rather than be afraid of it. We don't need to cringe behind our accent anymore.

I've experienced the same response to my return to swimming. People in the supermarket have patted me on the back and wished me well whatever happens, pleased that I've put myself on the line. But others have seemed annoyed by it, as if I'm being a greedy fool and putting my credibility at risk. Not only do they misunderstand my intentions but I suspect that I've upset their view of my career – the invincible Thorpe in the black suit.

But that was then and this is now. I just want to swim again. I don't really care about results. I was glad to expose myself by getting back on the starting blocks. It was much harder than I thought, but I knew I had to do it. And that isn't what makes it so important. I thought I could walk away from swimming and never go back. I was able to do that for four years but now I've realised that I need to swim. It's insane, but after a few laps I feel like the world is my oyster, that I can do anything.

In the end, I'm a swimmer.

MEDALS AND RECORDS

CR: Commonwealth record   OR: Olympic record
PB: Personal best   WR: World record
3:53.44 = 3 minutes, 53.44 seconds   SF: Semifinal

1997 Australian Championships, Adelaide

Bronze: 400-metres freestyle   3:53.44 (PB; WR for age)

1997 Pan Pacific Championships, Fukuoka

Silver: 400-metres freestyle
          4 x 200-metres freestyle relay
Notable: Youngest male ever to represent Australia; youngest
          ever Pan Pacific medalist.

1998 World Championships, Perth

Gold: 400-metres freestyle
           4 x 200-metres freestyle relay
Notable: Youngest ever male individual world champion.

1998 Australian Championships, Melbourne

Gold: 400-metres freestyle
           200-metres freestyle   1:47.24 (CR)
Silver: 100-metres freestyle

1998 Commonwealth Games, Kuala Lumpur

Gold: 400-metres freestyle   3:44.35 (PB)
           200-metres freestyle
           4 x 200-metres freestyle relay   7:11.66 (WR)
           4 x 100-metres freestyle relay

1999 Australian Championships, Brisbane

Gold: 400-metres freestyle
           100-metres freestyle
Silver: 200-metres freestyle

1999 FINA Short Course World Championship, Hong Kong

Gold: 200-metres freestyle   1:43.28 (WR)
           4 x 100-metres freestyle relay
Silver: 400-metres freestyle

1999 Pan Pacific Championships, Sydney

Gold: 400-metres freestyle   3:41.83 (WR)
           200-metres freestyle   1:46.00 (WR)
                                         (SF: 1:46.34, WR)

| 4 x 200-metres freestyle relay | 7:08.70 (WR) |
| 4 x 100-metres freestyle relay | |

Notable: Four world records in four days.

2000 FINA World Cup (short course)

| Gold: | 200-metres freestyle | 1:41.78 (PB, WR) |

2000 Olympic Selection Trials, Sydney

Gold:	400-metres freestyle	3:41.33 (WR)
	200-metres freestyle	1:45.51 (WR)
		(SF: 1:45.69, WR)

2000 Olympic Games, Sydney

Gold:	400-metres freestyle	3:40.59 (WR)
	4 x 200-metres freestyle relay	7:07.05 (WR)
	4 x 100-metres freestyle relay	3:13.67 (WR)
Silver:	200-metres freestyle	
	4 x 100-metres medley relay	

Notable: Most successful athlete at the 2000 Olympic Games.

2001 Australian Championships, Hobart

Gold:	800-metres freestyle	7.41.59 (WR)
	400-metres freestyle	
	200-metres freestyle	1:44.69 (WR)
	100-metres freestyle	49.05 (PB)

Notable: First since John Konrads in 1959 to hold all
Australian freestyle titles in 100–200–400–800-
metre distances.

2001 World Championships, Fukuoka

| Gold: | 800-metres freestyle | 7:39.16 (WR) |
| | 400-metres freestyle | 3:40.17 (WR) |

200-metres freestyle   1:44.06 (PB, WR)
4 x 200-metres freestyle relay   7:04.66 (WR)
4 x 100-metres freestyle relay
4 x 100-metres medley relay

Notable: First to win 6 gold medals at one World Championship; first since 1974 to win 200–400–800 distances.

2002 Australian Championships, Brisbane

Gold: 400-metres freestyle
200-metres freestyle
100-metres freestyle
100-metres backstroke

2002 Commonwealth Games, Manchester

Gold: 400-metres freestyle   3:40.08 (PB, WR)
200-metres freestyle
100-metres freestyle   48.73 (PB)
4 x 200-metres freestyle relay
4 x 100-metres freestyle relay
4 x 100-metres medley relay

Silver: 100-metres backstroke   55.38 (PB)

Notable: Matches Susie O'Neill's record of six gold medals in Games or world record times.

2002 Pan Pacific Championships, Yokohama

Gold: 400-metres freestyle
200-metres freestyle
100-metres freestyle
4 x 200-metres freestyle relay
4 x 100-metres freestyle relay

Silver: 4 x 100-metres medley relay

2003 FINA World Cup (short course)

Gold: 400-metres freestyle   3:34.63 (PB)

             200-metres freestyle   1.41.10 (PB)

2003 Australian Championships, Sydney

Gold: 400-metres freestyle

             200-metres freestyle

             100-metres freestyle (draw)

             200-metres individual medley   2:00.11 (CR)

             4 x 200-metres freestyle

2003 World Championships, Barcelona

Gold: 400-metres freestyle

             200-metres freestyle

             4 x 200-metres freestyle

Silver: 200-metres individual medley   1:59.66 (PB, CR)

Bronze: 100-metres freestyle

Notable: First to win three world titles in 400-metres freestyle; first medal in 100-metres freestyle at a global competition.

2004 Olympic Games, Athens

Gold: 400-metres freestyle

             200-metres freestyle   1:44.71 (OR)

Silver: 4 x 200-metres freestyle relay

Bronze: 100-metres freestyle   48.56 (PB)

Notable: First person to have won medals in the 100–200–400 combination in Olympic history.

ACKNOWLEDGEMENTS

At times it feels as if you're alone in the pool. There is a silence as you swim, following the black line, and the only noises are the thoughts inside your head. I have to remind myself sometimes that I'm not alone in my endeavours, and that I couldn't have achieved what I have without the interest, hard work and even love of those around me.

I have to start with my family, and my parents in particular. It might seem a cliché to recognise their efforts from early on when they drove my sister and me to and from our training sessions, often before and after light, but it's true – they did it willingly, day-in, day-out and without that commitment we would never have had the success in the pool that we did. As

ACKNOWLEDGEMENTS

I've said in the book, it wasn't only their physical efforts I'm grateful for, but their commonsense attitude to sport – where it might lead and where it might not.

Next are my coaches, from people like Jenni Ashpole and Chris Myers through to Doug Frost (even though we had our differences), Tracey Menzies, Milt Nelms and finally Gennadi Touretski. I learned something from all of them, as I did from people like Leigh Nugent, to whom I'm especially grateful for supporting my return to swimming.

Others have helped me in life outside the pool, like Dave and Michelle Flaskas, who have guided me and been my friend through the good and not-so-good years, Deidre Anderson, who helped me make some sense of a confusing world, and Jeff McMullen, for his wisdom in opening my eyes to another world and introducing me to the wonderful people and spirit of northern Australia.

I've had many colleagues from Australia and around the world, some well known and others not so well known, who have shared in the experiences I've described in chapters of this book. Some may call you rivals, I regard us as friends. The same goes for my Australian teammates with whom I've shared a camaraderie that would suggest swimming is not such a lonely sport. I acknowledge and thank you.

These acknowledgements are by no means complete, nor could they possibly be because so many people have an impact on our lives and shape the future in ways we cannot know at the time. To those people who have already done so and the ones who will have a positive effect on my life in the future, I also thank you.

Ian Thorpe

ABOUT ROBERT WAINWRIGHT

Robert Wainwright is a London-based Australian journalist and author. He has been a senior writer with *The Sydney Morning-Herald* for almost two decades and is a three-time finalist in the prestigious Walkley Awards for journalism. This is his sixth book.

INDEX

317